Redeeming the TIMES

Addressing Issues of the Church in the Present Age

Redeeming the TIMES

Addressing Issues of the Church in the Present Age

Editors:
Russell L. Dyer
Tommy F. Haynes
Jeff A. Jenkins

Clarity Publications
Oklahoma City, Oklahoma

Clarity Publications
P.O. Box 23384
OKLAHOMA CITY OK 73123

Printed in the United States of America

ISBN 0-9748241-0-0

APPRECIATION

We would like to express our sincere appreciation to:

The Southern Ridge Church of Christ
for providing assistance in the publication of this book,

Terry Walk for designing the cover and
For his invaluable work in typesetting,

Kathy Haynes, Dr. Fred Rhodes and Bill E. Smith
for proofing the chapters
and offering grammatical corrections

And

Last, but certainly not least to our wives & children for their
Support and encouragement in this effort

Redeeming the TIMES

Addressing Issues of the Church in the Present Age

Edited by Russell L. Dyer, Tommy F. Haynes and Jeff A. Jenkins

PREFACE

When I read the manuscripts of this book before its publication, I felt as if I had experienced a fresh breeze off a beautiful placid lake! Having read some of the books recently produced by teams of writers in our great brotherhood, I hoped that this one would not be as disruptive as many of them have been. I certainly was not disappointed.

Under the leadership of brothers Dyer, Haynes, and Jenkins, a group of gospel preachers, relatively young in years, but very mature in the faith, has confronted many of the issues that are disturbing the Lord's church today. They have also given us a work that appeals both to logic and scripture for answers to questions that trouble our brotherhood.

All of these writers have already proven themselves in their particular fields, and they have brought to this effort years of experience from study, writing, teaching, and preaching. Their reputations as men of strong convictions, and gentlemanly demeanor has proven to be valid, and will make this work appreciated even by those who may not always agree with the views they express. A look at their credentials is certainly inspiring. A look at their work is very enlightening.

As we learn well from the Old Testament, each new generation challenges the will and way of God, and if there is no one to confront that generation, it will be carried away into the captivity of sin. Our generation is no exception. Some in the Lord's church today question the validity of restoring the New Testament church, they would lead us into denominationalism. They have embraced the philosophies of those religious people around them. The group may not be large, but it is noisy, and it has captured some of our traditional instruments of communication. It is good that men like the authors of this book have raised their voice in protest. Let us give them the encouragement they deserve, and the help they need if they are to reach those who are confused.

Bill E. Smith
Oklahoma City, OK

INTRODUCTION

"Of the writing of books there is no end."
(Ecclesiastes 12:12)

We recognized that there was a need for a book about important issues in the church that has been written from a positive, loving, and Biblical spirit. It is our intention in the writing of this book to place good, Biblical reading material into the hands of Christians. We love the church and simply want to provide material that was beneficial to godly development. From the beginning of the project to its completion, it has been our goal to honor God and build up the church. We also wanted the book to address issues that are common within the church, and to address them with a spirit of encouragement. We know that there is no way that one book can address all of the issues we must confront. There is also no way that any singular chapter can answer all of the questions that might arise on a particular subject. It is our prayer that the chapters of this book will shed positive light in some very needed areas, as well as being clear, scriptural, and easy to comprehend.

Recent years have seen the production of what might be recognized as an explosion of religious books. Such books range from the fictitious novel to the inspirational stories of real life to the scholarly works of the highly educated to the life challenging and practical works written for the average reader. The written word remains a powerful instrument for the imparting of information, and the development of the human condition. In the church, we are often confronted with books that are directed mainly to members. Some of these books have the intention of pulling readers in a direction determined by the author rather than by scripture. Such books are undermining good leadership and causing division in the church. It is not our wish to divide, but to unify and strengthen the church.

As we chose the subject matter that we wanted to include in this book, we selected men who would be able to address each issue in a way that would bring about the most good. We asked that each writer present his material in a caring and considerate manner. We did not expect anyone to compromise his conscience or faith in any way. To the contrary, we desired that they present the very best of their study and understanding in a way that readers would get a clear picture of the matters being related. We are thankful to each man who agreed to take a part in this project. We are further indebted to each of the men for doing such a wonderful job of researching and producing the information in each chapter. The clarity and balance of their writing have given this book the character to be a valuable tool to any who will read it.

As contributing writers and editors, we have been blessed by working with this project. It has been a learning experience and we have truly received more than we have given. It is our prayer that this book will render service to the church of our Lord for many years. We hope that you will enjoy reading the various chapters of this book, but even more that you will be spiritually enriched by the content.

The Editors: Russell L. Dyer,
Tommy F. Haynes,
Jeff A. Jenkins

Why Should We Teach The Word Of God Today?

Jeff A. Jenkins

For the seventh consecutive year, record numbers of students have enrolled in public and private, elementary and secondary schools during the fall of 2003. College enrollment has broken the previous year's record for the fifth straight year. According to "Projections of Education Statistics to 2012," released by the U.S. Department of Education's National Center for Education Statistics, 53.6 million students entered K-12 classrooms during the fall of 2003, while 15.6 million students enrolled in colleges and universities. New enrollment records are anticipated every year during the first decade of the 21st century, since college enrollments have increased each year. By 2006, college enrollment is expected to reach 16.3 million, about 700,000 higher than in 2002. By 2012, around 17.7 million students are expected on college campuses, 13 percent more than in 2002.[1]

In spite of these staggering numbers, the rate of illiteracy in our nation continues to grow. One college English teacher reported attending a major summer workshop centered on how to teach writing. The primary method being touted at the workshop was the use of children's picture books such as *Click, Clack, Moo* and *Uncle Jed's Barbershop.* The college professor reacted by saying,

> "Surely, I thought, someone would question the approach. As a college English teacher who works daily with students who struggle mightily with college writing, I was certain someone, somewhere would suggest—maybe politely, maybe not—that with all of the other skills students needed to master, maybe picture books weren't the most effective use of time… Talk to teachers, review messages posted on e-mail groups and browse professional journals, and you'll find high school assignments that are long on fun and remarkably short on actual writing."[2]

Education is more accessible now than at any time in the history of our nation, yet the demands have become so watered down that education is becoming valueless. What is true about education in general in our world, is also true in regard to Bible knowledge. Gary Burge, professor of New Testament at Wheaton College, asserts that Biblical illiteracy is at a crisis level not just in our culture in general but in America's churches. "If it is true that Biblical illiteracy is commonplace in secular culture at large, there is ample evidence that points to similar trends in our churches."[3]

George Barna has spent the last several years researching religion. His assessment concurs with Burge. Barna says, "The Christian body in America is immersed in a crisis of Biblical illiteracy. How else can you describe matters when most churchgoing adults reject the accuracy of the Bible, reject the existence of Satan, claim that Jesus sinned, see no need to evangelize...and describe their commitment to Christianity as moderate or even less firm?"[4] Barna's research goes right to the heart of the matter. The results of his research are shocking. The bottom line for Barna is that there is a ***profound lack of belief in essential Christian doctrines.*** The most striking concern is the number of people in churches who deny the sinlessness of Christ. "Literally millions of Americans who declare themselves to be Christians contend that Jesus was just like the rest of us when it comes to temptation...guilty, impure, and Himself in need of a savior."[5] There is a direct link between the lack of belief and a lack of knowledge.Like Burge and Barna, George Lindbeck, a professor of religion at Yale, has commented on the decreasing knowledge of Scripture. "When I first arrived at Yale, even those who came from nonreligious backgrounds knew the Bible better than most of those now who come from churchgoing families."[6] David Wells, who has authored numerous books on what is taking place in religion in America, says in his book *No Place For Truth,* "I have watched with growing disbelief as the evangelical church has cheerfully plunged into astounding theological illiteracy."[7]

Are We Doing Any Better?

While some might contend that the previous quotes and statistics do not relate to members of the church of Christ, it seems as though we are not far behind the rest of the world. It appears that we have succumbed to the idea that our "study" of the Bible has to be fun. We have high school Bible classes viewing *Veggie Tales* videos and adult Bible classes viewing *Return To Mayberry, The Beverly Hillbillies, The Dick Van Dyke Show,* and *The Bonanza Bible Study* videos as a regular part of their "Bible" study. It is astounding when elders will allow young people to attend a youth event and hear a speaker who they would not allow to present a sermon from their pulpit! Worship services are also geared toward personal development and therapeutic wholeness. This emphasis has affected not just Bible classes and worship services in general, but also what is coming from pulpits. Sermons are shorter and often devoid of instructional information. They are more about what we feel and less about what we believe. We are living in tough times in relation to spiritual education. There may be harder days ahead. We have a responsibility to protect our spiritual children as well as our physical children. Without a strong view of Scripture neither we, nor they, will be prepared for the future.

Chuck Monan raises the astute question, "As a church do we know more about the Word of God than our ancestors?"[8] Brother Monan goes on to state, "I hear revisionist historians lam baste leaders in the Restoration Movement for their unenlightened views, but their critiques often fail to measure up to reality. When we compare the knowledge of God's Word these men possessed to that of church members today, there is no room for any of the current crop of critics to find fault."[9] Long ago God said of those who were His people, *"My people are destroyed for lack of knowledge. Because you have rejected knowledge, I also will reject you from being priest for Me; because you have forgotten the law of your God, I also will forget your children"* (Hosea 4:6). If it happened to God's people long ago, it certainly can happen to God's people during these postmodern days!

What is the Solution?

Once we become aware of the problem and admit the reality of its existence, the solution will come if we will commit to a return to the Bible. It is of paramount importance that we study the Word of God. When Paul wrote Timothy about the work of the Church in Ephesus, he filled both letters with admonitions focused on the Word. He said that elders must be able to teach (1 Timothy 3:2). The Greek word Paul uses is *"didaskatos"*. It means literally, skilled in teaching. Those who shepherd God's flock must skillfully teach the Word of God to the sheep. Paul further instructed the Church in Ephesus to *"...be diligent to present yourself approved to God, a worker who does not need to be ashamed, rightly dividing the word of truth"* (2 Timothy 2:15). He said the ministers are to *"Preach the Word..."* (2 Timothy 4:1) and that they are to preach it *"in season and out of season..."* (2 Timothy 4:1). That phrase, "in season and out of season", simply means that the Word of God is to be taught all the time. There is no time that elders, preachers, teachers, or anyone who is a part of the church has a right to change that commission. There is no time that we have the right to set aside God's chosen method of communicating His Word, and replace it with methods that we might prefer, or believe would work better. Paul said to the Corinthians *"it pleased God through the foolishness of the preaching to save those who believe"* (1 Corinthians 1:21). In Paul's letter to Timothy he discussed the need for teaching God's Word all the time. He also talked about how we are to teach. He said we are to *"reprove, rebuke, and exhort."* There is a negative teaching tone. We are to reprove and rebuke. We are challenged to allow God's Word to confront sin and error. There is also a positive teaching aspect. We are to exhort people to obey the Word of God and allow them to see how obedience to the Word brings joy to the Lord, as well as blessings to our lives.

We must understand the truth of what Jesus said, *"man does not live by bread alone, but by every word that proceeds out of the mouth of God."* People around the world, as well as members of the Lord's church in many places, are starving for the Word of God. People everywhere are hungry, they are reaching out, they are grasping for something to fill the hollow places in their lives. Many realize that there is a lack of understanding and insight. There is an inability to solve the problems and dilemmas of life, and a struggle with how to fix it. The sad reality is that in spite of the fact that God's Word contains the key to all of these problems, many hungry souls are being fed a steady diet of substitutes. God has ordained that His Word alone can feed the yearning of the hungry soul. This is true because it is in His Word that God is revealed. Our mandate comes from the Creator of man and the universe. It is not what any given culture would force upon us. In Paul's closing words to his young protégé, he gave compelling motivation for obeying this serious command.

Why Should We Teach the Word of God Today?

We are to teach the Word of God because we are living in dangerous seasons. Paul said that in the *"last days perilous times would come"* (1 Timothy 3:1). The "last days" is the Biblical phrase referring to the last dispensation of time that began when Christ brought the New Testament law into effect. The word perilous could be translated difficult, or even better, savage or dangerous. The word times could be translated season, epics, or movements. These savage seasons will threaten the Truth and the Church. According to 1 Timothy 3:15, times will increase in severity because evil men and imposters will proceed from bad to worse, "deceiving and being deceived." These dangerous times began during the days of the first century church and they continue to accumulate even to our day. In a real sense there is a greater spiritual danger now than there has ever been.

These dangerous seasons began with the Roman Catholic system that developed into sacramentalism. After hundreds of years of sacramentalism the reformation took place and sacramentalism began to decline. Out of the reformation came rationalism where men began to turn to their own thinking. Once man regained his identity he reasoned that he was greater than God. It was during this dangerous season that Thomas Payne wrote his famous book, *The Age of Reason,* a book that proclaimed the human mind to be god. To such thinking, the Bible became a slave to rationalism. It is rationalism that destroyed some of the greatest universities in the history of our nation, and unfortunately some of our Christian schools are falling prey to a form of rationalism.

Then came orthodoxism during the nineteenth century. Even though mass printing brought easy access to the Bible, many lost their zeal for God. Spirituality became either non-existent or at the very least shallow.

With the entrance into the twentieth century many new dangerous seasons came to threaten the church. During the 1950's ecumenism became very popular. There was a common call to lay aside all doctrine and focus on unity.

The prevailing attitude was, "let's not divide over these doctrinal issues." Ecumenism developed a new hermeneutic for interpreting scripture that was called the "Jesus Ethic." This new hermeneutic said that Jesus was a good man and that He would never say anything bad, so we should remove all of the bad from the Bible. Anything that discussed sin, hell, judgment, or retribution needed to be deleted. Any teaching that had the sound of doctrine began to be disdained. The legacy of ecumenism is a lack of discernment. This dangerous season began in the religious world in general, but it has now infiltrated the church of Christ. In a recent book, edited by two prominent preachers in the church, one of the authors presents the following thoughts,

> "Accepting ourselves in this way can give us courage to face other challenges which we have often failed to meet in Churches of Christ. For example, it can help us learn to overcome our sectarianism. When you feel you must conform to a specific list of criteria to be accepted by God, you expect others to do the same. But experiencing mercy in Christ can open us to showing mercy to other Christians (Matthew 18:23-35). We may still disagree with some of their beliefs, but we can accept them as Christians anyway—just as Christ accepted us while we were still sinners. Paul says, *'Welcome one another, therefore, just as Christ has welcomed you, for the glory of God'* (Romans 15:7). Embracing the God of grace in Christ can give us the courage to be a leader in ecumenical activity in the new millennium."[10]

Hal Hougey says the church has become a "Museum of the Status Quo," and he believes that drastic changes are imperative.[11] Others have stated that the church of Christ is a denomination and that the church of Christ was born of the American Restoration Movement.[12] All of these ideas appear to grow out of a worthy goal to bring about religious unity. This is not at all the type of unity for which the Bible pleads. Our Lord prayed in John 17:20-21, *"I do not pray for these alone, but also for those who will believe in Me through their word; that they all may be one, as You, Father, are in Me, and I in You; that they also may be one in Us, that the world may believe that You sent Me."* Our Lord's prayer for unity stands in stark contrast to ecumenism, where all doctrine is laid aside for the sake of being united.

On top of ecumenism you can place subjectivism, experimentalism, mysticism, pragmatism and paganism. We are fighting a war. According to Ephesians 6:12, it is a war of cosmic proportions. Francis A. Schaffer was right when he said, "Very few have taken a strong and courageous stand against the world spirit of this age as it destroys our culture and the Christian ethos that once shaped our country."[13]

In 2 Timothy 3:2-4, Paul describes more about what is taking place when he tells us something about those who are behind these dangerous seasons. He says that they *"will be lovers of themselves, lovers of money, boasters, proud, blasphemers, disobedient to parents, unthankful, unholy, unloving, unforgiving, slanderers, without self-control, brutal, despisers of good, traitors, headstrong, haughty, lovers of pleasure rather than lovers of God."* These are people who have no virtue or character. Paul says that we should turn away from people like this! He says they appear to be godly but really they deny the power of God. Paul goes on to say that they can destroy families! It becomes the responsibility of parents, teachers, youth leaders, preachers, elders, and anyone else in the church that loves the church, to protect the Truth of God's Word. We have been called to guard the Truth, to protect the Truth, to preach the Truth, and we cannot do any of these unless we know, understand, and love the Truth.

We should teach the Word of God not only because we are living in dangerous times, but also because of the devotion to the Scriptures shown by those who have lived before us. Paul discusses this very thing in 2 Timothy 3:10-11, *"But you have carefully followed my doctrine, manner of life, purpose, faith, longsuffering, love, perseverance, persecutions, afflictions..."* He is saying you have followed me. You not only have heard my teaching, you have also watched the way I have lived and endured through the trials of life. He later says, *"But you must continue in the things which you have learned and been assured of, knowing from whom you have learned them, and that from childhood you have known the Holy Scriptures..."* (2 Timothy 3:14-15). He is saying, "Timothy, you just do what I have taught you to do." In 1 Timothy 2:2, Paul instructed Timothy by saying, "And the things that you have heard from me among many witnesses, commit these to faithful men who will be able to teach others also." There are many today who are trying to re-invent ministry and change the church. John MacArthur, a prominent religious leader, says, "It is a studied effort to change the way the world perceives the church...Give them freedom, tolerance, anonymity. Always be positive and benevolent. If you must have a sermon, keep it brief and amusing...Above all, keep everyone entertained. Churches following this pattern will see numerical growth, we're assured; those that ignore it are doomed to decline...the whole point is to make the church user-friendly."14 It is astonishing to see church leaders and church workers discard the God ordained, scripturally mandated pattern, to invent one of their own. It takes a great amount of pride and a lot of audacity for a person to think he knows more than God knows and to think his way is better than God's Way.

The church today is what it is because of those who have labored before us. It is disturbing to hear some speak in unkind and unloving terms of those who have given their lives to teaching the unsearchable riches of Christ. We should be thankful for our heritage and give honor to those who have helped bring us to this point in time.

Paul further says we should teach the Word of God because the scriptures are dynamic. In 2 Timothy 3:15-16, he proclaims, *"...from childhood you have known the Holy Scriptures, which are able to make you wise for salvation through faith which is in Christ Jesus. All scripture is given by inspiration of God, and is profitable for doctrine, for reproof, for correction, for instruction in righteousness."* Paul states in clear terms that it is the Word of God that leads us to salvation. The Word of God is *"living and powerful, and sharper than any two-edged sword..."* (Hebrews 4:12). It is the power of the Word that produces salvation (Romans 1:16). It is the Word of God that *"converts the soul"* (Psalm 19:7). Peter said, *"having been born again, not of corruptible seed but incorruptible, through the Word of God which lives and abides forever"* (1 Peter 1:23). So the question becomes, why would we want to teach anything other than the Word of God?

Next, Paul says we should teach the Word of God because it is what God demands. *"I charge you therefore before God and the Lord Jesus Christ...Preach the Word!"* (2 Timothy 4:1-2). It has been my privilege to teach and preach God's Word for nearly 30 years and of all of the commands in the Bible this is the most frightening to me. Every time I stand before an audience to proclaim the Word of God, it is this verse that strikes me with Holy fear. This is a serious command. It is not our duty to make people feel good, or to make them happy. It is not our calling to fill church buildings to capacity. It is not our commission to make the church or ourselves more popular. We are not commanded to do our best to become more culturally relevant. It is our charge to bring God's Word to a starving world. In his book, *Losing Our Virtue,* David Wells poses some very insightful questions that all of us should consider. "Does the Church have the courage to become relevant by becoming Biblical? Is it willing to break with the cultural habits of the time and propose something quite absurd, like recovering both the Word and the meaning of sin? Is it sagacious enough to be able to show how the postmodern world is trapped within itself?"[15] These questions demand an answer from us. How we answer these questions may determine the future for our children.

The final motivating factor that Paul gives to Timothy and to us is the need to understand how deceptive our enemy really is. Paul informs us that there will be times when our enemy is successful. *"For the time will come when they will not endure sound doctrine but according to their own desires, because they have itching ears, they will heap up for themselves teachers; and they will turn their ears away from the Truth, and be turned aside to fables"* (2 Timothy 4:3-4). Paul is saying here that some will be driven by the sensual rather than the cognitive. We understand this when people talk about "what I want," or "what I like." This is also seen when decisions are made in churches because a majority of the members has voted on their choices.

The prevailing mood in the world of postmodern western culture is that everybody determines truth for himself, or for herself. In the age of tolerance everybody's opinion must be considered equally valid. There is no room for absolute doctrine. The only people who cannot be tolerated these days, are those who seem to be even a little intolerant. This danger being forced upon the church is called relativism. May we be reminded that our enemy, *"...the devil walks about like a roaring lion, seeking whom he may devour"* (1 Peter 5:8).

Francis Schaeffer called it "the great evangelical disaster—the failure of the evangelical world to stand for truth as truth."[16] He says that the "church has accommodated to the world spirit of the age."[17] Schaeffer further says that the church has accommodated the world on Scripture and on issues, "with no clear stand being taken even on matters of life and death."[18] It may indeed be necessary for us to draw a line between those who hold to a strong, uncompromising view of scripture and those who do not. We must be able to distinguish between subjective experiences and the objective Truth of God's Word. Friends, it is not our obligation to try to find what is culturally relevant—it is our duty to take the Word of God and bring it to bear upon our society. The truth is, wherever we live in this world and whatever language we speak, our lives are in the same needy condition. Only the Truth of God's Word can transcend all cultures and all generations. Apparently, there are many that believe we can not speak the Truth in a loving way. The Apostle Paul said not only is that possible, but it is necessary. *"Speak the Truth in love..."* (Ephesians 4:15). The idea that we will not confront sin, or rebuke error, because we love someone, is simply not true. If we love someone, we seek his or her best and highest good. All of this is completely connected to one's understanding of, and obedience to, Divine Truth. It is vitally important that we teach the Word of God to the heart and the mind. Only then can a lost world come to know God. Let us be kind and loving in our proclamation of the Word, but may we also be bold in presenting the unsearchable riches of Christ.

[1] National Center for Education Statistics. *Digest of Education Statistics,* 2002. <http://nces.ed.gov/pubs2003/digest02>

[2] Donna Harrington-Lueker, "Crayola Curriculum' Takes Over," *USA Today,* July 16, 2002, Editorial/Opinion

[3] Gary M. Burge, "The Greatest Story Never Read: Recovering Biblical Literacy in the Church," <www.christianitytoday.com/ct/9t9/9t9045.html.>

[4] Barna Research Online, "Religious Beliefs Vary Widely by Denomination," www.barna.org/cgi-bin/PagePressRelease.asp?PressReleaseID=92&Reference=B, June 25, 2001.

[5] Ibid.

6 George A. Lindbeck, "The Church's Mission to a Postmodern Culture," *Postmodern Theology: Christian Faith in a Pluralist World* (San Francisco: Harper & Row Publishers, 1989), 45.

7 David F. Wells, No Place for Truth or Whatever Happened to Evangelical Theology? (Grand Rapids: Eerdmans, 1993), 4.

8 Chuck Monan, Trends In Society In The Church, (A Sermon Preached September 23, 2002)

9 Ibid.

10 Paul Casner, *"Facing Our True Selves, The Transforming A Tradition: Churches of Christ in the New Millennium,* edited by Leonard Allen and Lynn Anderson, (Orange, CA: New Leaf Books, 2001), 99.

11 Hal Houghey, *The Quest for Understandable Hermeneutics,* (Concord, CA: Manna-Pacific Pub. Co., 1997)

12 This view has been in vogue for several years, and has been presented by a number of preachers, authors, and educators in Churches of Christ.

13 Francis A. Shaffer, *The Great Evangelical Disaster,* (Westchester, IL: Crossway Books, 1984), 37.

14 John MacArthur,

15 David Wells, *Losing Our Virtue: Why the Church Must Recover Its Moral Vision,* (Grand Rapids, MI: William B. Eerdmans Publishing Company, 1998), 199.

16 Shaffer, *The Great Evangelical Disaster,* 37.

17 Ibid.

Inspiration and Inerrancy

Dr. Kippy Myers

Inspiration is a very sticky subject these days, more than ever before. The scholarly world (and the world at large) is a mess when it comes to views of inspiration. The theological labels and beliefs are numerous, at times overlapping, and can be convoluted.

Many people who claim to be Christians will disagree on some very important issues: (1) what they mean when they describe what the Bible is supposed to be, (2) what purpose God intended for the Bible to serve (if He was involved with the Bible at all, in their view), (3) the specific way in which the Bible is authoritative, and other vital Bible topics that center on the inspiration of the Bible. For example, there are several positions on the meaning of biblical inspiration. Some think that the Bible writers were inspired only in the sense that a football team is inspired by their coach. Others think that they were only inspired in the sense that a comedian is inspired when he comes up with a particularly funny joke. Still others think that they were inspired in a supernatural way such that God was directly involved in both revealing His will to them as well as guiding their writing, ensuring a perfect product.

To get a basic picture of the situation, imagine a spectrum of beliefs about biblical inspiration with the extreme left labeled "All man, no God" and the extreme right labeled "All God, no man." What is commonly referred to as the liberal view would be located in the direction of the left side and the conservative view would be in the direction of the right side. That means that the fundamental tenets of liberal theology picture the Bible as more the work of human beings than God. The fundamental tenets of conservatism picture the Bible as more the work of God than human beings. But the more experiential or mystical views would be difficult to locate on such a spectrum. These views tend to de-emphasize the importance of what the biblical text says and place more focus on what it does as an instrument to encounter God personally.

Traditional View

I advocate the traditional view of the Bible (sometimes used synonymously with the high view of Scripture or the conservative view of inspiration). The traditional way of looking at the Bible is generally ". . . the Book *par excellence,* the recognized record of divine revelation."[1] More specifically, this view says that what the Bible presents as historical narratives are so in fact and occurred in space-time history in the places, at the times, and to the people it specifies. The traditional view usually includes corollaries like Mosaic authorship of the Pentateuch, Pauline authorship of several New Testament epistles, and early dates for most of the New Testament books.

The traditional view has its subcategories, however. (1) The "dictation" theory of inspiration avers that the writers were like dictation machines, computer printers. They wrote exactly what they were "told" by the Holy Spirit and had no leeway for their own vocabulary, ideas, and emotions. (2) The "dynamic" theory of inspiration says that the Holy Spirit gave the writers a general idea to write about and then left them to their own devices to work out the details. The basic ideas are from God, but there is significant leeway in the process for human beings to provide filler material and present the ideas in their own ways. (3) I accept the "plenary, verbal" theory of inspiration which says that the Holy Spirit supervised the writers very closely so that when each work was completed it was exactly the way God wanted it, although room was allowed for them to inject their own personalities, vocabularies, and emotions.

> One working definition of the traditional view of inspiration is, that mysterious process by which the divine causality worked through the human prophets without destroying their individual personalities and styles, to produce divinely authoritative writings.[2]

Thus, this view holds that the writers wrote under God's influence (although this work is generally attributed to the Holy Spirit) to the extent that they could not have produced these works by their human ability alone. When necessary, God miraculously informed the writers of what he wanted to be said and guided them to address properly the topics he wanted addressed. The Holy Spirit supervised the process in a way that excluded error (in the "autographs," i.e., the original written documents). Philosophically, the autonomy of each writer is respected, but the intervention of the Holy Spirit is allowed.

That is, Bible writers were inspired in a way that no other writers have been inspired. Although it seems clear that some of the writers accessed their own emotions, vocabularies, knowledge, experiences, and knowledge of secular writings, they believed that God was guiding their message so that the result was "the word of God," rather than simply their own ideas. The process of inspiration as the Bible describes it involved human beings, but because God was "running the show," the product was more than human. Thus, God controlled the *process* in such a way that he allowed the writers to draw from their backgrounds and vocabularies, while revealing the information and providing the guidance necessary to ensure a perfect *product* just as he intended.

Some people think that the Bible has errors in areas like history, geography, science, although not in doctrine. Usually, however, those who hold to a high view of Scripture (such as today's evangelicals), believe that the Bible is infallible in every way – no mistakes, no errors at all. It seems reasonable to believe that if a book is the product of God's omniscience, then it could at least be possible that it would be inerrant. After all, human beings make lots of mistakes ("To err is human"), but God does not work by trial and error. To this day, many attempts have been made to point out alleged biblical mistakes, but none has stood the test of time. Many times, even the foundations of the allegations themselves were found to be without factual basis. Archaeology continues to confound the skeptic and corroborate the Bible. I believe that the Bible as written by the men that the Holy Spirit employed, is without error in doctrine, morality, history, or in any other area.

The Bible's Own Claims

It should be noted that the traditional view of Scripture is traditional (i.e., it has a long history) for a good reason. It is what the Bible claims for itself. In hundreds, some say thousands, of cases Old Testament texts claim to be speaking God's words.[3] The prophets repeatedly claim God's inspiration with phrases equivalent to *"thus saith Jehovah."*

Someone might deny that Jesus and others in the New Testament held such a high view of the Old Testament because at times they appear to disagree with some of the Old Testament law. However, one must take into consideration the two major religious transitions in the Bible, viz., when the Mosaic law was given to the Jews, and when Christianity began.

For 1,500 years the Mosaic law had been in force. But as the Old Testament prophets had said, a harbinger would come, the Messiah would arrive, and a new age would begin. The New Testament presents John the Baptist as the harbinger, Jesus as the Messiah, and Christianity as the new age. Jesus lived and died as a faithful Jew, but being the focal point of a transitional period in religion, Jesus arrived on the scene preaching change. The New Testament says that his death effectively ended the period of the Mosaic law,[4] instituted a new law,[5] and thereby made Jews and Gentiles into one group of Christian people.[6]

Looking at their statements from this perspective, Jesus, Paul, and Peter never questioned the inspiration or accuracy of the Old Testament. Rather, they employed the Old Testament to prove that what it had said would occur, did in fact come to pass.[7] Jesus, Paul, and Peter were not manifesting unbelief in the Old Testament. Rather, they were saying that they *did* believe it and could see its teachings coming to pass in their time.

The Bible has Jesus saying[8] that God was the true author of the Old Testament texts that he quoted.[9] His statements about the Old Testament writings are considered a high view of Scripture because he says things like "Scripture cannot be broken" (John 10:35), and "not a jot or a tittle will pass from the law until all is accomplished" (Matthew 5:17-19). He also makes references to detailed circumstances in which Old Testament texts are being fulfilled literally.[10] He is famous for upbraiding the Pharisees with statements like, "Have you not read?" and "It is written . . ." as though what the Old

Testament texts said was authoritative and final. He responded to Satan's temptations with Old Testament quotes. He even made an argument based on the tense of one word as though even individual words of the Old Testament had significance.[11]

There are at least two hundred ninety-five New Testament quotations or direct references to the Old Testament and about six hundred thirteen allusions to it, totaling "about 10 percent of the New Testament text."[12] This is impressive for a number of reasons, not the least of which is that the people seemed to believe that the Old Testament words were authoritative in such a way that they used a proof text approach to confirm the legitimacy of what they said. That is how most of the New Testament uses of Old Testament texts occur.

The New Testament writings also say many times that God was speaking through both the Old and New Testament writers and speakers.[13] In keeping with this, Paul's epistles were being read and collected as authoritative documents very early. Misquoting his writings was like misquoting the other Scriptures and was just as self-destructive.[14] Therefore, canonization of the New Testament books was not something that occurred at a council in the fourth century. It had been going on for a long time on a grassroots level. Early Christians were quoting those books and using proof texts from the earliest times.[15] They occasionally quote other writings (poets, philosophers), but only as insights and not as divinely authoritative documents. These biblical quotes from both early non-believers and early Christian writings prove the antiquity of the high view of Scripture.[16]

As far as canonization of the Old Testament goes, "Contrary to prevailing critical opinion, there existed, prior to the Exile, a large body of sacred literature."[17] Aligned with this, the conservative maintains that Moses wrote all the words of the Lord in the "books of the covenant"(Exodus 24:4,7), and this was read to the Israelites upon their entrance into the Promised Land.[18] Joshua's farewell address was written *"in the book of the law of God"*(Joshua 24:26). Samuel spoke concerning the manner of the kingdom and "wrote it in a book" (1 Samuel 10:25). After the Israelites had neglected God for a long time, a priest named Hilkiah found the book of the law in the temple and King Josiah commanded that the people begin to learn it once again.[19] These texts further the idea that some of the Old Testament literature was produced very early and was considered to be from God.

Bible characters sometimes treat the Old Testament as a single, harmonious unit. For instance, when the Devil quoted an Old Testament passage (*"It is written . . ."*) as authority for Jesus to jump off the pinnacle of the temple, Jesus used another Old Testament passage which enlightened the meaning of the first one (*"Again it is written..."*) as though both were part of one unit, one contiguous body of consistent thought, harmonious throughout (Matthew 4:5-7).

New Testament writers and speakers also manifested a belief in the integrity and unity of the Old Testament when they used it in a holistic way as when the apostle Paul and the writer of the book of Hebrews quote a variety of Old Testament passages from different books to prove the points they were addressing.[20] Based on what the Bible says about itself and based on how the New Testament talks about and uses the Old Testament texts, it seems reasonable to conclude that the Bible itself teaches a high view of Scripture.[21] These are just a few of the times that the ancient writings are referred to in the writings themselves. Therefore, the Old Testament canon was similar to the later situation with the New Testament,

> This revelatory literature, although not reaching a fixed form until late in the second century B. C., was nevertheless regarded from the very first as the revealed will of God and therefore binding upon the people.[22]

Notice that I am *not* arguing the old circumlocution that "the Bible must be a revelation from God because it says so." As James Barr (although a liberal scholar) correctly notes, "How do we know that what the Bible teaches about inspiration is true?"[23] Just because a book claims to be something does not make it so. The point of these citations is to show that the high view of Scripture is an ancient view,[24] a biblical view, and not something from the modern era. Many liberal scholars inaccurately claim that the high view of Scripture originated with certain "fundamentalist" Presbyterians like Charles Hodge and B. B. Warfield at Princeton between about 1880 and 1920.[25] In reality, it is the critical methodology (which denies the traditional view) that is new, arising as recently as the nineteenth century.

Should the biblical claims for inspiration be taken seriously? To someone from the traditional perspective, it seems odd that a liberal scholar would say that the Bible is inspired and authoritative, yet reject it when it describes itself in such high terms.[26] But the presuppositions are numerous and divisive. Maybe the traditional view of inspiration does not make sense to some people. However, whether a person can understand the mechanics of this process of inspiration, which the Bible writers describe, should not preclude (1) the possibility that it actually happened, and (2) accepting the product without understanding the process. The Bible itself does not detail exactly how the human mind was influenced in the process of inspiration, or precisely how they recognized that God was the author of it. However, if the human mind/soul can control its physical body, why is it so difficult to think that God could do something similar with the human mind? If someone affirms that God exists and has acted in human history, it seems almost inevitable that God would eventually do some things that finite minds would have trouble comprehending.

Liberal View

Some scholars think that the traditional view is no longer tenable. They think that as the years have passed, more information disproving the traditional view has come to light about the history in the Bible and the background of the book itself. As the non-traditional Alan Richardson says, "The rise of biblical scholarship made necessary a new doctrine of the inspiration of Holy Scripture."[27]

This different way of looking at the Bible says essentially that the Bible is a compilation of writings that began as stories, sermons, legends, etc., and were eventually captured in written form by unknown writers for different reasons. Subsequently, the early versions of biblical works were,

> taken up by later authors or redactors who also incorporated, rewrote, and reinterpreted Israel's past for their own audiences, and . . . this process continued until the text received its present form.[28]

There is no single person whose particular formulation of this basic view fits everyone in the liberal camp. But Julius Wellhausen set forth such a cogent depiction of the process (generally referred to as the documentary hypothesis) that it set the standard for ages to come.[29] He believed that a Hexateuch was the product of a redactor editing, cutting, and pasting together the writings of four proto-Bible authors (J, E, P, and D). Each of the four original documents had its own identifiable characteristics (names used for God, stylistic differences, vocabulary, repetition, etc.). This became the standard way that source criticism (which emphasizes the nature of the original written documents), form criticism (which emphasizes the nature of the original oral traditions), and similar schools of thought identified the true origins of the biblical materials. With the advent of these critical methods of studying and explaining the Bible, "the traditional view of the Mosaic authorship of the first five books of the Bible . . . was fore ever [sic] disproved . . . ."[30]

Of course, Wellhausen's version of the documentary hypothesis did not remain static for long. Once scholars believed that by studying the biblical text they could discover things about origins of the Bible, others found sources within the sources, multiplying their own criteria for identification of sources, and subdividing each of the four segments into dozens of other authors, and earlier documents. Sections of the Old Testament other than the Hexeteuch were also investigated in this way, and this led to theories about multiple and late authorship which further undermined the traditional view. The prophets were subjected to the critical methodology of searching for the *true* Bible writers, and Isaiah, for example, was considered the product of at least two authors. More and more, study of the Bible in liberal circles shifted its emphasis from the study of doctrine to the study of religion from a scientific, anthropological approach. This approach inexorably spread to the New Testament. No matter which type of critical methodology a person chose to follow, the assumptions upon which the critical method was founded, combined with liberal theology, eventually created the main alternatives to the traditional view of Scripture.

Combine these attitudes with the changing face of religion through the years, and liberal theology ended up walking hand in hand with liberal views of Scripture. From the liberal position, theology "is conceived as essentially imaginative construction of a picture or understanding of God, humanity, and the world" rather than "essentially translation or interpretation of an authoritative Scripture or tradition . . . ."[31]

True Only in a Symbolic Way?

Therefore, the traditional and liberal views of Scripture obviously disagree about whether the Bible is historically accurate (or whether it was even intended to be). Part of the presuppositional wedge between them is the question of whether the Bible is *literally* true or only *symbolically* true.

The traditional conservative view ordinarily asserts that the Bible is an accurate historical record, miracles and all.[32] Thus, liberal scholars often refer to conservatives as "literalists." However, there are sections where symbolism is used to tell a story or make a point, just as people have always used symbolic language in their discussions. But the traditional view claims that the main story line is not simply symbolic; it is about actual events that occurred in space-time history.

In the lineage of Rudolf Bultmann and other liberal scholars, Spong has no patience with the traditional outlook. He says with great disdain,

> It is a pity that this truth cannot be heard until the Bible is freed from the hands of those who are in fact destroying Christianity with their literalistic claims even though in their naiveté they believe themselves to be serving the Bible faithfully.[33]

Those who agree with Spong think that the Old Testament is largely (though not all agree that it is entirely) a collection of myths, and that the New Testament is the same. For them, "more attention is given to [the Scriptures] as symbolic documents than as historical documents."[34] For example, the story of Christ's resurrection from the dead was not about an actual event, it is only a sort of parable, a story with some sort of religious truth connected to it. Marcus Borg thinks, "the meaning of the resurrection is that people within the early Christian movement continued to experience the 'empowering presence' of Jesus after his death." Hence, for Borg and those of similar belief like John Dominic Crossan (a participant in The Jesus Seminar), "The resurrection of Jesus has nothing to do with his corpse."[35]

Compare this with urban legends. Some think that urban legends are mythical but useful stories that comprise part of a culture's folklore. Although none of the stories is literally true, they are interesting, easy to remember, and thus continue to be told and retold. In this way, urban legends function as reminders of societal and ethical norms. For example, the legend of the couple who park in a lonely wooded area to "make out" is nothing but a cultural condemnation of teen pre-marital sex, preserved and disseminated in mythical form. The story did not occur in space-time history. But the story continues to transmit truths even though it might pick up additional details as it is retold in different cultural areas of the country. For example, in the South, the "Goat Man" kills the teens but in the North, the "Hook Man" does it. Anyone who takes this story for the literal truth and adds objective significance to the idea that Goat Man "means something" has made a big mistake.

This is essentially how liberal theologians, i.e., adherents of the symbolic, non-historical hypothesis, look at the Bible, except that they are working with spiritual truths, not just moral truths. The stories are not literally true as far as being events that occurred in space-time history, but they carry spiritual truths in the symbolism of their characters. They tell something about how people in different places and times have used the baggage of their own environment to communicate religious and ethical beliefs and principles.

This "psychoanalytic" or symbolic approach to the Bible shares similarities with the allegorical methods of Origen, Clement of Alexandria, and Philo of Alexandria. Rather than deal with straight line propositional statements like "there were four rivers in Eden," and think that it means four literal rivers existed in a literal place, these men could find all sorts of allegorical truths there about preaching the gospel, virtuous living, and other lessons. Some of the non-traditionalists' utilization of the critical method is like this in a way, except that they have a different philosophy about the Bible, they are far more widely accepted by scholars, and they take allegorization to a new level.

For instance, John Crossan reads that two men were making their way to Emmaus when the resurrected Jesus spoke to them,[36] but Crossan does not believe that this happened to anyone in actual fact. He thinks that it is rather "the metaphoric condensation of the first years of early Christian thought and practice into one parabolic afternoon." From this comes his oft quoted statement, "Emmaus never happened. Emmaus always happens."[37] So, do non-traditional thinkers really submit to a type of biblical authority, or do they claim authority over the text by recognizing authority only in the texts where their prior beliefs are stated? Compare this with scholars who presuppose that miracles cannot occur. Jarl Fossum says, "It can be asserted that Jesus really did raise the girl from the dead — which would only reflect fundamentalist naiveté."[38] Crossan holds a comparable belief when he says, "I do not think that anyone, anywhere, at any time brings dead people back to life."[39] It is very difficult to find common ground with such people to discuss biblical teaching unless we deal with the presuppositions first.

The Bible and Historical Accuracy

In contrast to this symbolic view of Scripture, the traditional view of Scripture puts tremendous emphasis on the Bible's historicity. The Bible is replete with historical details like cities, nations, genealogy, geography, politics, topography, government officials, ancient cultural practices, dates, etc. The Bible regularly deals with dates, names, and places that take the stories out of the realm of what is generally considered to be fiction, and put them at checkable places, at checkable times, and with checkable people in space-time history. Because of this characteristic of the Judeo-Christian holy books, Bible students commonly want to look into the history of Assyria, Babylon, Egypt, Syria, Palestine, Rome, Greece, et al.

How does a person go about testing the accuracy of a book which purports to have recorded events from the past? Secular historians can be examined for corroboration in some cases. Ancient manuscripts (official and unofficial documents), numismatics, architecture, ostraca, and other sources can also be checked for corroboration. Similar cultures and cognate languages sometimes show that recorded events and sayings which seem strange to twentieth century westerners were regarded as reasonable and normal occurrences in other parts of the world a thousand or more years ago.

Since the Bible employs the historical mode, historical verification is an important issue for those religious groups. That is not to say that conservatives think that all of the details in the Bible are checkable. Whereas the Bible has its historical core, it also has an emphasis on the miraculous. Verifying the accuracy of miracle accounts involves other issues like the trustworthiness of witnesses, the witnesses' proximity to the event, and whether they had a reason to distort the truth.

However, if a document can be shown to be completely accurate in its record of normal events, that should get a person's attention because it might lend credence to its accounts of abnormal events (like miracles) as well. If the Bible can be proven historically accurate, this does not mean that such in itself would prove that the miracles occurred. It does not. But those who assent to its historical accuracy would be encouraged to consider the miracles that it records right along with the historical details. Since in a theistic universe miracles are certainly possible (unless miracle accounts are to be dismissed out of hand), they should be investigated.

Barr makes it sound rather foolish for conservatives to be concerned about the history associated with the Bible. He thinks that even if the conservatives could prove that the books were written early and/or that certain recorded events were actually historical occurrences, it would not change anything. For him, the real issue is that "the understanding of truth and meaning as applied to the Bible has become thoroughly different" so that,

> the understanding of the Bible that has grown up in the tradition of modern critical scholarship and modern theology would remain totally different from that which conservative evangelicals want us to adopt.[40]

All of the conservatives' efforts are thus "a waste of time."[41]

Yet, if a book so unequivocally presents events that occur in historical settings, and does not represent itself as something else (except in certain cases where the text itself makes it clear), it makes sense to look at it in this light first and see if what it says about those events is accurate. So much of the Old Testament is built on remembrances of God's historical actions, that to make those actions into mere symbols would be to render a great deal of the Old Testament's inner logic at least irrelevant and perhaps worse.

Consider J. P. Moreland's story of a Jewish friend whose undergraduate degree was in classics from Harvard, his master's degree was in classics from UCLA, and his Ph.D. was also in classics from UCLA. When they first met, he told Moreland that he was a Christian. Knowing that he was also a Jew, Moreland asked him, "How did you become a Christian?" He said,

> Dr. Moreland, I have studied myth most of my education. I know the earmarks of myth; that's all I study. My undergraduate training was in mythology; my graduate training has been in mythology. And I was practicing Koine Greek reading the Gospel of Luke, and I got halfway through it, and as a Jew, I said, "My God, this man really did these things. What am I going to do? This is history. It reads like history. It doesn't read like myth. I know what myth tastes like because all I do is read it, and that is not myth."[42]

Nevertheless, Barr claims that although some who hold the traditional view of Scripture are well-informed scholars, generally speaking, it is a naive view, and well-informed people reject it.[43] It is interesting, however, that some people leave Barr's camp when they check the history for themselves and become more conservative when they find that it fits the facts better than they had been told in their university courses.[44] Removing any ambiguity about his fervor in this matter, Barr compares rejecting the critical method (the heart of the liberal view of Scripture) to rejecting the Copernican revolution.[45] Spong expresses his position with equal vehemence when he says that the traditional view is,

> an anti-intellectual approach to Christianity on the part of literal-minded, conservative Christians and a departure from the organized Christian church...[46]

He agrees with Barr and others that the conservative approach is naive. They do not think that it has kept up with the scientific age and Spong adds that the "few pseudoradical thinkers" who protect it will reduce Christianity to "one more ancient mythology that will take its place alongside the religions of Mount Olympus."[47]

Three popular reasons that liberals have offered for rejecting the traditional conservative view of the Bible, particularly the historicity, accuracy, and internal harmony of the Bible, have been, (1) contradictions "of known truth" as between the biblical account of particular historical events and secular records of those events, of such a nature that they could be considered mistakes on the part of the writers perhaps due to their pre-scientific understanding of things, (2) internal contradictions between biblical passages, and (3) morally questionable statements.[48] Reasons like these motivated S. R. Driver to say in 1897, "The price at which alone the traditional view can be maintained is too high."[49] Or, as Spong puts it, "A literal Bible presents me with far more problems than assets."[50]

Of course, a crucial question is how a person can recognize the contradictions. Principles must govern this procedure, including a proper definition of what constitutes a genuine contradiction.[51] For example, one should not simply look on the surface for merely apparent contradictions and jump to unwarranted conclusions because (as is true in life in general) sometimes apparent contradictions are only differences in word meanings, different settings, points of view, timing, different writers adding or leaving out details of the same event, translation problems, a lack of information on the part of the reader, or other matters that require thought and suspension of bias.[52] When conservatives respond in this manner, however, they are sometimes met with further allegations of "forcing" the biblical texts into strained explanations.[53] In reality, the truth sometimes sounds strained depending on the situation (as any police officer or parent of teenagers can attest). It should not be surprising that in a document as large, old, and multicultural as the Bible, this should happen occasionally.

Of course, there are also cases where,

> the biblical writers were not as accurate and precise as historians would be today. They give approximations, general identifications, and popular descriptions that those who

examine details may not always appreciate. However, when we discover the writer's main purpose and see how carefully he handles this, the failure to be preoccupied with minor details may then appear as an asset and not a liability.[54]

Judith Casanova and others add another reason to reject the traditional view. They say, "Nothing is infallible except God" and "To treat anything creaturely as infallible is to move dangerously close to idolatry, the worship of something that is creaturely."[55] First, just because God is infallible and something else is infallible, does not mean that the something else will be, must be, or is in danger of being idolized because it is infallible. There are always extremes, of course. Some people profane sacred things while others exalt the profane. But people's speculated reactions do not prove this point. Second, if God is infallible, it seems reasonable that he could deliver an infallible message even by the hands of otherwise fallible human beings. Is it impossible for an infallible God to deliver an infallible message to humanity? Third, if these authors take the position that there is anything at all in the Bible, any segment that is legitimately from God, it follows that someone could treat that particular section like an idol just as they think someone would treat an entire infallible book from God. Thus, there is nothing intrinsically wrong with thinking that God could produce an infallible book.

From that point, the argument could be filled in to show that it is reasonable to conclude that the Bible is such a book. Some begin with the internal characteristics of the Bible (like prophecy, harmony, practicality) and link that with external information (like early church history, transmission of the biblical text through history, comparison to other holy books, archaeology, science). Others begin with prior considerations. For example, if God exists, and if he created human beings, it makes sense that he would reveal himself to them.[56] If he revealed himself to human beings, it makes sense that it would be more than a purely subjective, one-person-at-a-time method of communication. Otherwise, although intuitional communication would benefit each person who received it, it would not be beneficial to others who had not received it. It could also be a constant source of division, since in a time when miracles (in the biblical sense) have ceased, there would be no objective means of establishing which person has received the genuine message from God.

However, if the communication were more objective in oral and/or written form, this would benefit both the reader/hearer and the people to whom the message could be passed along. If God's message were in an objective format as oral and/or written rather than wholly subjective, then it would be propositional. If it were propositional, then principles of critical thinking would apply to it. This means that conservatives believe that they can look at the Bible and apply rules of critical thinking and interpretation. By this, they can discover some basic principles about how God wants people to think about animal *telos* by carefully examining the Bible's statements about animals, the implications of those statements, and the appropriate biblical examples that relate to the same. There are dozens of monographs about evidences for the divine origin of the Bible. This paragraph just points to a couple of approaches.

Conclusion

Would it not be more reasonable to conclude that the Bible came about in almost any other way than to say that God is its ultimate author? Given the limitations of certain paradigms, yes it would be more reasonable. In such a case, the options listed earlier (precognition, etc.) might seem to be more reasonable explanations of the Bible phenomenon even though they stretch one's concept of mathematical probability. But given a certain set of reasonable presuppositions, a good case can be made than God exists, that God could and would communicate with humanity in a variety of media, and that God could and has seen to it that a book was written which is composed of a divine message to humanity. Therefore, it is not simple claims that should be accepted at face value, but good claims, as noted in Locke's discussion of revelation claims.

Thus, if the Bible is inspired of God in the traditional sense, that implies that it is God's very word, the standard of all that is good and evil. It has objective meaning and establishes an absolute point of reference for all of reality. Thus, we are obligated to love, study, and obey it.

[1] R. H. Mounce, "Bible," *Evangelical Dictionary of Theology Walter A. Elwell,* ed. (Grand Rapids: Baker Book House, 1984):136.

[2] Normal L. Geisler and William E., *A General Introduction to the Bible* (Chicago: Moody Press, 1986):29.

[3] For a list of several hundred of these, see A. Berkeley Mickelsen, *Interpreting the Bible* (Grand Rapids: Wm. B. Eerdmans Publishing Company, 1963):81-84.

[4] Colossians 2:14

[5] Romans 3:21-22, 28; 7:6; Galatians 3:15-29; Hebrews 8:1-13, et al.

[6] Ephesians 2:14-16; Galatians 3:26-28

[7] 1 Peter 1:10-12. Peter's writings contain many Old Testament references and quotes.

[8] Of course, for those who reject the traditional view of Scripture, there is the question of which/how many statements Jesus actually made and which were later supplied by the early church, copyists, redactors, storytellers, and others. For example, see Robert W. Funk, ed., and The Jesus Seminar, *The Acts of Jesus: The Search for the Authentic Deeds of Jesus* (San Francisco: HarperSanFrancisco, 1998).

[9] Matthew 15:4; 22:31-32; Mark 12:36; 13:24-27, et al.

[10] Matthew 26:31, 54; Mark 9:12-13; Luke 4:14-40; 24:44-47; John 13:18

[11] Matthew 22:31-32

[12] Rene Pache, *The Inspiration and Authority of Scripture* (Chicago: Moody Press, 1969):97.

[13] For example, see Acts 1:16; 4:25; 28:25; 1 Corinthians 2:10-13; Galatians 1:10-11; 1 Thessalonians 2:13; 2 Timothy 3:16-17; Hebrews 1:1-2; and 2 Peter 1:20-21.

[14] 2 Peter 3:15-17

[15] For example, see "The Epistle of Polycarp to the Philippians" and similar letters in which the writers make reference after reference and use quote after quote from New Testament gospels and epistles as early as late first century and early second century.

[16] See Geisler and Nix 99-112.

[17] Mounce 136.

[18] Joshua 8:35

[19] 2 Kings 22:8

[20] Romans 9-11; Hebrews 1-4

[21] Consider Brian S. Rosner, *"'Written for Us': Paul's View of Scripture,"* A Pathway into the Holy Scripture Philip Satterthwaite and David Wright, eds. (Grand Rapids: William B. Eerdmans Publishing Company, 1994):81-105. There are also a number of excellent responses to recent trends in how to think about Scripture as another article in A Pathway . . . where Kevin Vanhoozer addresses Karl Barth's "indirect identity" and James Barr's "non-identity" views in "God's Mighty Speech-Acts: The Doctrine of Scripture Today" 143-181.

[22] Mounce 136.

[23] *James Barr Fundamentalism* (Philadelphia: Westminster Press, 1978):264.

[24] See also, John D. Woodbridge, *Biblical Authority: A Critique of the Rogers/McKim Proposal* (Grand Rapids: Zondervan, 1982).

[25] Examples of this view can be found in: Barr, Fundamentalism 261ff.; and in Jack B. Rogers and Donald K. McKim, *The Authority and Interpretation of the Bible: An Historical Approach* (San Francisco: Harper & Row, 1979).

[26] This is true of the numerous claims by speakers and writers in both Testaments that their messages are from God, New Testament references to Old Testament inspiration, and New Testament references to people like Paul as having written authoritative literature (2 Peter 3:15-16).

[27] Alan Richardson, *A Preface to Bible Study* (Philadelphia: Westminster Press, 1944):33.

[28] Steven L. McKenzie and Stephen R. Haynes, *To Each Its Own Meaning* eds. (Louisville: Westminster/John Knox Press, 1993):30.

[29] Julius Wellhausen, *Prolegomena to the History of Ancient Israel* (New York: Meridian, 1957).

[30] Richardson 25.

[31] Gordon D. Kaufman, *"Doing Theology From a Liberal Christian Point of View"* in Woodbridge and McComiskey 410.

[32] See R. Douglas Geivett and Gary R. Habermas, eds., *In Defense of Miracles: A Comprehensive Case for God's Action in History* (Downer's Grove, Illinois: InterVarsity Press, 1997).

[33] John S. Spong, *Rescuing the Bible From Fundamentalism: A Bishop Rethinks the Meaning of Scripture* (San Francisco: Harper Collins, 1991):226.

[34] Donald E. Miller, *The Case for Liberal Christianity* (San Francisco: Harper & Row, 1981):36.

[35] Paul Copan, ed. *Will The Real Jesus Please Stand Up? A Debate Between William Lane Craig and John Dominic Crossan* (Grand Rapids: Baker Books, 1998):119.

[36] Luke 24

[37] John Dominic Crossan, *Jesus: A Revolutionary Biography* (San Francisco: Harper, 1994):197.

[38] Jarl Fossum, *"Understanding Jesus' Miracles," Bible Review,* 10:2 (April 1994):50.

[39] John Dominic Crossan, *Jesus: A Revolutionary Biography 95.*

[40] Barr, Fundamentalism 159.

[41] bid.

[42] J. P. Moreland and Kai Nielsen, *Does God Exist? The Great Debate* (Nashville: Thomas Nelson Publishers, 1990):60.

[43] Barr, *Beyond Fundamentalism* (Philadelphia: Westminster Press, 1984):174.

[44] For example, see W. M. Ramsay, *The Bearing of Recent Discovery On the Trustworthiness of the New Testament* (Grand Rapids: Baker Book House, 1953). For his background and change of mind, see especially pages 3-31.

[45] Barr, Fundamentalism 173.

[46] Spong 9.

[47] Spong 31-32.

[48] Paul J. Achtemeier, *The Inspiration of Scripture: Problems and Proposals* (Philadelphia: The Westminster Press, 1980):42.

[49] S. R. Driver, *An Introduction to the Literature of the O. T.* (New York: Meridian Books, 1956):viii.

[50] Spong 24.

[51] As suggested in texts like Bernard Ramm, *Protestant Biblical Interpretation* (Boston: Wilde, 1956):184-195.

[52] For examples of explanations for the most common allegations of contradictions and/or discrepancies in the Bible, see Gleason L. Archer, *Encyclopedia of Bible*

Difficulties (Grand Rapids: Zondervan Publishing House, 1982); George W. DeHoff, *Alleged Bible Contradictions Explained* (Murfreesboro, TN: DeHoff Publications, 1975); and John W. Haley, *An Examination of the Alleged Discrepancies of the Bible* (Nashville: B. C. Goodpasture, 1951).

[53] Books like Ruth Green's seem to do a lot of this. With a little consideration for the importance of context, many of her alleged contradictions would disappear. Ruth Hurmence Green, *The Born Again Skeptic's Guide to the Bible* (Madison, Wisconsin: Freedom From Religion Foundation, 1979). For lists of the more commonly alleged contradictions, see Barr Fundamentalism 40ff. and Spong 15ff.

[54] Mickleson, 93

[55] Judith Casanova, John B. Cobb, Jr., Lewis Ford, William Beardslee, and Joseph Deegan, *"What Can We Believe About the Bible?" in What's A Christian To Do?* David P. Polk, ed. (St. Louis: Center For Process Studies, 1991):18.

[56] The argument in the following paragraph comes from Ralph Gilmore and David Lipe, *"The First Principles of Hermeneutics"* in The Freed-Hardeman Lectures (Henderson, Tennessee: Freed-Hardeman University, 1986):153-160.

WHEN GOD IS SILENT

Russell L. Dyer, Tommy F. Haynes, & Jeff A. Jenkins

It is true. Silence can speak loud and clear. When I was a teenager my car broke down several miles out of town. I was able to catch a ride to my home and a couple of days later my father took time from his busy schedule to help me go get my car. When we were almost there I realized that I had failed to bring the keys and when I told dad he simply pulled into the next turn-off and headed back toward home. He didn't say one word to me the entire rest of the trip. He didn't yell or scream; he just didn't say a word. By his silence it was easy for me to ascertain how upset he was with me. We know how it feels to be given the "silent treatment." Whether one is angry, hurt, disappointed, or upset we know that silence speaks volumes.

For hundreds of years the debate about silence in the Word of God has raged on. When God's Word is silent about a given issue what does it mean? Is God's silence permissive or prohibitive? There are many things about which our Father has not spoken. God has not revealed everything to us, and it would be highly presumptuous for us to make lame attempts to pierce the silence of God. Several years ago brother Jimmy Jividen made this astute observation about the silence of the Scriptures.

> "The silence of the Scriptures may be understood in three ways: (1) Silence is sometimes the unrevealed will of God that a man cannot know and does not need to know. (2) Silence sometimes pertains to incidentals – the ways and means of doing something that is commanded in the Scriptures but about which details are not revealed. (3) Silence is sometimes exclusive. It would disallow anything beyond that which is clearly revealed." [1]

It is incumbent upon those of us who want to be diligent students of the Word of God to determine how silence is to be understood. The Apostle Paul reminded all of us that, *"All Scripture is given by inspiration of God, and is profitable for doctrine, for reproof, for correction, for instruction in righteousness, that the man of God may be complete, thoroughly equipped for every good work."* (2 Timothy 3:16-17) When we misunderstand silence it is not the fault of God's Word, it is our fault.

Often, our inability to understand the Word of God is because of our own stubbornness. For instance, when some man or church wants to incorporate some act or teaching into their worship that has no biblical authorization he says, "THE BIBLE DOES NOT SAY NOT TO DO IT." Because Scripture does not specifically prohibit the practice or teaching in question, some presume to know that this signifies God's approval. Among the many problems with this reasoning is it presumes to know the mind of God. Are we really at liberty to do anything we desire, so long as the Bible does not condemn it? Does the silence of God prohibit us from doing such? From a practical standpoint, God could not have included every prohibition in His Word, for we could not carry a copy if He did.

Restoration leaders, as well as Scripture itself reflected the importance of silence. In 1809 Thomas Campbell said, "We speak where the Bible speaks and remain silent where the Bible is silent." If the Bible is inspired we cannot ignore this adage that has been held dear throughout the history of the Church.

What Does the Bible Say About Silence? The Scriptures themselves affirm the restrictive force of their silence.

Biblical History Of Silence

Paul was very concerned about the restrictive nature of the scriptures. He wanted the Corinthian church to know how they should approach scripture. *"Now these things, brethren, I have figuratively transferred to myself and Apollos for your sakes, that you may learn in us not to think beyond what is written, that none of you may be puffed up on behalf of one against the other"* (1 Corinthians 4:6). However, the history of the silence issue in scripture does not reveal prohibition as the only view we should take. Silence is both prohibitive and permissive, depending on the particulars of the command involved.

Noah was to build an ark (Genesis 6:14-16). This command is restrictive in that God states some particulars. The ark is to be built of gopherwood, it was to have rooms, be pitched in and out, have a window, and a door, and was to be a certain length, height, and width. These requirements by God were not up for negotiation. When God fell silent on the particulars, there was no more to be said by Noah on the issue. However, Noah was going to have to use tools in the construction of this massive ship. God allowed Noah to use whatever tools he needed to accomplish his task. Noah preached to people while the ark was being prepared (2 Peter 2:5). So far as we know, God had not commanded him to do this. Noah was given freedom to do whatever was necessary within the parameters of righteousness to get the job done. Noah is a perfect example of obedience in this instance as the Bible states, *"And Noah did according to all that the Lord commanded him"* (Genesis 7:5). He did not go beyond what was said to him by God, and yet was not weighted down with worry about how to get it done.

Virtually all commands in the scriptures are both restrictive and permissive. Restrictive when God states specifically what He desires for us to do. Permissive in getting the task accomplished within the framework of righteous living (i.e. A man could not steal money to give to the work of Christ).

One of the most cited Bible events, when it comes to the issue of silence, concerns Aaron's sons, Nadab and Abihu. *"Then Nadab and Abihu, the sons of Aaron, each took his censer and put fire in it, put incense on it, and offered profane fire before the LORD, which He had not commanded them. So fire went out from the LORD and devoured them, and they died before the LORD"* (Leviticus 10:1-2). What was the Lord's issue with these two men? God had specifically commanded priests to kindle their fires for the incense in a certain way and from a certain place (Exodus 30:1-10). There was to be no offering except when God told them to make offerings. Apparently, Nadab and Abihu did not kindle the fire correctly, and may not have been told to kindle any fire at all! The literal translation of the word here is "strange" fire. The root of this word has to do with one who commits adultery, or turns aside from what he was to accomplish. These men kindled that which was foreign to the Lord's will. They paid the ultimate price for so doing.

Two more sad examples of those who spoke where God was silent are found in the writings of Samuel. Israel was in trouble with Philistia. They had not yet repented of the prevailing attitudes during the time of the judges when *"...everyone did what was right in his own eyes"* (Judges 21:25). This headstrong persuasion had lead Israel into frequent destructive tendencies. As Philistia began to again assert power over Israel, the people determined that if they brought out the Ark of the Covenant, they would certainly win. God was the only one who could tell the people when to move the ark (Joshua 3). God tells Joshua to carry the ark before the army in preparation to defeat Jericho (Joshua 6). God would also ask leaders of Israel to come before the ark as a place of consultation (Joshua 7:6,7). However, when faced with possible defeat by the Philistines, Israel presumptuously took the ark and carried it before them like a good-luck charm (1 Samuel 4:1-9). God defeated His own people for such presumption, and the ark is captured and taken away from them for a time. God had not spoken to them about using the ark in this way. King Saul was also guilty of viewing the silence of God as permissive. Saul gave sacrifices that had not been commanded at Gilgal. Not only did he sacrifice, he did it himself without the permission or accompaniment of a priest (1 Samuel 13:9,10). God had Samuel proclaim to Saul that the kingdom was now to be taken from him (1 Samuel 13:14). Viewing the scriptures solely as permissive when it comes to what God has commanded and not commanded has always yielded disaster.

Moving to the New Testament, one does not travel far before we realize that Jesus respected the silence of His Father. *"Most assuredly, I say to you, the Son can do nothing of Himself, but what He sees the Father do; for whatever He does, the Son also does in like manner. For the Father loves the Son, and shows Him all things that He Himself does; and He will show Him greater works than these, that you may marvel"* (John 5:19,20). Jesus Himself was sensitive to every word His Father had spoken. Jesus did not presume to go beyond God's word. In the face to face confrontation between Jesus and Satan, Satan took scripture out of context to tempt Jesus. Jesus answered with scripture, and in the first temptation said, *"Man shall not live by bread alone, but by every word that proceeds from the mouth of God"* (Matthew 4:4). This statement reflects honor toward what is stated, and respect for God's silence.

The epistles are filled with many commands and examples for our learning and application. We should use what we have learned from the examples in the Old Testament and by our Savior to realize both the restrictive and permissive nature of God's silence (Romans 15:4). When God has spoken directly to the things we are to do, we must do exactly what He has specifically told us. When it comes to getting the thing done, we are allowed to use the tools necessary to produce what God requires within the limits of righteousness.

When we develop this attitude, we will find a freedom of conscience that is not possible when we follow our own will. Habakkuk said, *"But the LORD is in His holy temple. Let all the earth keep silence before Him"* (Habakkuk 2:20). Respect for the authority of God's silence is a matter of humble attitude toward the sovereignty of God.

John recorded the words of Jesus as the Bible comes to a close. These very words imply the respect we should maintain toward the silence of scriptures. *"For I testify to everyone who hears the words of the prophecy of this book: If anyone adds to these things, God will add to him the plagues that are written in this book; and if anyone takes away from the words of the book of this prophecy, God shall take away his part from the Book of Life, from the holy city, and from the things which are written in this book"* (Revelation 22:18-19).

Put the Principle of Silence to Work

Children often have a grasp of the devious while maintaining an appearance of naiveté. Consider a common situation. Siblings have been given a specific job by their mother. As they debate the fairness of the work they are to do, and bemoan the fact that they cannot do whatever it was that they wanted to do, they conspire. One of the siblings grabs enough fortitude of desperation that a plot is designed and expressed. "Mom said that we cannot do this, but she did not say that we cannot do that. She can't get mad at us for doing what she did not tell us that she did not want us to do. After all, we are only children." The logic is adorable, and at the same time dishonest. Those of us who have been children and have used that logic know the truth. Trouble is the result. Accountability is held. Hopefully a lesson is learned.

The dynamics involved in an interpretation and especially the application of silence can be complex. As has already been stated, there are times that silence is prohibitive, and there are times that silence is permissive. What is said, and the context in which it is said determines the meaning of what is not said. Knowing the source of information is an absolute necessity. For it is in knowing the character of the authority that we begin to grasp how to appropriately apply the information that is clearly given, as well as what is not so specifically stated. The consistency of application is tied to a consistency of character. When the nature of God is more clearly discerned there is a far greater propensity to properly apply His desires. Silence will always be consistent with what is specifically stated.

There has been a lot of information disseminated regarding general human behavior as it relates to brain side control. It is not really fair to limit all of the study of such things to a few token statements, but I will. Left-brained people are typically controlled, detail oriented, structured, and results based. Right-brained people are more free spirited, unstructured, artistic, and flowing. These patterns of behavior often affect how we try to interpret and apply what God has stated, and the things that he has not specifically stated.

The confluence of silence from permissiveness and restriction is never more obvious to the inquirer than it is when it is applied to the character and exacting details of doctrine. For what is taught is governed by the principle of applied knowledge. Even theory is given with the character of a limited application. Thus a specified body of teaching or doctrine carries with it expectations of application that call for an understanding of how what is stated affects what is not stated.

The ongoing debate concerning the implications of the Constitution of the United States is a pointed application of the principle of silence. For the question of intent is at the heart of the debate. The prescription preventing the "state" from establishing a "church" has been discussed with increasing vigor. There are those who take the wording and seek to apply it as a limitation of governmental power over religious practice. Others have seen in it the opportunity to remove any hint of religious matters from anything to related to governmental practices. It could be that both arguments miss the point. For it is more what is not said than what is said. We can understand and agree that the government is not to establish a state religion. Where implication becomes application it turns to debate an intention that has not been stated in words. We can only look to the nature of our ancestors, who wrote and ratified the language into law to determine the larger scale of application in the general society. Still, it is the context of an open and free society into which the application is made. Telling such a society what it cannot do, will always be met with debate, protest, and even revolt.

Applying Silence to the Common Activities of the Church

Where there is silence from God, He has already spoken. Silence is marked and recognizable because of existent and obvious expression made by God. Considering the stated nature of silence, it can readily be inferred that any command or teaching example in the Bible will be contrasted against a background of silence. Limited space makes it impossible to address every point. Considering a few instructional commands and examples as they are applied should suffice to give at least some showing of the practical and necessary use of silence.

The Great Commission

Jesus gave the command: *"Go into all the world and preach the gospel to every creature. He who believes and is baptized will be saved; but he who does not believe will be condemned"* (Mark 16:15-16). We often refer to this passage as "The Great Commission." It appears to be an encompassing command. Notice that Jesus includes the entire world, leaving no place to be excused. He further involved all people in the phrase "every creature." There is a definite message that is to be preached or taught. That message is the gospel. Activities on the part of the recipients are stated and connected to salvation or condemnation. The command is simple, direct and marked with silence.

Within the command of the "Great Commission" there is prohibitive silence. For there is no audible or graphically recorded statement here that claims no other message can be used. There is simply the command to go and this message to obey. There would be no purpose in the command or the message if salvation could be attained in some other way. *"Nor is there salvation in any other, for there is no other name under heaven given among men by which we must be saved"* (Acts 4:12). That no other way is mentioned at this point does not open the door to multiple choice salvation. A mode is stated. Belief and baptism are the given mode of obtaining the desired salvation. An unwillingness to believe is tied to condemnation. There is no reason to state that other methods or designs will be futile. The clearly stated principle is complete within itself. What is not stated is prohibitive by the nature of what is stated.

There is also some silence in this commission that is permissive. It is in the area of incidentals. There is no description of exactly how to go, or how the message is to be preached. There are open areas of silence that allow judgement to be used. Still, such judgement must be consistent with the message. They could walk, ride, or sail (or even a combination of all of these) to many places. No method of travel is mentioned. They could personally visit or send letters to proclaim the gospel. There are means of communication and travel that are available in this age that were not even a possibility of thought in the first century or for many centuries thereafter. Whether it is taken and preached by personal travel, bounced off a satellite in digital format, short (or long) wave radio, email, or any other of multiple means of communication is of open possibility. The silence here allows freedom to work in consistency with the specific of the command to go and preach the gospel.

Worship Assemblies

The church is to assemble with specific purposes. The activities of assemblies for worship are taught by command and example. We are to be "speaking to one another in psalms and hymns and spiritual songs, singing and making melody in your heart to the Lord," (Ephesians 5:19). We are to "break bread" (Acts 20:7), or "eat the Lord's Supper" (1 Corinthians 11:20). There is teaching in the worship assembly (Acts 20:7). Collections to apply to the works of the church are a part of the worship (1 Corinthians 16:2). Prayers are also to take place in the assemblies of the church (1 Timothy 2:1, 8). Each of these passages denotes an activity that can be done under the authority of scripture.

There is silence in several points. Where, when (other than the day of the week), how we are to assemble is not stated. There are Bible examples of meetings in homes, outdoors, and even in the Jewish temple. Through the years, the church has assembled in every sort of structure or non-structure imaginable. Sitting or standing is not mentioned. The order of activities is not listed. Details that flow from the main principles are not given. There must be some latitude in these areas, and thus make such silence permissive.

These areas of silence become prohibitive as they relate to the nature of the things that are stated. Singing cannot become whistling. The Lord's Supper cannot become the turkey and dressing meal of the Thanksgiving holiday. I read a statement from my father the other day. He said,

> "If we bring an instrument of music in, we have another kind of music. Like I stated a little while ago, if we have little bits of lamb on the plate we have another kind of food. We might use silver trays or a china dish or we might use a tree stump for the table instead of this nice oak table. That wouldn't change the food on the table at all. We would still have the bread and the fruit of the vine. But if you start putting jelly on the bread or you start putting lamb on the plate with the bread you are bringing in different elements. Now do you see the difference? When you bring an instrument you are bringing in another kind of music. Just like the lamb's meat on the table would be another kind of food. The only two foods authorized for the Lord's Supper are the bread and the fruit of the vine. The only kind of music authorized in the word of God, for God's praise in worship today is vocal music. That means that the music that is made with your mouth and your vocal chords. That is the only kind of music that is authorized." (Hershel L. Dyer – Sermon: Instrumental Music)

When it comes to music in the New Testament church, we would naturally go to the examples and commands for the New Testament church. The Holy Spirit reveals that we are to be *"...singing and making melody in your heart to the Lord"* (Ephesians 5:19). The scriptures specify singing and making melody, but nothing else is specified. The tools necessary to be able to sing might include a song leader, a tuning fork or pitch pipe, perhaps a sound system, a song book or overhead projection. It would not, however, include an instrument of music, for such would alter to the nature and character. An instrument is not a tool to assist singing; it is an addition to the singing. God's Word is silent on the church ever having used instruments in worship. This would hold true for adding anything to the Lord's supper other than fruit of the vine and unleavened bread. These are the specifics. The silence here would allow the use of a tray, men to pass the emblems, etc. We could not, however, add sweet tea and pretzels to the supper. This is also the case with the use of our women in active leadership in worship. The Bible is silent on this subject. The examples and commands lead us the specific direction of male spiritual leadership (1 Corinthians 14:34, 1 Timothy 2:11,12). These are not cultural statements, for no command would be associated with them if they were. God has been very specific about what He wants us to do. We must respect, honor, and obey the silence of the Lord.

Making Good Judgments

The question of silence is the question of how we determine the authority of God as we apply it to the things we do. More consideration may be given to the collective applications for the church, but it is just as important to an individual life. Either God has full authority or He has no authority at all. If we submit to His authority, the application of silence is at issue. Our relationships to our spouses are given in principle, command, and example. We are told that our children are to be trained and developed in the *"nurture and admonition of the Lord."* As citizens and workers we have commands to be conscientious. The exacting details of how to do these, and other obligations, are not stated. We are left with some latitude to apply actions that are consistent with the stated commands and principles.

Making scripture based judgements regarding actions, as Christians, is not always easy. Our personal inclinations may run contrary to the demand of consistency. There may be pressure from generational peers to be like them. Frankly, it is easy to recognize the commands and know the exacting boundary of what is stated, but the challenge of the unstated things is a bit more complex. We have the opportunity to choose from an array of possibilities. The silence may then be permissive and prohibitive at the same time. For the possibilities of choice, though varied, must remain consistent with what has been stated.

Some will declare that the door of liberality was opened when the Lord did not expressly state that something could not be done. Arguments of this nature have been most noticeable in the areas of worship activities. Again, it is the matter of how we recognize the authority of God and scripture that determines the application. A rebellious child may immaturely excuse behavior by claiming that a parent or authority did not expressly forbid the activity. The wise and mature person grasps not only for the "letter of the law", but also for the spirit of it. Seeking the desire of God and submitting to his recognizable authority, will cause us to find the limitations placed within silence. That God *"cannot lie"* (Titus 1:2), means that He cannot be untrue or inconsistent to Himself. Application of actions derived from His Word cannot be inconsistent to that Word.

Jesus stated, *"He who believes and is baptized will be saved"* (Mark 16:16). Some might want to place other things in the place of baptism. The logic may be that since he did not say that other methods would not save. It may be a little like defusing a bomb. The expert may have explained, "The bomb will be defused when you cut the green wire and then the black wire." The expert did not say that another way would not work. It was just stated that this is the way that works. If another approach is being used, it might be good to stand at a safe distance. Faith in Jesus Christ that is expressed and confessed in baptism is the action to take for the remission of sins and the promise of eternal life.

Theories can be batted from one pattern of logic to another. The thought processes and discussions may be enjoyable. When push comes to shove, and something of value is at stake, there is no room for unsubstantiable ideas. The applications of silence made in the actions of the church and by individual Christians must always derive authority from what is clearly stated in commands or revealed in examples.

Conclusion

God's method of revealing His message to us in our day is the New Testament (Hebrews 1:1-2). We can only know the Truth that will set men free by reading God's revelation. Jesus was very clear when He said, *"Sanctify them by Your Truth. Your Word is Truth."* (John 17:17) The only way for us maintain the purity of Christianity is for people everywhere to return to the guidelines of the New Testament authority. That can be done only when the principle of the "silence" of the Scriptures is revered.

We conclude this chapter with these comments made several years ago by Winford Claiborne when he spoke on this vital topic,

> "Millions of honest people have not even thought about the silence of the scriptures. They have accepted whatever their churches do without any thought of their scripturalness. I am not for one moment questioning anyone's honesty. I am asking

you to think seriously about the topic...Compare what your church does with what the Scriptures teach. If you find your church to have introduced into its worship some practice without any scriptural authority, I plead with you to use your voice in opposing it. You need to realize that not just church leaders – but all church members will have to give an account in the day of judgment. Will you please study these matters openly and honestly?"

[1] Jimmy Jividen, *"The Bible Doctrine of Silence"*, Gospel Advocate, January, 1996 (Nashville: Gospel Advocate) 1996, p. 12

Wrestling With Our History

Chuck Monan

> Our culture is in that recurrent phase when, for good reasons, many feel the urge to build a wall against the past. It is a revulsion from things in the present that seem a curse from our forebears. Others attack or ignore selected periods in this latter mood, national, religious, or cultural ancestry becomes a matter of choice; people who feel the need to "dig for roots" wherever they fancy. The storehouse of traditions and creeds offers an over-abundance, because the culture is old and unraveling.
> ~Jacques Barzun, *From Dawn to Decadence*

If you didn't know better you might think that Barzun has been reading our mail. Churches of Christ are going through a great struggle in coming to terms with their history. Some have seen the Restoration Movement as successful in restoring the one true church. Others claim it has only produced three more denominations. Some find satisfaction in the numerous positive contributions of reformers like the Campbells, Stone and Scott. Others maintain that the only heritage these left is hopelessly flawed and negative, which continues to be an albatross to us today. Some point to Churches of Christ having more right about them than wrong. Others seemingly find very little good and a myriad of bad in today's church. Some see a bright future, others forecast only doom and gloom.

So which is it? As you might imagine, the question is a bit more complicated than that. For a variety of reasons, though, let me state at the outset that my assessment is that the former view is more compelling than the latter. This is not to say that we have perfectly restored or modeled what was in the mind of God before the world was created. Any organization comprised of people is destined to be imperfect. Our failings have been legion. Our flaws have been obvious. Our lack of fervor and commitment has borne witness against us. But the effort to restore the ancient order of things has not been entirely in vain. A wise person notes that the anecdote to feel-good history is not feel-bad history but honest and inclusive history. In the remainder of this chapter this is my goal in offering up a brief analysis of our past.

Some Alleged Problems

A frequent charge made by many critics today is that Churches of Christ have been both ignorant and dismissive of the ebb and flow of religious history, and the subsequent contributions others have made to what and where we are today. They maintain that this view sees our development as taking place in a vacuum, immune from all forces and influences that might have tainted us. It has been disdainfully expressed as the belief that there was originally this perfect church, and then it disappeared, only to appear again a couple of hundred years ago. And while there are some simple enough to believe such a notion, to project such provincialism on all of us is inaccurate and irresponsible.

If the discussion of our strengths and weaknesses is to be credible it must begin with the person who influenced the American Restoration Movement more than any other: Alexander Campbell. If current critics are correct, and churches of Christ have been warped by Campbell's flawed hermeneutical approach, it must be accepted that this approach sprang from his own disdain of history. For even as Campbell endeavored to read the Bible "as if for the first time," he did not ignore the towering contributions of countless ones who had gone before. His attempt to produce a fresh hearing of the biblical text apart from domination by traditional dogma should not be equated with condescension toward the work of other reformers. He recognized that he was not the first to suggest reform or restoration. All of us are influenced by a variety of factors, and Campbell was no different.

Those familiar with Campbell's writing in *The Christian Baptist* and the *Millennial Harbinger* will recognize his obvious familiarity with issues, arguments, controversies and personalities that shaped religious discourse from ancient times to his own day. This knowledgeable appreciation was especially evident in Campbell's many debates. In his contest with skeptic Robert Owen, Campbell made a brilliant twelve-hour speech defending Christianity. Of this speech Campbell biographer Robert Richardson said, "For cogency of argument, comprehensive reach of thought and eloquence, it has never been surpassed, if ever equaled." Debate moderator Jacob Burnet, a member of the Ohio Supreme Court, observed: "I have been listening to a man who seems as one who had lived in all ages." This hardly sounds like a man ignorant and/or dismissive of religious history. Further evidence of Campbell's admiration of previous reformers is seen in the naming of his son, Wycliffe, in honor of the great English reformer John Wycliffe. Sir Isaac Newton, whom Campbell greatly admired, said, "If I have seen further than Descartes, it is because I have stood on the shoulders of giants." There is every reason to believe that Campbell felt the same way concerning his contributions to biblical issues.

Campbell also receives the lion's share of the blame for our hermeneutical underpinnings. They are blasted for being poisoned by Baconian inductivism and Scottish common sense realism. The alleged problem with this method is that it reduces the Bible into an inert object that we can study empirically, thus easily pulling out its clear and obvious meaning. There are several errors in this charge.

First, it fails to appreciate the rather deplorable state of exegesis and interpretation among many of Campbell's contemporaries. The famed Cane

Ridge Camp meeting of 1801 is a vivid illustration under the direction (or lack thereof) of Baptist, Methodist and Presbyterian preachers, folks were behaving in all manner of bizarre ways. Falling, jerking, dancing, barking and laughing uncontrollably were but a few of the supposed proofs of conversion by the Holy Spirit. This doggerel captured the feeling of the time about salvation:

If you seek it,
 you can't find it.
If you find it,
 you can't lose it.
If you lose it,
 you never had it.

In such a confused atmosphere Campbell's premise that God was not the author of confusion was a needed corrective. He maintained that faith involved a decision based on evidence, and was therefore distinguishable from the chaotic, mystical happenings at Cane Ridge.

Second, even the more thoughtful examiners of Scripture made no distinction between the Old and New Testaments. Campbell's Sermon on the Law in 1816 clarified that Christians look to the New Testament as their source of authority. Scholars have noted that he seems to have been influenced by the Glas-Sandeman churches in Scotland on this point, but no one would be more associated with this approach than Campbell. Charges that churches of Christ ignore the Old Testament date back to this sermon, even though they are inaccurate.

Third, Campbell's method of interpreting Scripture – which has greatly influenced churches of Christ to the present – is much sounder, more balanced and responsible than most modern critics concede. Those who assail our supposedly flawed Campbellian interpretive approach seem to forget how Campbell's hermeneutic was (and is) worthy of emulation. Few, if any, relevant considerations necessary for accurate interpretation are ignored. He set forth his principles of interpretation in *Christianity Restored:*

Rule 1. On opening any book in the sacred Scriptures, consider first the historical circumstances of the book. These are the order, the title, the author, the date, the place, and the occasion of it…

Rule 2. In examining the contents of any book, as respects precepts, promises, exhortations, etc., observe who it is that speaks, and under what dispensation he officiates.

Rule 3. To understand the meaning of what is

commanded, promised, taught, etc., the same philological principles, deduced from the nature of language; or the same laws of interpretation which are applied to the language of other books, are to be applied to the language of the Bible.

Rule 4. Common usage, which can only be ascertained by testimony, must always decide the meaning of any word which has but one signification…

Rule 5. In all tropical language, ascertain the point of resemblance, and judge of the nature of the trope, and its kind, from the point of resemblance.

Rule 6. In the interpretation of symbols, types, allegories, and parables, this rule is supreme: ascertain the point to be illustrated; for comparison is never to be extended beyond that point – to all the attributes, qualities, or circumstances of the symbol, type, allegory, or parable.

Rule 7. For the salutary and sanctifying intelligence of the Oracles of God, the following rule is indispensable: *We must come within the understanding distance.*

There is a distance which is properly called the speaking distance, or the hearing distance; beyond which the voice reaches not, and the ears hear not. To hear another, we must come within that circle which the voice audibly fills.

Now we may with propriety say, that as it respects God, there is an understanding distance. All beyond that distance cannot understand God; all within it, can easily understand him in all matters of piety and morality. God himself, is the center of that circle, and humility is its circumference *(CR 3-5)*

Even a critical observer like Disciples of Christ scholar M. Eugene Boring acknowledges that criticism of Campbell's objective, mechanical style of interpretation is lacking in fairness. In his book *Disciples and the Bible* he writes,

> …(T)his was not the only dimension. His climatic "Rule 7" should not be overlooked. Here, the supposed objectivity of interpretation and the tendency to make the Bible into an object

> is overcome, and the living word of the Bible is appropriated as direct personal address from God, dependent on the receptivity and humility of the reader. Campbell's insistence on the public, objective nature of biblical interpretation is not to be contrasted with personal existential appropriation, but with clerical presumption which supposes that only an initiated elite can interpret the Bible's "mystical" non-obvious meaning. Campbell's method of interpretation was both populist and personal. (p.87).

Understanding these thoughts is important because much of the debate today in churches of Christ centers on the issue of hermeneutics. Critics claim our "method" (as if a body with no hierarchy or headquarters could ever succeed in mandating a rigidly uniform style on autonomous congregations) has led us into the theological wilderness. But when pressed for examples of specific errors induced by our hermeneutic, they hem and haw in their attempts to provide such. Has our hermeneutic led to wrong positions on the nature of the church? Its organization and governance? God's plan of salvation? The nature, form and function of true worship? The Christian's manner of life? When these and other subjects arise, the charges by the critics fall flat.

The Mainstream of Biblical Thought

No intelligent observer would deny that there is much room for improvement in churches of Christ. At the same time, and almost without exception, our shortcomings are due to causes like worldliness, greed, and lukewarmness more than an flawed interpretive process. Blaming Francis Bacon and John Locke for our problems would be laughable if it weren't so pitiful. Whatever axe the nattering nabobs of negativism have to grind, even they should be able to see that, ignorant pockets of blatant sectarianism aside, we have been in the mainstream of both biblical interpretation and historical opinion.

Take the subject of baptism as an example. The development of "mourner's bench" religion has blossomed into salvation by belief alone. Teaching that remission comes simply by accepting Jesus "into your heart" runs counter to the teaching of Scripture as well as centuries of church history. Careful exegetes have known that marginalizing the significance of baptism in conversion cannot be harmonized with either. While virtually every denomination has capitulated to popular opinion, churches of Christ have refused to retreat from the insistence that the Bible teaches baptism to be the line of demarcation between the old life of sin and the new life of salvation. Increasingly there are stirrings among some denominationalists that the importance of baptism needs to be emphasized again. In his book *Paul's Idea of Community*, Fuller Theological Seminary professor Robert Banks notes:

> What does water baptism signify? Paul does not regard it as a solely symbolic action or as an inexplicably magical one. It is not an outward representation of an already concluded inner decision, i.e., God's covenantal election of the person involved and the latter's individual commitment to God (Acts 16:33-34). Nor is it the mechanism by which God's benefits are automatically guaranteed to whoever undergoes it. Paul's linking of faith with baptism suggests that it was by means of baptism that the individual or family actually committed themselves to God. It is precisely because the believer is a physical being, and because God's relations with him or her take place within a physical environment, that the whole person (not merely inner self) and water (an element of God's material creation) are involved. Baptism, therefore, is a genuinely dynamic affair. Through it a person becomes an individual in the full sense for the first time – by becoming aware of their own true position vis-à-vis God and being drawn into intimate relationship with God.

It would be ironic and tragic for brethren to abandon the teaching that baptism is essential to salvation just when others are beginning to return to the Bible's position.

Another illustration is seen in the area of church organization. The Henderson Hills Baptist Church in Edmond, Oklahoma, is one of the fastest-growing churches both in that city and among Baptists in America. They recently appointed elders. This is a significant addition, given their pastor-driven structure. They did so, because they realized that the New Testament taught a pattern they weren't following so they decided to attempt to return to the Bible's teaching – just as churches of Christ have overwhelmingly done in having elders/shepherds pastor the flock.

Still another example might be taken from our aversion to instrumental music in worship. Campbell said,

> ...that all persons who have no spiritual discernment, taste or relish for spiritual meditations, consolations, and sympathies of renewed hearts, should call for such aid is natural...so to those who have no real devotion or spirituality in them, and whose animal nature flags under the oppression of church service, I think that instrumental music would be only a desideratum, but an essential prerequisite to fire up their souls to even animal devotion. But I presume to all spiritually-minded Christians such aids would be as a cow-bell in a concert.

There are members among us who have determined that the absence of the instrument is but another peculiarity bequeathed to us by Campbell's flawed hermeneutic. They would be wrong. Campbell's conclusion that *a cappella* singing was the practice of the early church is corroborated by history, authorized by the New Testament, and is in agreement with the views of religious leaders such as Thomas Aquinas, John Calvin, Huldreich Zwingli and Charles Spurgeon. It should be noted that at least a couple of these people predate Francis Bacon and John Locke. Without elevating this issue to the importance of the deity of Christ, it should be noted that our understanding and practice here occupies safe, responsible ground on three levels: biblical, historical, and practical. Noted scholar Everett Ferguson expresses why:

> There never would've been a sermon preached against instrumental music if no one had ever advocated introducing it into the assembly. To make out the opponents of instrumental music as the bad guys is to fail to understand history. The Restoration Movement was unified on the subjects of music and activities in the assembly until the instrument was introduced; to accuse opponents of instrumental music of being divisive is to ignore the united common practice in the first place. Actually, the *a cappella* practice is the ecumenical common ground – nearly anyone will say that unaccompanied singing is acceptable. The criticism of us concerns our insistence on the exclusive use of vocal singing; but a unity movement should not abandon the common ground. This position is agreed to be biblical and to have historical precedent behind it. If something is right, it cannot be wrong to teach and practice. The advocates of the instrument still have to make a case for their position.

A Fundamental Debate

One of the most-discussed issues in Churches of Christ today is the role of grace in salvation. Going back to the famed "five-finger exercise" of Walter Scott on the Western Reserve, a hallmark teaching among us has been the *ordu salutis* or plan of salvation. Boring describes Scott's contribution to this subject:

> According to an anecdote (legend?) prominent in Disciples history, when Scott entered a new town on his evangelistic tours, he promoted the evening preaching services by engaging children on their way home from school and teaching them the "steps of salvation" as faith/repentance/baptism/remission of

sins/gift of the Holy Spirit and promise of eternal life. The final two "steps" were combined in order to fit the fingers of one hand, for in reality there were six steps: three that human beings were to take and three that God would take in response. While Scott begins with the steps that human beings must take, he assumes that these three steps are in response to the divine initiative of sending Christ and confronting human beings with the gospel. Thus, Scott's schema retains the divine initiative despite its appearance of making God's act a response to human "steps." This "plan of salvation" was in stark contrast to the understanding that prevailed in his context, according to which human beings could do nothing for their own salvation, until the work of the Holy Spirit generated faith and repentance in their lives and made them know that they were among God's elect.
~ *Disciples and the Bible, p.41.*

It is worth noting the results produced over the years by the path chosen by the Disciples of Christ. Boring comments, "There is something tragic about the way contemporary Disciples have neglected their traditions at this point, making us more tongue-tied when it comes to explaining what it means to become a Christian, and consequently one of the factors in our tendency to avoid evangelism altogether. Without diminishing our emphasis on the primacy of the love and grace of God, we need a practical, sane, biblical way to respond to the question, 'What must I do?'" Whatever our failings, we can be thankful we haven't sunk to such a low point.

Accusations that we have made salvation a matter of slavishly following a prescribed checklist have been launched against restorationists since Campbell's time. He even included one of their doggerels in the August 1831 *Millennial Harbinger:*

"Though your sins be black as jet,
Never mind to mourn or fret –
Come to me, no longer dream,
I will plunge you in the stream,
Up you'll come in garments white,
Holy as a saint of light,
Come to me each son and daughter,
Here's the gospel in the water."

Those articulating this view have never successfully explained why baptism is a "work" while belief, repentance and confession are not. For most of us it is repentance – the process of "changing our minds" – that is the most difficult work of all. It demands that we bend our will to the Lord's, a process that takes a lifetime.

Teaching what the Bible teaches about baptism in no way nullifies the value of grace. The Bible's emphatic position that salvation is by grace through faith is unassailable. Few have improved on Campbell's understanding of this great truth:

> Grace is favor, and not right or obligation, and, therefore, all grace is free, unmerited favor. If we spoke of sovereign grace we should imply that there was a grace not free and sovereign, and of such grace I cannot form a single conception.... We are saved by grace, from its alpha to its omega, and anyone who sins that grace may abound is as self-deceived as any pagan in the world. Grace is the most active, operative, working principle in the universe.
> - *Millennial Harbinger,* September 1850

If we had a dollar for every time we hear that churches of Christ have never preached grace or that "the only thing I learned about grace in the church is that you could fall from it," we'd all be rich. Is such an accusation true? For some preachers and congregations, perhaps. A blanket indictment of everyone, though, seems harsh and unfair. Campbell unequivocally states that, "Grace is the most active, operative, working principle in the universe." Yet some would have us believe that during the last two hundred years that it was only when K.C. Moser and Jimmy Allen started writing, teaching and preaching that grace was discovered to Churches of Christ. Propagating such ideas is to engage in boldly unsupportable exaggeration or caricature, and ought to stop.

Some Actual Weaknesses

Robert Burns wrote, "Oh wad some power the giftie gie us, to see oursel's as others see us!" If we had the ability to see ourselves as others see us we would notice a few areas where we have been lacking.

One weakness has been the way we have too often isolated ourselves from others in Christendom. Without compromising biblical doctrines there have been numerous opportunities for friendship with those outside of churches of Christ that have been neglected. Most of our religious friends would likely characterize us as isolated and aloof. It was said of Campbell that no other person ever made such inroads into denominations. And this was not accomplished by treating others as if they were unclean. LeRoy Garrett describes how Campbell was able to wield such influence.

> His wide circuits placed him among the high and the lowly, whether in homes, churches, schools, courthouses, legislative halls, sails, or conventions of sundry types, and such contacts helped his cause to "struggle into life," as he once put it.
> - *Stone-Campbell Movement,* p. 356

Admittedly, Campbell's brilliance and position as the most recognizable religious leader in America opened some doors that may prove difficult for us to replicate. We may not preach before Congress or to the President, or have Henry Clay moderate one of our debates. We can still improve our accessibility and affability, increasing our level of contact with those outside churches of Christ. On the occasion of opening a new building in York, Nebraska, on May 19, 1957, Roy H. Lanier, Sr. stated, "...the church of the Lord seeks to join hands with all the other moral forces in the community to oppose all that tends to lower the moral standards of the community." A generation later, we still have much room for improvement in this area.

Another albatross in our history is found in the area of race relations. The rise of the Restoration Movement in America coincided with the institution of slavery moving from a "peculiar institution" to a supposed force for moral good to the wedge that would rend asunder the Union. Most of the reformers were godly, balanced men whose actions mirrored their beliefs. Thomas Campbell, for instance, moved from Kentucky when he was forbidden by law to teach a slave to read. Alexander Campbell freed the slaves he inherited from his father-in-law, John Brown. In 1829 he worked with the Virginia Constitutional Convention in an attempt to end slavery there. Setting aside these and other examples, churches of Christ would mirror the United States in struggling with the racial question for the next century.

David Lipscomb was outspoken in his belief that Christianity demanded that the hand of brotherhood be extended to former slaves and their descendants. He understood that what course the nation – and the church – took in the aftermath of the Civil War was largely the responsibility of white people, Southerners in particular. He wrote,

> ...The Negroes are here helpless and ignorant, perishing for lack of proper care and attention to their comfort. We have been their lifelong associates, have played with them in childhood, toiled side by side with them in manhood, have provided for their wants in common with our own, have regarded them as members of our own households, have nursed them in sickness, have followed their relatives as they ours, to the same burial ground, have wept around the same grave, have attended together the same meetings, sang the same songs, sat

around the same communion table of our common Lord, and looked forward to one common hope of rest in the same blessed Heaven, and shall we suffer ourselves to be alienated from them or them from us for no act of theirs or ours?

Lipscomb's view was not shared by the majority. Blatant Jim Crow discrimination, segregation and marginalization became a way of life in the South. Things were only slightly better in the North. At a time when Christians had a golden opportunity to be counter-cultural, most were content to observe the status quo. In his book *A Distant People* historian Robert Hooper relates an exchange between Foy E. Wallace, Jr. and Marshall Keeble that took place in Wallace's *Bible Banner* paper. A Wallace editorial expressed dismay at whites attending black meetings, with Keeble obviously the target:

> The manner in which the brethren in some quarters are going in for the negro meetings leads one to wonder whether they are trying to make white folks out of Negroes or negroes out of the white folks. The trend of the general mix-up seems to be toward the latter. Reliable reports have come to me of white women, members of the church, becoming so animated over a certain colored preacher as to go up to him after a sermon and shake hands with him holding his hand in both of theirs. That kind of thing will turn the head of most white preachers, and sometimes affect their conduct, and anybody ought to know that it will make fools out of the negroes.
> I am very much in favor of negro meetings for the negroes, but I am just as much opposed to negro meetings for white people, and I am against white brethren taking the meetings away from the negroes and the general mixing that has become entirely too much of a practice in the negro meetings.

One month later, Wallace published a letter from Marshall Keeble:

> Dear Sir and Brother in Christ:
> For over thirty years I have tried to conduct my work just as your article in the *Bible Banner* of March suggested. Taking advice from such friends as you have been for years has been a blessing to my work. So I take the privilege to thank you for that instructive and encouraging article. I hope I can conduct myself in my last days so that you and none of my friends will have to take back nothing they have said complimentary about my work or regret it.

Please continue to encourage me in my work and *pray for me.*
Fraternally yours,
M. Keeble

It is impossible not to feel ashamed that important leaders (and no doubt a significant number of members) in churches of Christ thought and behaved in such a way. Apologists can excuse this attitude but it does not change the fact that it is antithetical to the teachings of Scripture. This kind of racism, both covert as well as overt, was responsible for our colleges remaining segregated. Stating, "that's just how things were" does not excuse the church for its actions during this time. The fallout from this failing continues to be felt in Churches of Christ which remain largely segregated along color lines to the present. Who among us would argue that two churches – one white, one black – is God's plan for his people?

Yet another weakness is the tendency we have had to imagine that every doctrinal issue is of equal importance. Most of us are too familiar with our fractured status. We are so divided that there is a key in Mac Lynn's *Churches of Christ in the United States* in order to determine whether we are Mutual Edification, One Cup, Non-Institutional, etc. It strains the bounds of credulity to believe that such issues are worth causing and perpetuating division. It should be noted that these disagreements originate in our high view of Scripture. This view is not a weakness, but a strength. The weakness has been in our occasional inability or unwillingness to distinguish between law and expediency. Sometimes our own ignorance and pride have fueled regrettable partings. Barton W. Stone and his brethren resolved, "We will, that preachers and people, cultivate a spirit of mutual forbearance; pray more and dispute less; and while they behold the signs of the times, look up, and confidently expect that redemption draweth nigh." *(The Last Will and Testament of the Springfield Presbytery)*. All of us could do with a little more of this spirit. A movement to unite Christians works much better when the ones calling for unity don't divide at the drop of a hat.

Conclusion

The premise of restoration is not flawed, unnecessary, or hopeless, but eminently biblical. As far back as Jeremiah's time the call was sounded:

> This is what the Lord says: *"stand at the crossroads and look; ask for the ancient paths, ask where the good way is, and walk in it, and you will find rest for your souls." (Jeremiah 6:16)*

The very next line is significant: *"But you said, 'We will not walk in it.'"* We must be sure to understand that the refusal of many to walk in the old paths does not negate the principle of restoration itself. The theme of returning to God and forsaking our own ways is a needed corrective every generation must hear.

Butler University professor F.D. Kershner recognized the appeal and importance of restoring the ancient order of things. He points to the following as chief features of the Restoration Movement:

1. The acknowledgement of the New Testament Scripture as the only authoritative rule of faith and practice for Christians.
2. The renouncing of all human creeds and the acceptance of Jesus the Christ, the Son of God, as the only creed binding upon members of the church of Christ.
3. The restoration of the apostolic, or New Testament, church with its ordinances and life as originally practiced in apostolic times.
4. The union of all Christians upon the basis of the platform laid down in the preceding propositions. The plea has sometimes been regarded as primarily a plea for Christian union, but it was upon the basis mentioned that union has been advocated.

This is what the matter boils down to today in churches of Christ. Will we pursue a path of restoration – or will we deem the enterprise untenable and unnecessary and go a different direction? All the current wrestling with our history is taking place against this backdrop. Those who see us as merely one denomination among many will eventually follow the path taken more than a century ago by the Disciples of Christ as the American Restoration Movement splintered into three parts. Those of us who believe that Christianity is undenominational will continue to pursue the goal of restoration.

Law Or Love

Greg Clark

The story is told of a woman who lived with a perfectionist husband who always criticized her. She never kept the house clean enough nor did she dress up to his unrealistic standards. He even gave her a list of 25 rules to be obeyed if she wished to keep him happy. When she failed in any of them, he responded with verbal abuse. Eventually, he died and as time went by she fell in love with another man who was kind and loving. Her heart's desire was to please him in any way she could. His patience and encouragement rebuilt her self-esteem and enriched her life. One day while going through some old papers, she came across the list of 25 rules from her first husband. She couldn't believe her eyes. Everything on the list he had demanded, she was now choosing to do out of love for her husband. The rules had produced resentment, love brought joyful submission.

For many people today this story illustrates their sentiment about submission to God. They believe it ought to be their own decision to respond to His will out of love rather than command. In our choice-obsessed society, people would rather select (based upon their perceived needs) which parts of God's will they wish to apply. If application of His word is not of their initiative, then the Bible becomes "a rule book." To insist that one be accountable to a spiritual law is, in their mind, similar to living with an arbitrary and abusive husband who demands certain behavior.

It is this viewpoint that is contributing to an increasing tentativeness toward preaching on the authority of God and His word. The preference is for heavy doses of love and grace and less emphasis on the demands of God and the duty of man. One might wonder if this theological shift has not manifested itself as well in a different preaching style. A *"Thus says the Lord,"* along with a barrage of scriptures to prove the point, is seldom heard today. Increasingly popular is a style of storytelling with fewer quotations of book, chapter, and verse. Preachers with soothing conversational tone and political correctness stand in stark contrast to biblical examples.[1]

Neglect of teaching on the authority of God and His demands has produced confusion in Bible classes as Christians wonder what, if anything, is required to "remain faithful?" With blurred vision, Bible class teachers often fail to differentiate between cultural preferences (which are open to change) and the things to which the church must adhere in obedience to the Lord and God-given apostolic authority. Command, example, and necessary inference are traded in for a more simplistic approach of just loving Jesus.[2] The biblically illiterate find joy and comfort in the repetitive messages of freedom, unity, and love while little or nothing is said about covenant obligations. Obligation becomes a byword for legalism. Those who take a stand on scriptural demands are accused of being judgmental. Reoccurring issues such as instrumental music, the role of women in worship, baptism for forgiveness of sins, and divorce and remarriage become mere intellectual gymnastics. Neglected issues such as the *duty* of a disciple, the *command* to evangelize, and personal *responsibility* in the local church are deemed even more irrelevant.

Those who travel this dangerous path believe the end of the Mosaic Law is tantamount to the end of any law. The New Testament (and some would argue the entire Bible) is viewed as a collection of "love letters" rather than a "constitution." These letters or "collection of stories" come from a heavenly Father who doesn't expect much out of fallen mankind other than the desire to have a relationship with Him. He's like the dad every teenager wants. He doesn't care how late you stay out or what you do when you're away from home as long as you feel love toward Him. The "logophobic" finds a new and improved presentation of a God who is more personal and less institutional.[3] The God who was oppressive and demanding is traded in for a close friend who accepts more than we as "five steppers" ever imagined.

Like the Bereans we need to *"examine the Scriptures"* (Acts 17:11) carefully. If we have become anthropocentric in our preaching on salvation, we need to repent. If the main attraction has become *"What shall we do?"* (Acts 2:37) rather than look at what He did, then let's change our approach. Perhaps a contributing factor to the low number of conversions seen today is that we haven't presented a very compelling portrait of the One to whom people need to respond. We cannot allow our worship to be known only for the fact that it is different. We must always reflect Christ in our worship. Our approach to scripture must strike a balance between law and love.

Change in itself is not wrong. The book of Acts is full of change for the growing body of Christ. Those who reject change of any kind stifle our freedom in Christ and often cause others to go beyond where they had originally intended. There is only one way a congregation of any size can know how to redeem the times and that is by continually going to Scripture. God has revealed everything we need as His people to do His work.

A clearer perspective on God should always be our goal. Unfortunately, many are depending upon the latest feel good devotional book for their understanding of who God is and what He desires. The true portrait of our heavenly Father can be found in the Bible in greater detail and beauty than any best seller at the bookstore. In it, we can behold a more complete picture of both the *"kindness and severity of God"* (Romans 11:22).[4] We can stand in awe of His lovingkindness and bow in submission before His holy throne. The Bible does not present law and love as antithetical when the obligations are given by the authority of God.

The Authority Issue

Not too many people care for "speed traps." My personal respect for law enforcement officials causes me to think there are loftier pursuits for them (at least when I am in a hurry!). Nevertheless, my choice in the matter is to either respect their authority and adjust my speed or do my own thing and face the consequences. Personal feelings don't change the reality.

Children have authority issues with parents and teachers. Teenagers often are at odds with those who set the rules. As adults we still struggle with the idea of someone else being in control. Authority is a delicate issue. We want it, but most of the time others have it. The one area where this should be relatively easy is in the demands God makes on my life. However, when every man does what is right in his own eyes, it feels liberating. This is the real issue when it comes to the disassimilation of law and love. What feels right to me ought to be right.

God has never abdicated his authority to the wishes or emotions of man. He is eternal and unchanging. Moses proclaimed to a new generation, *"He is God; there is no other besides Him... He is God in heaven above and on the earth below"* (Deuteronomy 4:35,39). The basis for his authority is His incomparable nature. He alone is morally perfect.

Therefore, he can require mankind *"to fear the Lord your God, to walk in all His ways and love Him"* (Deuteronomy 10:12). David wrote, *"The law of the Lord is perfect, restoring the soul... the precepts of the Lord are right, rejoicing the heart; the commandment of the Lord is pure, enlightening the eyes"* (Psalms 19:7,8). The children of Israel had a wonderful future ahead of them under the leadership of Joshua if they would *"be careful to do according to all the law which Moses My servant commanded you; do not turn from it to the right or to the left"* (Joshua 1:7).

The authority of God's Word is clearly taught in the New Testament. His word is inspired (2 Peter 1:20,21), all sufficient (2 Timothy 3:16,17) and will be the standard of judgment (John 12:48). Through our obedience to truth we are *"born again not of seed which is perishable but imperishable, that is, through the living and abiding word of God"* (1 Peter 1:22,23). Faith comes by hearing the word of Christ (Romans 10:17) and in it we can *"know that you have eternal life"* (1 John 5:13). No one has the right to modify truth to their own interests, even when these interests are accompanied by commendable motives. Jesus proclaimed only one truth and one way.

The current societal trend toward relativism rejects definitive statements of truth. Anyone, including God, who claims to know right and wrong, pure and impure, truth or error, is dismissed as a radical fundamentalist. Making our message more palatable by de-emphasizing God's authority and the exclusive claims of Christianity may very well bring an increase on the attendance board. After all, people don't want to hear their church-going relative is lost. They struggle with the idea of only one way to the Father and only one church (the body of Christ). But if our allegiance is first and foremost to pleasing God rather than men, the proclamation of God's authority must not be silenced. Let us not forget He is the one who loves the world so much that He sent His Son and provided hope to all. A perusal through the pages of both the Old and New Testaments is helpful in keeping the connection between His authoritative law and His amazing love secure.

Patriarchal Expections

Long before the Mosaic Law, there were obligations placed upon those who wished to enjoy a relationship with God. Law in a general sense is any command, direction, or constraint imposed by a recognized authority.[5] When God spoke to the fathers of families and made His will known, He delivered law. Obedience to the divine instructions was based upon the Creator's inherent right to specify to His creation His desire in worship and daily life. Man, as the created, was tempted from the beginning to pursue personal will over God's. Adam and Eve sought enlightenment and found shame and banishment from the garden. When Cain offered a vain sacrifice, he may have very well carried it out in great sincerity and devotion for God. However, his fruit basket was an affront to the demand God had made for faithfulness. His countenance fell, but it was not because of a lack of love on God's part. He had failed to master sin. God's grace allowed him to live even though his brother's blood was crying out from the ground.[6]

For 120 years the love of God superceded his own rage over the depravity of man in the days of Noah. Every sermon from Noah was a call to repent before it was too late. Peter noted it was the "patience of God" that kept the door of the ark open as long as it did (1 Pet. 3:20). Like today, the moral demands were rejected by the corrupted hearts of a sinful world. Personal pleasure seemed like the better choice until the raindrops started to fall.

A watermark of the Patriarchal age is God's promise to Abram to bless all families through Him. Can the love of God be seen any clearer than in the Messianic promise? Abraham received the promise because of his obedience to God (Genesis 22:18: 18:19). Had he not left his hometown, he would not have experienced his incredible friendship with God. If he would have chosen to keep Isaac at home rather than taking him to the mountain as God commanded, he would have never enjoyed the faith walk we admire. Abraham's faith was demonstrated in works of obedience to the demands of God.[7]

Mosaic Law

To cast God in the role of a killjoy who gave his rules at Mount Sinai is to overlook the fact that God chose Israel before giving the Law.[8] The Law did not begin the relationship, but obedience to it preserved it (Exodus 19:5). The giving of the Law was a demonstration of God's love for His people (Deuteronomy 6:24). Obedience to it was a demonstration of Israel's love for God. It was possible to fear God, keep His commandments, and love Him all at the same time. *"And now Israel, what does the Lord your God require from you, but to fear the Lord your God, to walk in all His ways and love Him, and to serve the Lord your God with all your heart and with all your soul, and to keep the Lord's commandments and His statutes which I am commanding you today for your good"* (Deuteronomy 10:12,13). Deuteronomic theology was not to be taken lightly. An abundance of blessings awaited the faithful and curses and defeat could be expected by the disobedient.[9] The covenant relationship came with conditions.

Moses highlighted the heart in obedience to these conditions when he said, *"I command you today to love the Lord your God, to walk in His ways and to keep His commandments and His statutes and His judgments, that you may live and multiply, and that the Lord your God may bless you... But if your heart turns away and you will not obey... I declare to you today that you shall surely perish"* (Deuteronomy 30:16-18).[10] Notice again, the emphasis on the authority of God to bless and to punish. God expected them to pay attention to every directive. *"You shall therefore keep every commandment which I am commanding you today, so that you may be strong and go in and possess the land"* (Deuteronomy 11:8).

In the book of Romans, Paul reminds us that the stipulations delivered at Mount Sinai were designed to educate men about their sin and call for a higher standard (Romans 3:20; 5:20; 7:5,7ff). By design there was a daily reminder of man's uncleanness and imperfection. This knowledge of sin created a battle between the flesh and the demands of the Law. Similar to the law of other Near East nations, the Law specified how to apply the standard to a variety of real life situations.[11] The Law reached into all areas of life. In all facets, the message was the same - man was falling short.

By highlighting man's inability to obtain righteousness on his own, the Law educated men in the holiness of God. Because He was holy, His people were to be holy. God knew first hand that only One would be able to obey the Law fully. Obedience in faith, brought forgiveness of sin (based upon the blood of Jesus yet to be shed). When His people were stubborn and rebellious, God's love, as great as it was, did not excuse their unacceptable behavior. For the idolatrous nation of Israel, God poured out His heart through the prophets. Their continued disobedience brought about the Assyrian captivity. Judah faced Babylonian exile for their continued rebellion even after periodic revival from faithful kings and passionate prophetic preaching. Judgment upon both was not the result of being forsaken by God, but rather it was the outcome of their guilt (Jeremiah 51:5).

God told Hosea, "*When Israel was a youth I loved him, and out of Egypt I called My son... I took them in My arms... I led them with cords of a man, with bonds of love... I bent down and fed them... My heart is turned over within Me, all my compassions are kindled"* (Hosea 11:1-8). Through Joel, God proclaimed, *"Return to me with all your heart, and with fasting, weeping, and mourning; And rend your garments. Now return to the Lord your God, for he is gracious and compassionate, Slow to anger, abounding in lovingkindness"* (Joel 2:12,13). Seeking to become like the nations around them, it was difficult for Israel and Judah to understand the coexistence of law and love.

God's love for Judah was made even more evident even while judgment was enacted. Through Jeremiah he spoke of the return of a remnant. For those who would seek Him with all their heart, he had *"plans for welfare and not for calamity to give you a future and a hope"* (Jeremiah 29:11). He spoke of the time when He would make a new covenant with them even though they disobeyed the old. He proclaimed, *"I will put My law within them, and on their heart I will write it"* (Jeremiah 31:33).

Even Gentile nations were amenable to God's authority. Nineveh had the choice to repent or face the wrath of God. During the preaching of Jonah, they chose to repent. Jonah knew ahead of time that this could happen. What was his clue? *"I knew that Thou art a gracious and compassionate God, slow to anger and abundant in lovingkindness"* (John 4:2). Jonah's perspective of God was much different than those today who accuse God of being unyielding and less loving in the Old Testament.

During the restoration period of Judah, Ezra helped ignite a renewed zeal for the "book of the law of Moses." With great emotion, the people committed their lives to its authority and took difficult steps to realign their lives with the commandments of God (Nehemiah 8,9; Ezra 9-10). Writings of the post-exilic prophets reveal much work to be done. But even as the period of Bible history came to a close for some 400 years, the final exhortation called for them to *"Remember the law of Moses My servant, even the statutes and ordinances which I commanded Him"* (Malachi 4:4).

Law In The New Testament

Between the testaments the understanding of the Law underwent major changes. Ritualistic observance of the externals and an ever growing oral tradition produced a legalism based upon the piety of man. Rabbis took upon themselves the authority to modify the Law to their own desires. Transgressing the commentary of the scribes was a greater offense than neglect of the Law.[12] Righteousness was defined as the strenuous *effort* to keep the Law.[13] Emphasis was placed on the ability of man to attain or earn God's favor through righteous works as prescribed by men.

The teachings of Jesus confronted this erroneous application of the Law. Religious leaders were asked, *"Why do you transgress the commandment of*

God for the sake of tradition?" Jesus labeled them as hypocrites who were "teaching as doctrines the precepts of men" (Matthew 15:3,9). They were "fools and blind guides" who had *"neglected the weightier provisions of the law; justice and mercy and faithfulness"* (Matthew 23:17,23). Their law was an odd and confusing mixture of Mount Sinai and man.

At the cross, the Mount Sinai Law came to its foreordained conclusion. Jesus had fulfilled the Law. The Law, as schoolmaster, had fulfilled its duties of educating men about sin and the holiness of God. This education was not to be thrown out simply because a new covenant was being made. Nothing changed concerning the holiness of God or His authority as Creator. The ultimate answer to man's sin problem, which was concealed in the Law, would be revealed in the gospel. Jews were released from the incompleteness of the Law to find answers and spiritual fulfillment in Christ. Gentiles were no longer hindered from coming to God, but had the same access through the blood of the Lamb. The promises to Abraham to bless all mankind through his seed had come to fruition. Justification would come through faith in Christ.

One can imagine why many Jews had difficulty with this concept. The faulty leadership of the rabbis had skewed their thinking on pleasing God. Since they believed justification would come through their own righteous works of the Law, many *"stumbled over the stumbling stone"* (Romans 8:31-33). Perhaps no one was more aware of the sincerity of the scribes and Pharisees than Paul, and yet he proclaimed there is none righteous and *"by the works of the Law no flesh will be justified in His sight"* (Romans 3:10,20). He warned that seeking justification through a syncretism of law-keeping and faith in Christ would sever one from Christ. It is *"by grace you have been saved through faith; and that not of yourselves, it is the gift of God; not as a result of works, that no one should boast"* (Ephesians 2:8-10). While Paul denied the role of meritorious works, he included the human faith response as a condition to receiving the gift of remaining in the relationship. His rebuttal to self-righteous law-keeping must be taken in the context of first century Judaism.

It is further obvious from the teaching of Jesus that the passing of the Law would not mark an end to authoritative expectations of disciples. Jesus expected His words to be heard and obeyed (Matthew 7:21-27). His commandments included denial of self and confessing Him before men. Disciples were *commanded* to love one another (John 13:34,35). By keeping His commandments man abides in His love and proves his loyalty to Him (John 15:10-17). According to Jesus, *"He who has My commandments and keeps them, he it is who loves Me; and he who loves Me shall be loved by My Father"* (John 14:21). In whatever sense His message may have been a "love letter," His point was clear - God expects obedience. *"If you love Me, you will keep My commandments"* (John 14:15).

The apostle John continued this thought in his discussion of walking in the light under the New Covenant. With amazement, he writes, *"See how great a love the Father has bestowed upon us"* and then with piercing clarity stated, *"By this the children of God and the children of the devil are obvious; anyone who does not practice righteousness is not of God, nor the one who does not love his brother"* (1 John 3:1,10). John taught by inspiration of the Holy Spirit conditions to remaining in God's love. *"And the one who keeps His commandments abides in Him, and He in him"* (1 John 3:24). The harmony between commandments (not of the Mosaic Law, but of those under the New Testament) and love cannot be more clearly stated than when he wrote, *"By this we know that we love the children of God, when we love God and observe His commandments. For this is the love of God, that we keep His commandments; and His commandments are not burdensome"* (1 John 4:2,3). One who truly has a love for God will not reject the loving guidance given by God for our own good. *"This is love, that we walk according to His commandments"* (2 John 6).

If there are no covenant conditions in Christ then the apostle Paul was an alarmist and his writings should be discarded. He was concerned with the possibility of moral failure that would cause him to be *"disqualified"* (1 Corinthians 9:27). Paul proclaimed the *"grace of our Lord was more than abundant"* (1 Timothy 1:14) and yet warned that if Christians continued to live in unrepentant sin they should not be deceived into thinking God would overlook their rebellion (Galatians 5:19-21; Col. 3:5,6). Grace is not an escape clause for immoral behavior. *"Are we to continue in sin that grace might increase? May it never be!"* (Romans 6:1). The church of God at Corinth had a hard lesson to learn concerning an immoral member. His faithful attendance and God's amazing grace did not give them the luxury of overlooking his sin. He wrote, *"you have become arrogant, and have not mourned instead, in order that the one who had done this deed might be removed from your midst"* (1 Corinthians 5:2). The proper love response was to point out the violation of God's will. According to Paul, those who fail to respond to the kindness of God and *"obey the truth"* are *"storing up wrath for yourself in the day of wrath and revelation of the righteous judgment of God, who will render to every man according to his deeds"* (Romans 2:4-8).

Conclusion

No amount of obedience to God's Word obligates Him to save us. Our salvation rests upon His grace. Asking *"What shall we do?"* and then doing it in faith separates those who would receive the free gift of God and those who reject it. From Genesis to Revelation, God's love is clear. He desires universal salvation, but He also placed upon man the privilege of choice. The choice to "obey the gospel" in no way obligates God. He chooses by His grace to forgive us of our sins and count us as righteous in Christ Jesus.

The "five steps to salvation" were never identified with such a title, but neither were they condemned individually by Paul as meritorious works. He preached the gospel as the power of God for salvation. His focus was on Christ crucified. Without Christ, there is no offer of salvation. Without a response, there is no reception of salvation. No amount of love or ecumenism can change the multiple accounts of conversion in Acts.

Just as God revealed how to be cleansed of one's sins through the blood of Jesus Christ, He also made known that our obligation is to *"walk in a manner worthy of the calling"* (Ephesians 4:1). Both moral behavior and doctrine are salvation issues in the New Testament (1Timothy 4:16; Gal. 1:8,9). God's love for mankind has never resulted in the absence of law. Through His word, He lovingly directs and corrects (Hebrews 12:6-11).

The current emphasis on the Gospels and pursuing Jesus is overdue. True spiritual formation among our members isn't possible with an epistle-only diet. We need to know Jesus if we are to follow Him and share Him. This emphasis however, has implied a tension between the instructions given by Jesus and that of the apostles. The debate overlooks the simple fact that Jesus planned for the apostles to be the extension of His teaching.[14] The promise of the Holy Spirit was to instruct the early church in God's will for daily life and worship under the New Covenant. Disciples devoted themselves to the apostles' teaching because they recognized their teaching and example as authoritative (Acts 2:42; 1 Corinthians 11:1; 1 Thessalonians 2:13). To know their *"pattern of sound words"* (2 Timothy 1:13) is to know the Father's will.

If we throw out God-authorized standards for worship and behavior we do so in disrespect for God's authority. The intent might be to love others into our fellowship, but when they arrive what will they learn? God's grace covers all moral failures regardless of your heart? God's grace will take care of all doctrinal errors regardless of what the Bible says? God's grace means there is no law in Christ? If they learn this from us, it will be a message from man, not God.

Let us seek the blessings, not the loopholes, of living under the law of Christ. To serve others is to truly understand the heart of the Master (Galatians 6:2; Matthew 20:28). May we be people of mercy *"who are to be judged by the law of liberty"* (James 2:12) and *"speak the truth in love"* (Ephesians 4:15). Our churches need action, not apathy. Disciples should constantly strive for spiritual formation and not be content with stagnation. As James said, the *"one who looks intently at the perfect law, the law of liberty, and abides in it, not having become a forgetful hearer but an effectual doer, this man shall be blessed in what he does"* (James 1:25).

[1] It's hard to imagine how Peter would have preached the first gospel sermon in today's non-confrontational style. How would he say "you nailed him to the cross?" Stephen's sermon in Acts 7 would have definitely been different if he would have left out, "You men who are stiff-necked and uncircumcised in heart." Both sermons contain a great amount of what some call "proof-texting," as they bring in a variety of passages to make their point. All would agree that careful attention must be given to the original context from which a passage is pulled.

(All Scripture quotations are taken from the New American Standard Version.)

[2] An excellent discussion on the shift to the so-called "New Hermeneutic" is found in Dave Miller's book, *Piloting the Strait* (Sain Publications: Pulaski, TN., 1996), pp. 113-124.

[3] Ibid., p.117.

[4] Rom. 11:22. Paul's point in this passage was that his "fellow countrymen" were losing out on eternal life because they had not obeyed Christ. Gentiles were being "grafted in" because of their faith. If the Gentile Christians lost their faith, they too would face condemnation. "For if God did not spare the natural branches, neither will he spare you" (Rom. 11:22). Both the kindness and severity of God are conditional. The faithfully obedient experience his kindness, the disobedient fall into his severe judgment.

[5] Both the Hebrew, torah, and the Greek, nomos, can express law in general as given by any authority "distinguished from the free action of its subjects." When nomos is preceded by the definite article it usually is referring to the Law of Moses. It is also used to refer to the stipulations of the New Covenant as will be discussed later in the chapter. John McClintock and James Strong, *"Law" in Encyclopedia of Biblical, Theological, and Ecclesiastical Literature*, vol. 5, (Grand Rapids: Baker, 1969), 284.

[6] Gen. 4:1ff. The assumption is made that God had specified what kind of sacrifice was necessary. Why else would God have no regard for a sincere offering and refer to it as a transgression of his will?

[7] Jas. 2:21-24. Paul's discussion on the faith of Abraham in Romans is in the context of works of the Law for justification. Even though the Jews emphasized circumcision, Abraham was justified before circumcision. The promise given to him would not be fulfilled in the Law (Rom. 4:1ff).

[8] God's decision to choose the descendants of Abraham was not based upon their population, strength, or intellect. Moses preached, "Because He loved your fathers, therefore He chose their descendants after them." Deut. 4:37,38. Cf. Deut. 10:15.

[9] Deuteronomic theology is also referred to as the doctrine of retribution. Deuteronomy chapter 28 is considered the premier passage in outlining this principle to Israel. Bill T. Arnold and Bryan E. Beyer, *Encountering the Old Testament* (Grand Rapids: Baker, 1999), p. 147.

[10] Deut. 30:16-18. In verses 19 and 20, Moses further stated, "So choose life... by loving the Lord your God, by obeying His voice, and by holding fast to Him." Legalism focuses strictly on obedience without giving proper attention to the intent of the heart.

[11] Chapters 21-23 of Exodus are an excellent example of this style. God expected the general ethical principles to be rightly applied to a variety of situations. Arnold and Beyer, p.106.

[12] cf. Talmud, Erubin 21b; *The Mishnah,* Sanhedrin 11:3.

[13] The Jews understood that no one was fulfilling the Law perfectly. They in effect lowered the standard by pronouncing one righteous who was outwardly extending great effort to keep the Law. George Ladd, *A Theology of the New Testament* (Grand Rapids: Eerdmans, 1974), p. 542.

[14] Michael Weed points out that some who are calling for an emphasis on the gospels are doing so "to find in Jesus a freedom from structure - order and tradition - a freedom which is necessary to evolve into large generic Protestant evangelical communities." However, the gospels were written after the epistles and "presuppose the existence of a faith-community or church." Weed further states, "While the Gospels record the life of Jesus, they do so with a constant eye toward presenting the founding events of the Christian church (e.g., the last supper, the cross, resurrection) in a way that illuminates the present circumstances of the life of the church in the world." Michael Weed, *"Gospel vs. Epistle, Jesus vs. the Church - A Misplaced Debate" in Directions for the Road Ahead - Stability in Change Among Churches of Christ,* ed. by Jim Sheerer and Charles Williams (Yeomen: Chickasha, 1998), pp. 144,147.

The Church: Cultural Or Scriptural?

Tommy F. Haynes

There are strange sounds coming from some sectors of the Lord's body today. The very possibility of someone being able to go all the way back to the Bible and imitate the things discovered there from the first century church is being questioned. In fact, one recent book claims, "...as humans we have no choice but to begin where we are. No one can begin at the beginning. God is timeless and he is truth, we are neither. When we come to the Bible, we come from where we stand although God's Word lays a claim on us to transform us, it is a claim we appropriate from where we are in history and culture."[1] There are frightening implications in this statement. It leads to the conclusion that no matter what the Bible says, we can only interpret it through the traditions and habits of our culture and history. This necessarily means that the Bible would be interpreted differently by every generation, for the culture, traditions, and history would change. Such ideology leads us into ambiguity and meaninglessness. This kind of thinking also calls into question whether God can deliver to us a message that can be understood and does not change.

I was in my office when the call came. A young lady who had been coming to our assemblies for a couple of weeks wanted to visit with me. As we talked she began to chronicle her experience with religion. She was raised in a denomination, but during her college years had visited almost every kind of religious group imaginable. Her education was in religion, but from a secular institution. The young woman went on to explain what she had discovered in the Bible. Detailing faith, repentance, baptism, and faithful living, I listened intently as she also discussed her discovery of the kind of leadership the Bible teaches the church to appoint. She asked me what we believed on these doctrines. Our discussion covered worship, organization, evangelism, the role of women, and other matters of biblical importance. Each of these she had studied and concluded on her own. Until this time she had not found anyone who believed these things. After three hours, we went to the baptistery and she was immersed for the remission of her sins. She had found the church of Jesus, and had discovered the scriptural body of Christ.

It is of paramount importance to explore the validity of the claim that we can go all the way back to the Bible for the entrance, organization, worship, and work of the church of Christ. If such is not possible, then the church simply becomes a denomination among denominations, and a branch on a denominational tree that does not resemble at all the scriptural teaching of our Lord, *"I am the vine and you are the branches"* (John 15:5 NKJV). Is the church a culturally driven institution or a scripturally ordered identity? This is a question that must be answered. The answer is vital to our survival in the doctrinal storms we must face.

Can We Go All The Way Back To The Biblical Designation and Formation of the Church?

John would write, *"Therefore let that abide in you which you heard from the beginning. If what you heard in the beginning abides in you, you also will abide in the Son and in the Father"* (1 John 2:24). John not only says that we can go all the way back to the beginning, but if we are to abide in the Son and Father, we must go all the way back. Paul would encourage the Corinthians *"Imitate me, just as I also imitate Christ"* (1 Corinthians 11:1). It was possible for the Corinthians to observe in the life of Paul those Christ-like habits that they should then imitate. He is telling them to do that very thing. One can follow Christ in spite of the examples of the culture surrounding him. The determination to follow Christ must be pressed in spite of the fallacies of our age. As Peter prepared the members of the "dispersion" for the suffering they would endure, he tells them, *"For to this you were called, because Christ also suffered for us, leaving us an example, that you should follow His steps"* (1 Peter 2:21). If we are doomed to follow the culture in which we find ourselves, and must obey Jesus within the dictates of history and culture, Peter's encouragement can never be fully realized in our lives.

We can go back to the Bible for our leadership. We can divorce ourselves from the control of the culture in which we live, with regard to the essentials, in order to obey Christ. Making our goal to strive to become like Him, is what the church is to encourage. This is the vital purpose of the body of Christ. The Bible affirms that the footsteps of Jesus are discernable. We can find them. We can follow them.

The footsteps of Jesus are clear and so are the details of His church. There are those who hold a very modernistic position and would have us pattern ourselves after the discoveries of reformers and restorationists. Christ declares that the church belongs to Him (Matthew 16:18). He instructs us that to gain entrance into that kingdom one must be born again of the water and spirit (John 3:5). Jesus promised to send *"the Spirit of truth"* Who would guide us into all of the truth (John 16:13). The Spirit was given to the apostles on Pentecost (Acts 2:1-4). Speaking through these men the Spirit proclaims concerning Jesus, His fulfillment of prophecy, miraculous works, death, burial, resurrection, and ascension to the right hand of God (Acts 2:16-36). His church was established on Pentecost as a result of the gospel message (Acts 2). Those who heard entered the church by means of repentance and baptism for remission of sins (Acts 2:38). Jesus added them to His body, which necessitates the conclusion that there is a well-defined, discernable, recognizable body (Acts 2:47). That church remained steadfast in the apostle's doctrine (taught principles), fellowship, breaking of bread, and in prayers (Acts 2:42). The church worshipped on the first day of the week (Acts 20:7). They sang vocally, using only the instrument commanded by inspired word, the human voice in concert with the heart (Ephesians 5:19). The church was led in prayer by men in the assembly (1 Timothy 2:8). They gave as they were prospered (2 Corinthians 8 & 9). The assembly was also used for teaching, which in the time before the written word necessitated miraculous teaching (1 Corinthians 14; Acts 20:7ff.). We can know how the church was started and how it functioned from the plain teachings of the Bible.

Additionally, we can go back to the Bible in order to grasp the meaning of the relationship that the church sustains with Christ. The church is described as *"the body of Christ"* (I Corinthians 12:27; Ephesians 1:22,23; 4:12; Colossians 1:24). The church therefore "belongs" to Christ just as our bodies belong to our heads. This requires that the body, the church, take its complete direction from the head, Christ! The church is also pictured as the bride of Christ (Ephesians 5:22-33). In this relationship we stress the qualities of oneness and faithfulness. There are things that are expected of a wife because she and the husband are one. She must be faithful to him. There cannot be an "identity crisis" concerning who she is in relationship to the husband. If the bride fails to maintain her part of the commitment, unfaithfulness will soon come into that relationship. The unfaithfulness of the church will bring about a divorce from the husband. Christ will remove the candlestick from the church if apostasy (spiritual adultery) results (see the seven churches in Revelation 2 & 3). We may not be in a position to know the exact point when that takes place, but no church should run the risk of coming to that point. As the bride, we must remain faithful and true to our bridegroom, Christ. Faithfulness involves more than a lack of adultery. Dr. J.D. Bales wrote, "Faithfulness to Christ does not mean only faithfulness in doctrine, although it involves it...the call is not only to be the bride faithful, but the bride in love."[2] The church is not just about the keeping of rules. It is the deep involvement of each member in the love of Christ and the advancement of His body.

Decisions have to be made on the part of a congregation about the way worship and work will be enacted. Over time, some activities undergo change, but the basics must never change. In none of the declarations that we need to be more sensitive to our culture do we find any replicable pattern for our practice. There are some claims that the active elements of work and worship of the church are as much cultural as they are scriptural. From that perception, there is a call for tolerance and acceptance of denominational practices upon the grounds that our "traditions" and practices are no better being merely the result of following men. "Should those in the body act as if there is no such distinction and, thus, lead those outside of Christ to believe they are perfectly safe and need no further response to God?"[3] God teaches us how to live and what to do by means of His word. That word does make distinctions between vain lip service and actual spiritual living. Men muddy the water with modernistic language leading to destruction while God gives us clear direction for life. We can go all the way back to the bible for the identity and function of the church of Christ.

Is It Hard To Be A Scriptural Church In Our Culture?

"The differences between the secular and sacred are rapidly blurring in American Society."[4] "Our culture today holds "tolerance" as one of its highest virtues."[5] In this tolerant society to claim that one can know truth and act on it is considered ignorant and arrogant. The more "enlightened" America becomes, the greater the clamor to lay claim to loving ignorance in the name of tolerance. "Our relativistic thinking has fostered a blind tolerance among us for many beliefs and practices which are unbiblical."[6] This makes our task even more difficult, for we accept the teaching of Jesus that *"You shall know the truth and the truth shall make you free"* (John 8:24).

Our claims to be the church of the New Testament are not founded on a desire for elitism or exclusion. The Lord will accept all who obey His will (Matthew 11:28-30). We readily accept the understanding that God hold the position of eternal judge of mankind (Revelation 20:12). The Father has determined to judge us through His Son (Acts 17:31). Laying claim to being the church of the New Testament requires a foundation set firmly on the word of God. Jesus established *"His church"* (Matthew 16:18) and this demands that we search the scriptures to identify that church, replicating it in every generation.

While we do not have the right to determine who is saved and who is lost eternally, we must hold ourselves, and everyone else who claims to be a Christian, to the biblical standard of redemption. If one has not claimed the blood of Jesus through baptism, he cannot be added to Christ's body. If one is not going to practice the "apostle's doctrine" he is not part of the "called out." We do not have the right to admit anyone into the fellowship of the saints who has not obeyed Christ. Through God's revealed truth, we can make certain that one has met at least the basic criteria laid out by divine teaching. We can know, and should ask, if one has believed that Christ is the Son of God, repented of past sin, confessed Jesus, and been baptized for the remission of sins. This is simply the proof that the rule of God has been accepted in their lives. Until Barnabas verified certain things to the disciples concerning Paul, they were not willing to accept him (Acts 9:26-28). The disciples were not wrong to ask for such assurances. The Bible gives no indication that this was wrong on their part. This attitude on the part of the church is not excluding anyone. Anyone can obey these simple truths and be added by the Lord to His church. When we do not hold people to the truth of salvation, we are doing them great harm. How else will they know what Jesus requires of them to become his disciple?

The pressure on the church to intertwine popular culture is enormous. "More and more Americans are opting for 'full service churches' that can offer quality and variety in music, extensive youth programs, diverse educational opportunities, a counseling staff, support groups, single's ministry, athletic activities, multiple Sunday morning services, a modern nursery, and other services and programs only available in larger churches."[7] Anderson believes that churches must do what he here proclaims. Many of these expectations are a numeric impossibility for the average church. Not only do such cater to the selfish nature, they are wholly impractical. This pursuit for what satisfies self makes the biblical message a hard one to swallow. Jesus said, *"If anyone desires to come after Me, let him deny himself, and take up his cross daily, and follow Me"* (Luke 9:23). Jesus could not accept the discipleship of the rich young ruler because he had much and was not willing to give it up (Mark 10:21). With churches pandering to every whim of the masses, many will miss the message of Jesus. The selfless pursuit of the cross will not be seen. Bowing to the pressures of culture will sound the death knell of the church in any age. "American culture has triumphed. It was supposed to happen the other way, but too many people got comfortable with culture because it's easier to give in to current and be carried along, than to swim upstream."[8]

This clamor for change is not the fault of the message or the nature of the church. It is the work of a powerful evil entity that wants Christ's message and His body to change. Satan is reaching deep into the body and wrapping his filthy fingers around the very heart of the church. We must awaken to the extreme damage that has been done, and repent (Revelation 2:5, 16, 21, 22; 3:19, 20, 21).

Have We Made Mistakes?

We certainly have, and we must not argue that we have not. One of the first axioms of logic is that the abuse of a thing does not argue against the thing itself. John Gipson said it well, "I resent some aberration being held up as the norm among preachers, elders, and deacons. I resent some emotionally-ill person being described as an example of what "our" Christianity does to people. I resent the caustic insinuations that the brotherhood can't tell a metaphor from a gate-post, or a parable from a poem. To hear some tell it you would think we have never put a passage in its historical setting, or discovered that there is narrative in the Bible."[9]

The church for several decades has suffered a lack of growth and ineffective ministry. This has led to the argument that the basis of the church itself must be wrong if such exists. The "crux" and "flat bible" theologies have developed as a reaction to our failures. Proponents of extreme changes argue for the church to be whatever we want it to be so long as it respects that Jesus Christ is the Son of God, and the gospel narrative (death, burial, and resurrection) is believed. The theory of essential doctrines being determined by the "closeness to the cross" is foreign to scripture.[10] Given this philosophy, the design, worship practices, leadership, and works of the church are simply whatever we want them to be because they are not in close proximity to the cross. Some are going so far as to even say that entrance into the church does not have to include baptism for remission of sins. One popular writer and radio personality stated, "Just pray the sinners prayer with me and you will be saved…" He would later on suggest that one be baptized because you are saved, but no mention was made of the biblical purpose and efficacy of baptism. Baptism for the remission of sins is not viewed as being in close proximity to Jesus.

The answer to our mistakes and apathy is not to change our message and the nature of the Lord's church. Instead, we need to re-ignite the fire we are to always keep burning in our hearts. The Lord was going to remove the candle from the church in Laodicea if they did not repent of their lukewarmness (Revelation 3:14-22). Jesus did not tell them to re-examine everything they held and be tolerant of the pagan religions around them. The changes He wanted effected in Laodicea were to re-start the flame of truth that had once existed among them. Jesus in fact tells them to *"…buy from Me gold refined in the fire…"*(Revelation 3:18). This very statement of Jesus teaches that they were going to have to go back to what they had been in the beginning and replant those seeds in their lives.

We must restart the drive that seeks souls, fellowships the saints, and works hard to keep the bright light of Jesus shining through our lives. We must get back to every member being involved in personal evangelism and edification, every member attending the assemblies of the body, and every member using their God-given talents in ministries to strive for perfect love in the church (Ephesians 4:15,16). This is the real answer to our problems. Tolerance and change for the sake of change will not have the needed effect. The radical changes being promoted today would cut us loose from the anchor of biblical authority, and send us adrift in a cultural storm (Ephesians 4:14; Hebrews 6:19).

Is There Any Proof That We Can Go All The Way Back To Scripture For What We Believe?

Yes there is! There are prisoners locked away for life who are coming to the truth with only their bibles. Prison ministers often discover men and women who have arrived at the truth and are simply waiting for someone to assist them in obeying that teaching. There are individuals who study on their own and arrive at the same conclusions that we have accepted. Such was the case with the young lady we mentioned at the beginning of this chapter. She is not unique, and I have personally experienced similar situations several times in more than twenty-five years of preaching. If we are always tied to our culture, unable to divorce past religious influences that exist between us and the first century, this would never be possible.

By requiring that we obey a set of commands, Christ is telling us that there is a knowable and provable plan of salvation. He requires that we be a united body. We are challenged to, *"speak the same thing, and that there be no divisions among you, but that you be perfectly joined together in the same mind and in the same judgment"* (I Corinthians 1:10). The church can exist as it did in the first century. The very warnings against apostasy are enough to teach us that there is a body of doctrine, which we must uphold. *"For I know this, that after my departure savage wolves will come in among you, not sparing the flock. Also from among yourselves men will rise up, speaking perverse things, to draw away the disciples after themselves"* (Acts 20:29,30). In Paul's letters to Timothy there is frequent discussion of those who had made shipwreck of the faith, and warning him to avoid such things (I Timothy 1:19; 4:1-3; 6:11; 2 Timothy 3:1-9). Timothy is encouraged to avoid doctrinal as well as moral transgressions.

What Is The Scriptural Church?

The scriptural church is that church, which recognizes itself as the body of Christ. The scriptural church will teach what the New Testament teaches about entering the body of Christ (Acts 2). The scriptural church will strive to obey the "form of doctrine" presented by the inspired apostles in the epistles (Romans 6:17). The scriptural church will seek out the elements of worship and praise that graced the first century church. The scriptural church will seek to enact ministries that meet the descriptions of the work of the Christians of the first century. The scriptural church will strive to evangelize the world (Matthew 28:18-20; Mark 16:15,16), and follow up on those who obey by edifying them through daily contact and opportunities to study and grow. The scriptural church expresses concern for the poor by administering to their needs (2 Corinthians 8 & 9). The scriptural church will demand that every member strive to be holy, consecrated, and sanctified. The lives of members will reflect this in a discernable way by their function in the body (1 Corinthians 12). The scriptural church will know that her origin is rooted deeply in the Pentecost event, and not from a split in a denominational organization.

Everett Ferguson writes, "Our distinctives are for the most part not distinctive. They are mostly items everyone agrees are all right; others only say that something else is all right too."[11] It is sad when those who say that other things are all right are coming from brethren who ought to know better. Such divisive messages harm the body of Christ, and all but delete the unique message of the Savior. The church is not a cultural product. It is the unique and distinctive product of the redemptive plan of God through the powerful blood of Jesus. The church is the body of believers who get their identity and mission statement from Jesus. The church is of Christ, and is reproducible in every century.

Conclusion

A dear friend encouraging my wife and me in the child-rearing years said, "It is a great life if you don't give up." Those words mean even more today as they apply to the life of the church of Christ. When the winds of unscriptural change blow around us, we must fight to stay on course. We must stand up for a knowable and discernable body of truth, the scriptures, as the only standard by which the church can be measured. May God help us to never give up, and to enjoy the great life that is provided by Christ through His church.

[1] J. Childers, D. Foster, J. Reese, *"The Crux Of The Matter"* (ACU Press: Abilene, TX, 2001), 74.

[2] J.D. Bales, *"Modernism, Trojan Horse In The Church"* (Searcy, AR, 1971), 18.

[3] Dr. Stafford North "Review Of The Crux" (Presented at Harding Graduate School of Religion – Memphis, TN, 2003) , 7.

[4] Leith Anderson, *"Dying For Change"* (Bethany House Publishers, Minneapolis, MN, 1990) p45

[5] North, 8.

[6] Dr. Dave Miller, *"Piloting The Strait" (*Sain Publications, Pulaski, TN, 1996) p19.

[7] Anderson, 51.

[8] Cal Thomas, *"It's True: In Dow We Trust"* (Daily Oklahoman, Oklahoma City, OK – October 4, 2003) , 6A.

[9] John Gibson, *"Gimme' A Break"* (Bulletin article – 1991).

[10] Crux, 194.

[11] Dr. Everett Ferguson, *"The Church of Christ – A Biblical Ecclesiology For Today"* (William B. Eerdmans Publishing, Grand Rapids, 1996), 48

From Faith To Faith: Encouraging Intergenerational Ministry

Tim Pyles

The Great Divide?

The summer of 2003 saw a nationwide farewell tour by country music mega-group Alabama. After more than two decades of live performances and forty-two #1 hit singles, they were finally taking their act off the road. I bought tickets to their show in Dallas for my wife, Kim, and daughter, Hannah, so that they could enjoy a well-deserved "girls night out." However, the outing became a father-daughter date when Kim ended up in a knee-high cast on her left leg the week of the concert and chose not to brave the crowd on crutches.

Sitting in front of us at the show was a three-generation family: two teenage daughters with dates in tow, a Baby Boomer mom and dad, and a pair of grandparents. It was hard to tell which of them had more fun, although I probably would have awarded that prize to Grandpa, whose Texas-sized cowboy hat kept blocking my view of the stage. Though fifty years likely separated those squealing adolescent girls from their toe-tapping grandparents, they all found common enjoyment and pleasure in a shared experience. Their mutual admiration for an accomplished musical group bridged the generational differences that invariably existed between them. *Should not our common faith in Jesus Christ and our shared experience of spiritual life and ministry in His church span generational divides as well?*

Only the hopelessly naïve would attempt to deny the existence of "generation gaps." Such age-defined differences are a psychological, sociological, and cultural reality. If you need further convincing, just make a brief visit to a shopping mall. Be sure to take in the mayhem of the music store and the relative serenity of the cafeteria. Look, listen, and learn! Though specialists might disagree on the precise years of birth that delineate them, American society consists of several distinct generations. The G.I. Generation, born between 1901 and 1924, endured the Great Depression and fought World War II. They are followed by the Silent Generation (1925-1942), which produced many technical professionals and social activists, but no U.S. President. Numbering some seventy-five million are the Baby Boomers, born between 1943 and 1960, the oldest of whom are now nearing retirement age. The center of intense cultural focus in recent years has been Generation X or the Baby Busters (1961-1980). The up-and-comers in our society are the Millennials (1981-2000), also known as Generation Y or Echo Boomers, the first generation to reach adulthood in the new millennium. Those currently being born are forming Generation Next, the Cyber Generation, or whatever it ultimately may be called.

Generations have become increasingly more isolated from one another in our society. In 1950, one in every two homes had a live-in grandparent. In more recent times, such three-generation families constitute only two percent of U.S. households.[1] James W. White attributes this widening generational isolation to what he describes as "almost a conspiracy" of social patterns (mobility, divorce, increase of families with no children at home, individuality) and institutions (work, schools, residence, clubs and organizations, sports, the entertainment industry).[2] Advertisers have identified and targeted increasingly narrower bandwidths of age and other demographic criteria, communicating that our culture's constituent parts are so vastly different from one another that they cannot be approached on the same basis. We are living in what Dean Merrill calls Niche Time.[3]

One Body

As society has gone in regard to generational segregation, so the church has gone, frequently for ill rather than good. It is another unfortunate instance of the cultural tail wagging the Christian dog. While most churches would never dream of encouraging ministries or activities that unduly separated members by race, gender, or socio-economic status, little problem has been seen in consistently segmenting the body of Christ on the basis of age and/or marital status. The result has been a validation and accommodation of generational and demographic rifts within the one organism on this earth that is divinely suited and equipped to bridge them, the church of the living God.

Recognition of the tendency toward isolation of age groups from one another has led to a renewed call for an intergenerational approach to Christian faith and the life of the church. The concept is variously referred to as trans-generational, cross-generational, multi-generational, or age-integrated Christianity. In a sense, all of these designations are redundant, much as the phrases "lifestyle evangelism" and "friendship evangelism" merely describe evangelism as the Lord intended it, discipleship that permeates our walk of life and our relationships. Similarly, the only model of church life that we have in Scripture is intergenerational. However, the above terms will be used for the sake of contrast with strict homogeneous-age divisions that often exist within the ministries of the church.

God designed His church as a place where worldly barriers could be overcome on the basis of the peace established by the atoning blood of Christ (Ephesians 2:11-22). In Jesus, there was to be *"a renewal in which there is no distinction between Greek and Jew, circumcised and uncircumcised, barbarian, Scythian, slave and freeman"* (Colossians 3:11 NASB). Though gender roles are delineated in the New Testament in certain matters of church leadership and worship, notions of male superiority were not to be tolerated or allowed to threaten the unity of the body of Christ (Galatians 3:28). Walls were to crumble, and gulfs were to be bridged. However, as evidenced by the book of Acts and the epistles to the churches, these goals were not readily accomplished by first-century Christians. The challenge remains just as great for the contemporary church. We must add age-oriented issues to the already large bag of prejudices and suspicions that would hamper the unity of Christ's church.

At the heart of intergenerational efforts is a desire to demonstrate coherence and harmony between our ministries in the church and biblical theology about the body of Christ. "The educational strategies of a faith community need to demonstrate consistency with the essence of 'church.'"[4] Concisely stated, we must practice what we preach. *The church is one body!* Romans 12 and I Corinthians 12 describe an interdependent body made up of diversely gifted, individual members. Just as various organs and systems function in complementary fashion in our *"fearfully and wonderfully made"* physical bodies, so, too, has God composed the church of His Son. Age is a vital component of congregational diversity. There are no age-defined vestigial organs or generationally unnecessary or irrelevant members. No age group should be caused to think, "Because I am not older (or younger), I am not a part of the body." Nor should one generation ever intentionally or unintentionally communicate to another, "I have no need of you." The goal of the intergenerational paradigm is "to build cross-generational relationships that strengthen faith formation in the community and at home."[5]

Before further discussion is given to intergenerational approaches to ministry, the value of homogeneous-age relationships and settings in the church needs to be affirmed. To allay any premature or unwarranted fears, it should be understood that no one is advocating that we disband the Sunday morning four-year-old class and scatter its members throughout the congregation's education ministry. Common sense demands that we recognize and address the stages of human cognitive development and socialization in our teaching of the Word of God. Children's ministry, youth ministry, singles ministry, and seniors ministry each fill important and useful places in the body. The spiritual song *Blest Be the Tie* affirms that "we share our mutual woes, our mutual burdens bear." This mutuality of life experiences, both joyful and sorrowful, frequently centers around the phases of life: adolescence, young adulthood, marriage, starting a family, raising teenagers, adjusting to an empty nest, and coping with aging and declining health. It is only natural that we are drawn to people in the church who are walking where we are walking.

Barriers to congregational unity are raised, however, when homogeneous-age or like-demographic divisions exist exclusively, perpetually, and unquestioningly in churches. One's entire Christian life can be spent successively transitioning through the youth group, college class, singles ministry, young married class, pray-for-me-I-have- teenagers class, console-me-my-children-left-home class, and the Golden Years class. This systematically conditions Christians to feel that they can only learn and serve effectively and comfortably with those whose dates of birth are within five years on either side of their own. Class members bristle when someone significantly older or younger (and uninitiated in our ways) innocently wanders into "their class." In some churches, Bible classes have grown old together over two or three decades. While this results in having class members who are extremely "close" to one another, the classes are frequently "closed" to relationships with newcomers or outsiders. LaGard Smith laments this compartmentalization of Christians as "generational apartheid."

> For all their advantages, there are also inevitable down sides to carving up the family in "singles ministries," "seniors ministries," and "the college group." Once such categories are created, at some point the wholeness of the Lord's body begins to get lost in much the same way that focusing on minorities in society can actually produce more strife than unity. Generational apartheid is not to be desired any more than any other kind of apartheid.[6]

Though valuable, these specialized ministries must be designed and implemented in an integrated fashion in order to facilitate intergenerational ministry and learning. Allan Harkness identifies a sad irony that exists in churches where "a strong affirmation of 'the family' is made while concurrently the bulk of the communities' programs practically deny genuine intergenerational interaction!"[7]

Building bridges across age-defined lines can be accomplished by debunking some of the myths about generational differences, working to overcome cultural conditioning, and questioning conventional wisdom that may be incompatible with God's will for His church. Generational distinctions do not have to define us or divide us. We often have far more in common than we care to admit. In exposing the myth that the needs of Generation X are irreconcilably different from Baby Boomers, James Emery White writes:

> We have found that once twenty-somethings get married and have a child, they begin to look and act very much like boomers. When they start a family, those who wanted the music café and coffee bars become much more interested in the nursery. I cannot overemphasize the massive change that occurs in the Gen-Xers' tastes and demeanor and schedule and priorities when they walk down the aisle and start a family.[8]

Another misconception is that people do not desire spiritual cross-generational relationships, when, in fact, many do. Erik Johnson describes a prototypical twenty-three-year-old Baby Buster with bleached hair and a goatee who joined a Bible study group whose members were in their fifties and older. His parents had divorced when he was sixteen and his father had been a workaholic. On his first visit to the study group, he said, "I'm looking for a mentor."[9] Only someone of an older generation could fulfill that need in his life.

Unconventional Wisdom

"Great is the Lord, and highly to be praised, and His greatness is unsearchable. One generation shall praise Your works to another, and shall declare Your mighty acts" (Psalm 145:3-4). The principle of proclaiming faith from one generation to another is the foundation of God's call and charge to parents to impart the knowledge of God to their children (Deuteronomy 6:4-7, 20; Ephesians 6:4). While this responsibility for teaching and training younger generations lies primarily in the hands of fathers and mothers, it is a supplemental responsibility that falls upon the entire community of faith.

Children need the involvement and influence of older Christians in their lives, and the burden for initiation of such relationships lies with adults. Youth and young adults need access to the counsel and wisdom that come from many years of life's experiences. Dennis Sawyer provides a compelling rationale for those who would question the need for intergenerational relationships in churches. "Because 'common sense' isn't so common anymore. The wisdom that used to be shared around the supper table in America, from older to younger, isn't happening."[10] Samuel the prophet was mentored as a youth by Eli the priest who was able to draw upon the reserves of experience, and even failure, in raising his own sons. An aging apostle Paul, though nearing the finish of his race of faith, remained an effective source of wisdom and counsel to his young spiritual sons, Timothy and Titus, who were just hitting their stride in ministry. A church that I visited in Alabama included among their learning centers a station in which the young children learned the faces and names of the congregation's elders. They were taught from an early age that these men were their shepherds, too!

Conversely, older saints need to be challenged and energized by the vitality and fresh insights of younger hearts and minds. Though it is generally the case that *"age should speak, and increased years should teach wisdom,"* Elihu demonstrated that it is sometimes the young who must supply instruction for the old (Job 32:7). A retooling of thinking needs to take place in adults who view adolescents as "pathological," "almost like creatures with diseases," and "at an age that can be 'dealt with' only by setting them apart in their own program in a kid-proof and soundproof wing of the church."[11] There is a tendency for parents to be involved with younger generations only when their own families are in those stages of life. They staff the nursery, teach children's classes, and serve as youth group sponsors and chaperones as long as they have children who take part in those ministries. Once their offspring doff caps and gowns, many march off the field of involvement and take their seats in the stands. When asked to serve further, they make smug pronouncements about having "done their time and paid their dues," as if responsibility in the body of Christ has a statute of limitations or can be quantifiably fulfilled and paid off.

Beyond Demographics

From its inception, the Jerusalem church bore a distinctive quality of *koinonia,* a "togetherness" in one body. Thus, they continued in *fellowship* (Acts 2:42) and had all things *in common* (Acts 2:44). This oneness of the early church extended across generational and demographic lines. When Luke reported that the Jerusalem church grew to a body numbering five thousand men (Acts 4:4), he left it to the reader to mentally supply the estimated number of women and children that were an essential part of that extended spiritual family. Love and ministry were extended to the oldest members among them, especially widows. Even then, cultural and social barriers had to be overcome that stood in the way of equitable treatment of those in need (Acts 6:1-7). Paul's letter to Titus included instructions relative to Christian character and relationships among young and old, men and women, in the churches on the island of Crete (Titus 2:1-10). As Paul's letter to the Ephesian church was read in their assemblies, the children must have felt a sense of importance and inclusion as the Spirit-inspired apostle addressed them directly (Ephesians 6:1-3). While I Corinthians 7 has generated much debate, one thing is certain. Demographically, the church in Corinth included those who were married, not yet married, divorced, widowed, and those like Paul who would never marry. Yet, they all were a part of the same body whose unity and interdependence is described in I Corinthians 12.

Most congregations are involved in some type of intergenerational ministry already. Smaller churches have historically accomplished this with ease. Without sufficient numbers to unnecessarily fragment, most activities of the body are congregational in nature. Even in larger churches, programs may not be so much in need of an overhaul as in a good tune-up. Remember, the goal is not to abolish homogeneous-age and like-demographic groupings in churches, but to balance them with intergenerational settings and opportunities that integrate these groups into the life of the body as a whole. Vacation Bible Schools can serve as microcosms of multi-generational involvement. The problem is that they generally last only three to five days annually. Efforts are needed to develop, expand, and initiate such experiences of shoulder-to-shoulder, multi-generational learning and service throughout the year.

Youth ministries are particularly prone to isolation in congregations. The blame for this lack of inclusion lies primarily with older Christians. When our youth commit their lives to Jesus, are baptized in His name for the forgiveness of their sins, and are added by God to His church, how often do we make efforts to integrate them into the ministries of the church? We generally consign them to being "youth group Christians." Do we think to give them the involvement forms that are immediately put into the hands of adult converts or members coming from other congregations? More often than not, we get from youth exactly what we have expected of them. At times, those expectations have been embarrassingly low. By what we communicate and fail to communicate to our youth, we can reinforce the unbiblical notion that they are the church of tomorrow, rather than a vital part of today's church.

Youth may desire to be included, but are seldom asked. Young Christian men need to be encouraged to serve and lead regularly in the church's worship assemblies, not just on one designated Sunday night a month. Otherwise, we subliminally communicate that, as yet, they remain adjunct members of the body. Young men and women who have become disciples of the Lord need to be mentored and trained as teachers of others, working alongside older, experienced teachers. While youth ministries are doing great work through mission trips and service projects, these activities can be greatly enhanced by including parents and other members of older generations. A study by the Search Institute released in 1990 found significantly higher "faith scores" among adults who could remember as a child (ages five to twelve) doing something for others with their parents. A sampling of thirty-three thousand ninth to twelfth graders indicated that such "serving youth" are "less likely to be involved in at-risk behaviors, more confident of their worth, stronger in their leadership skills, and better equipped for social situations."[12]

Integrated youth ministries seek to be involved in the every aspect of church life in addition to the activities and settings in which they naturally and understandably share time with those their own age. A failure to integrate them as teens can leave young Christians unprepared and ill-equipped for assimilation into the body as a whole once they leave school, especially if the youth program has been more activity-driven than spiritually focused. David Ng writes:

> Often the long-term effect is that young people find no reserves of faith to draw upon once the party is over, once the young people have graduated from high school and go away to college or work. They have been the recipients of exciting programming without dealing with Christ's claim on their lives or having to assume any responsibility for the life of the group. They have no ownership in the group or in the Christian

> faith...By participating in the life and mission of the church rather than being mere recipients, the young people come to know who they are and what the church is.[13]

Singles may also find difficulty in being accepted into the mainstream of the church. Dean Merrill notes that many church leaders and members "view singles the way Congress views soybean farmers – a special interest group with a one-item agenda to push – a population to be placated by giving them a Friday-night meeting in a side room and a small provision in the annual budget."[14] While focused ministries can provide much-needed encouragement and fellowship, they need not entirely isolate singles from the rest of the body. Most congregations have enough of a challenge resisting the formation of "special interest groups" without further exacerbating the problem along generational and demographic lines.

Churches can further widen generational divides by making assumptions about entire groups of people based on age and concluding that radically different approaches must be used in sharing the message of Christ with them. An adverse side effect of offering a variety of worship formats designed to appeal to different generations is that, thereafter, it becomes extremely difficult, if not impossible, for those groups to ever comfortably and meaningfully worship together as one body. Frequently, preferences in worship style are not generational at all. I have several older brothers in Christ who never met a contemporary praise song that they did not like. I have fellow Boomer/Buster Borderliner brothers who would be as pleased as punch if we never sang anything composed after 1850. Their taste in hymns defies age. Yet, we all worship together each Lord's Day, incorporating both old and new (voices and songs) in our praise to the Father. Worship needs to bring generations together, not further separate them.

Making assumptions about individuals and developing programs based on their date of birth can come across as patronizing and impersonal. One size does not fit all, even within generations. People want to know that they are valued for who they are, not for their generational affiliation. For example, small group ministries have proven themselves extremely effective, but it is erroneous to assume to that a small group format will appeal to everyone in a given generation for whom it may have been designed. James Emery White writes:

> We have found that small groups are very much needed by those who need small groups. Read that sentence again slowly. The truth is that many do not need them, and may not be best served by them...In fact, small groups can become just as much a sacred cow to the contemporary church as Sunday school was to earlier generations.[15]

Congregations that are attuned to individual needs will ensure that ministries and programs are designed so that square pegs will not be forced into round holes based on generational assumptions.

Generations Together

How can churches take steps to intentionally bring generations together? Set up a mentoring program involving older members and youth. Periodically offer a variety of Bible classes based on subject/text rather than accommodating perpetual, age-based, adult class divisions. (Note: if the offerings include "Finding Mr./Ms. Right," "Coping with Toddlers," and "Maximizing Medicare," little intergenerational ground will be gained.) If homogeneous-age classes rule on Sunday mornings, offer cross-generational options on Wednesday nights. If home-based small group studies are utilized, make sure that the members have not been cut from the same demographic cookie cutter. Encourage diversity in these groups, integrating nuclear families, single parents, singles, widows, childless couples, seniors, and teens whose families may not attend the congregation. Promote the same kind of diversity on ministry teams and committees. Have a quarter of Bible study in which parents and youth are involved in a class together. Re-inventing the wheel is unnecessary. Just make adjustments to ministries and systems that are already in place.

If there is hesitancy to implement a broad-based program, start small. Offer a Sunday morning intergenerational adult Bible class. Invite a few members from each of the other age-defined classes to form the nucleus of the group. Ask for a commitment from them for one quarter. Open it up for others to attend, but limit the class size in order to facilitate discussion. Be sure that you cover the entire spectrum of members in the congregation. Invite some spiritually maturing high school juniors and seniors to join the study. They will only be away from their peers for three months, and their insights will contribute greatly to the class.

Intentional efforts to facilitate more age-inclusive and cross-demographic classes and activities will likely meet some resistance. This is to be expected. *"The cultural norm, common in schools and most church environments, is to separate people, and especially children, by age. Cultural norms aren't amended easily."*[16] If the church has been equipped by God to transcend generational differences, why have we so often failed? *"Because faith communities too often have followed rather than led."*[17] It is time for us to lead. The anxieties of some will be eased when it is adequately communicated that what is being sought is a harmonious co-existence between homogeneous-age and intergenerational approaches. It is not an either/or proposition. It is a marriage of the best of both methodologies. *"Blending ages keeps the old younger and the young wiser."*[18] The church cannot afford to rob itself of the blessings of cross-generational life.

[1] James W. White, *Intergenerational Religious Education* (Birmingham, Alabama: Religious Education Press, 1988), 2.

[2] Ibid., 1-11.

[3] Dean Merrill, "Not Married-with-Children," *Christianity Today* 41 (July 14, 1997), 34.

[4] Allan G. Harkness, "Intergenerational Christian Education: An Imperative for Effective Education in Local Churches," *Journal of Christian Education 41* (July 1998), 11.

[5] Drew Zahn, "Connecting the Generations," *Leadership 23* (Spring 2002), 38.

[6] F. LaGard Smith, *Radical Restoration* (Nashville: Cotswold Publishing, 2001), 225.

[7] Allan G. Harkness, "Intergenerational Education for an Intergenerational Church," *Religious Education 93* (Fall 1998): 435-436.

[8] James Emery White, "Gateway Country," *Leadership 22* (Summer 2001), 35.

[9] Erik Johnson, "Stepping Over the Gap," *Leadership 20* (Spring 1999), 107.

[10] Dennis Sawyer, quoted by Dean Merrill, 35.

[11] David Ng, *"Rethinking Youth Ministry," Rethinking Christian Education,* ed. David S. Schuller (St. Louis: Chalice Press, 1993), 86.

[12] Merton P. Strommen, *"Rethinking Family Ministry," Rethinking Christian Education,* ed. David. S. Schuller (St. Louis: Chalice Press, 1993), 70.

[13] David Ng, 95.

[14] Dean Merrill, 35.

[15] James Emery White, 36.

[16] Drew Zahn, 39.

[17] James W. White, 14.

[18] Erik Johnson, 108.

Is Ecumenism What Jesus Meant?

Lindsey D. Warren
Thomas Bart Warren

It is important to declare that this effort is limited in scope. Due to the number of different individuals and organizations that are included in the Ecumenical perspectives we will only be able to examine an extremely small percentage of people, thoughts, and positions of this movement. This material will be influenced by the great diversity, division, and complexity concerning a large portion of the doctrinal positions discussed in the chapter. That will be seen in the large number of lengthy quotations that will be referenced in these pages. This methodology will be utilized in part because of limited space, but primarily due to the desire to let the views being considered be put forth in the most accurate manner possible. This particular chapter will examine the following points of consideration:

I. Introduction material and background information
II. The Ecumenical Movement faces both struggles and progress
  A. It faces struggles concerning:
    1. Membership
    2. Finances
    3. Doctrine
    4. Total opposition
  B. Progress in the Ecumenical Movement?
    (The Community Church)
III. Examining the Ecumenical Movement from the New Testament

Introduction Material and Background Information

This effort will focus primarily on the concept of ecumenism. This doctrine is said to be "the attempt to bring about unity among believers. It may take the form of either cooperation between separate groups or actual merger into one organism" (Erickson 48). William J. Richardson sites William Albert Visser 't Hooft identifying "...seven usages of the term ecumenical (oikoumene) in the course of history" (153). This chapter will be limited to the following concepts:

> The noun "ecumenism" and the adjective "ecumenical" are derived from the Greek word *oikoumene,* which is used in the New Testament to mean the Roman Empire or, more generally, the whole inhabited world. Gradually, the term came to refer to the whole church (as opposed to that which is divisive) or to the whole faith of the church (as opposed to that which is partial or defective).

> It is not surprising, therefore, that the word would be used to designate a modern Christian movement concerned with the unity, renewal, and universal mission of the church. Specifically, the ecumenical movement has used the term with reference to (1) the unity and renewal of the entire Christian community (i.e., the growing relationship among the now-separated churches and their common effort to be the one, holy, catholic, and apostolic church), (2) the worldwide mission of the church (i.e., the work of the church throughout the *oikoumene*), and (3) the unity of all humankind—indeed, of all creation—and the relationship of such unity to the church. (Musser 142-143)

"The twentieth century probably exceeds any others in the extent of overtures for Christian union it has witnessed" (Richardson 153). For a very brief historical background concerning the Ecumenical Movement[1] please notice that:

> By the beginning of the 20th century, Christianity was a genuinely international religion. The 19th-century missionary expansion, notably in Africa and Asia, gave birth to the ecumenical movement, which generally is reckoned to have begun at the World Missionary Conference at Edinburgh, Scotland, in 1910. Various transdenominational bodies had been formed during the 19th century, such as the Evangelical Alliance (1846), and international youth movements such as the YMCA (1844), the YWCA (1858), and the World Student Christian Federation (1895). (Douglas 285)

While being very much aware of the above-mentioned precursors, "the modern ecumenical movement conventionally dates itself from the World Missionary Conference at Edinburgh in 1910" (Hastings 189). "The Edinburgh assembly endorsed a proposal for a World Council of Churches, which came into being, after delay occasioned by World War II, at Amsterdam in 1948" (Ferguson 219). The World Council of Churches' initially stated that it was,

> The WCC's original basis declared it to be 'a fellowship of churches which accept our Lord Jesus Christ as God and Savior.' This limited (and easily criticized) confession was enlarged at New Delhi to read 'a fellowship of churches which confess the Lord Jesus Christ as God and Savior according to the Scriptures, and therefore seek to fulfil together their

> common calling to the glory of the one God, Father, Son and Holy Spirit.' (Ferguson 219)

The Ecumenical Movement of the 20th century maintained a primary emphasis on global evangelism and ecclesial unity. It was an effort to follow the prayer of our Lord Jesus Christ in John 17: 21, "that they all may be one" with a goal "that the world may believe" (Hastings 189).

The unity of the followers of our Lord is certainly a worthy goal. The words of Jesus Christ in John 17 indicate His strong desire for complete harmony among His followers. Jesus states His interest in Biblical unity in verses 13-26 of John chapter 17 (according to the updated New American Standard Bible):

> *"But now I come to You; and these things I speak in the world so that they may have My joy made full in themselves. I have given them Your word; and the world has hated them, because they are not of the world, even as I am not of the world. I do not ask You to take them out of the world, but to keep them from the evil one. They are not of the world, even as I am not of the world. Sanctify them in the truth; Your word is truth. As You sent Me into the world, I also have sent them into the world. For their sakes I sanctify Myself, that they themselves also may be sanctified in truth. I do not ask on behalf of these alone, but for those also who believe in Me through their word; that they may all be one; even as You, Father, are in Me and I in You, that they also may be in Us, so that the world may believe that You sent Me. The glory which You have given Me I have given to them, that they may be one, just as We are one; I in them and You in Me, that they may be perfected in unity, so that the world may know that You sent Me, and loved them, even as You have loved Me. Father, I desire that they also, whom You have given Me, be with Me where I am, so that they may see My glory which You have given Me, for You loved Me before the foundation of the world. O righteous Father, although the world has not known You, yet I have known You; and these have known that You sent Me; and I have made Your name known to them, and will make it know, so that the love with which You loved Me may be in them, and I in them."* (John 17:13-26).

It would seem reasonable that anyone or any organization attempting to follow the plan of God would treasure these words of Our Lord. However, neither our Heavenly Father nor His Son will accept anything other than complete obedience to Him and His plan of obedience. Jesus Christ supports just such a position as found in Matthew 7:21: *"Not everyone who says to Me, 'Lord, Lord,' will enter the kingdom of heaven, but he who does the will of My Father who is in heaven will enter."* Therefore, pleasing our Redeemer will require that we accept only Biblical authority instead of any human guidelines. The Lord intends for us to "package" our response to Him with both good intentions and, as pointed out in the second chapter of James, with proper actions. It is not an either/or situation for us or any other follower of His. So we must have God pleasing actions coupled with pure hearts and goals (Matthew 5:8, 13-20). Please note verse 19 of Matthew 5: *"Whoever then annuls one of the least of these commandments, and teaches others to do the same, shall be called least in the kingdom of heaven; but whoever keeps them and teaches them, he shall be called great in the kingdom of heaven."* In this passage Jesus says that for anyone to receive God's approval we must KEEP His commandments as well as TEACH them. In other words, one out of two in this matter will not be well received by the Son of God. He expects the "TOTAL PACKAGE" from each of us.

The Ecumenical Movement Faces both Struggles and Progress

It appears to be a challenging task to get a clear understanding of the Ecumenical Movement for a number of reasons. A primary reason would be the diversity within individual denominational groups. Diversity can be found in such matters as doctrine, worship, mortality, and ecumenical activities, just to name a few.

The confusion only multiplies when you begin to include denominational and broader organizations. We will very briefly consider some of the struggles that the Ecumenical Movement has faced and continues to face. Notice just a small portion of the Ecumenical Movement's membership:

> A flurry of new acronyms is appearing on the ecumenical stage: ACR (The Association for Church Renewal); CCT (Christian Churches Together in the U.S.A); FCFONA (Foundation for a Conference on Faith and Order in North America); GCF (Global Christian Forum). All affect evangelicals.
>
> These acronyms represent attempts to transcend and to some extent replace, redefine, or reconfigure the older acronyms of the NCC (National Council of Churches) and the WCC (World Council of Churches), the carriers of ecumenical vitalities and viruses during their last 50 years.

> The Global Christian Forum appears to look beyond the WCC to include evangelicals, Pentecostals, Roman Catholics and, in a more prominent way, the Orthodox. (Oden 1)

Oden gave an example of such organizations struggling with membership when he expressed that North American Evangelicals tend to respond to summaries of: "…ecumenical activities with a wary eye, even if they intend to be inclusive of evangelicals and Pentecostals and more respectful of ancient ecumenical teaching" (Oden 1). Further, Oden provides some telling insights when he suggests that:

> Evangelicals within the mainline long for a deeper expression of the unity we share in our confession of Jesus Christ as the only Lord. We lament the divisions that ecumenism itself has caused and continues to reinforce. We long for the broken body of Christ of to be made whole, but not apart from moral teaching on marriage and the family that honors God. Evangelicals lament the lack of unity at the Lord's Table. But God will not bless such efforts if they begin with a wrong step.
>
> The organizations that compose the Association for Church Renewal see little of the repentance required to begin such a journey. They will have their first grassroots meeting in Indianapolis on October 24-26, and we will then see how the reconfiguration of evangelically informed ecumenical vision will more realistically develop. (2, 3)

Another example of struggling with doctrinal matters and still being less than totally pleased with the outcome of the negotiations can be found in the 2.5 million member denomination of the Presbyterian Church (U.S.A.) concerning divisiveness. The 214th General Assembly of the Presbyterian Church during their June gathering of 2002, Clerk Clifton Kirkpatrick stated in regard to the 214th General Assembly that: "There's a real hunger in this assembly to focus on things that unite us in Christ" (Guthrie 1). Some delegates desired unity to the point that Stan Guthrie wrote about one vote at the convention:

> Meeting in Columbus, Ohio, delegates endorsed a statement affirming Christ's lordship in a 497-11 vote. "Hope in the Lord Jesus Christ" calls Jesus "the only Savior and Lord" and says that "no one is saved apart from God's gracious redemption in Jesus Christ." But the document refuses to "restrict the grace of God to those who profess explicit faith in Christ" and reserves the fate of non-Christians to the "sovereign freedom" of God.

> Conservatives expressed relief. "It's not as strong as I would like it, but it will do," said Parker Williamson of the Presbyterian Lay Committee, which accused delegates at last year's assembly of apostasy. (1)

Opposition to the Ecumenical Movement can be found in both varied and stronger forms. For example, the European Union has created problems for some religious people and groups that include both neglect and doctrinal demands (Olsen 1). In the United States, civil liberty organizations stand ready to bring lawsuits agains almost any religious activitu that disturbs their beliefs ("Walking" 1). Even efforts to help their own cause can produce something less than support.

Sociologist Alan Wolfe recently published a book entitled The Transformation of American Religion. Wolfe attempted to soothe the organizations that have been bringing these lawsuits. However, Wolfe has succeeded in disturbing the believers he was attempting to help. Wolfe encourages the liberals to relax, "...because the conservative Christians' rhetoric of biblical inerrancy and moral stringency is belied by their actual practice" ("Walking" 1). The subtitle of the book by Wolfe is, "How We Actually Live Our Faith." The author indicates that religion is now privatized and lacks confidence. Therefore, American Evangelicals are attempting to avoid offending other groups altogether (1-2).

Wolfe suggests that the culture has influenced religion to the point of reversing the desired goal (which is to influence culture with God's word) of Evangelical denominations. He refers to this as "toothless evangelicalism" and offers several reasons for this "gummy" state of affairs. The book presents the idea that:

> This toothless evangelicalism, Wolfe says, is the result of market forces and peculiarly American cultural habits. "Christians and Jews...have ignored doctrines, reinvented traditions, switched denominations, redefined morality, and translated their obligation to witness into a lifestyle."
> Doctrinal ignorance is one feature of American religion that amazes Wolfe most. But he sees such egregious ignorance as a parallel to American politics, in which few voters bother to learn the details before they vote.
>
> Likewise, Wolfe notes the way in which market forces have combined with the ethic of expressive individualism to secularize religion. Savvy pastors take what the unchurched

want most and offer a religious path to their desires. After interviewing a prominent Cincinnati pastor, Wolfe concluded: "Religion is [for him] not the alternative to such modern ideals as individualism, but a more effective way to realize them." And a nationally known megachurch pastor from Houston told him, "I take what is worldly and baptize it."

Indeed, the reshaping of the suburban landscape has largely erased truly public spaces for witness and has made it necessary for churches to offer incentives for people to come to them. "That process," Wolfe writes, "inevitably transforms the balance of power between institution and individual" as the unchurched "know that they have something the megachurches want." Some megachurches have made a serious attempt to reorient themselves against the prevailing cultural winds, but drifting with the current—"practicing the culture" rather than "practicing the faith" as one of Wolfe's critics put it—is surely a constant temptation.

By making religion not only attractive but easy, Wolfe says, we are experiencing "salvation inflation." The reference is to the well-known phenomenon of grade inflation, in which teachers give so many A's that top grades become meaningless. Likewise, as evangelical Christians expect less of people "to achieve salvation, the blessings of salvation are offered with fewer strings attached." Wolfe quotes another sociologist, who writes that most megachurches provide "high-instensity experiences of communality with relatively weak systems for insuring individual religious accountability—the assurance of right without the punishment of wrong."

Many features of contemporary American religion appeal to Wolfe's sensibilities: the way in which the desire to get along with others has created an ethic of tolerance and niceness; the way that Bible study has been so personalized as to effectively block its implications for radical social transformation; the way the fear of offending others has reduced most witness to "lifestyle evangelism." Wolfe also thinks the high degree of "religious switching" is "a kind of insurance policy against bigotry." It is harder to hold prejudices about Catholics or charismatics if you've spent a few years in each of those circles. ("Walking" 2-3)

In opposition to the sociological findings of Wolfe, other studies have indicated that members of the postmodern generation have strong desires to be identified with and follow orthodox religion. Agnieszka Tennant interviewed journalist Colleen Carroll concerning research conducted on Generations X and Y. These young adults are thought to be reacting against a large portion of their life experiences in both culture and church life. Carroll's research suggests that even if these people might be moving into a mainline denomination they still are supporting the basic fundamentals of evangelicalism. They seek religious safety and believe they must attend a church that preaches and teaches the word without compromise in order to find such. Concern is expressed that these younger generations may have the best of intentions without achieving the best results. The journalist (Carroll) is fearful that such desire for safety will lead the X'ers and Y'ers in an inward direction as opposed to an evangelistic outreach (Tennant 1-3).

Michael S. Hamilton and Jennifer McKinney have supplied a sociological study that applies to this discussion. There are some younger evangelicals that believe that there is an excellent opportunity to see a renewing of mainline Protestant denominations returning from their waywardness. Hamilton and McKinney are reporting such even though in most cases individuals or institutions find themselves gliding "...down the slippery slope from orthodoxy to infidelity. Once down the slope, there's usually no climbing back up. It's a one-way street from evangelicalism to liberalism..." (1). Such efforts have been attempted but they have failed each time. Additional studies show:

> Contemporary renewal groups have greater staying power and more supporters than ever before. They are committed to remaining within their denominations rather than leaving. For the first time, the renewal movements are also cooperating with each other across denominational lines. Opposition by denominational officials, though strenuous at times, has been less consistent and less effective than in the past. Renewal clergy are actually younger than liberal clergy, raising the possibility that liberals are living on borrowed time.
>
> Perhaps the most significant development of all is that, this time around, the renewal movements within the denominations are being fueled by evangelical parachurch movements that stand outside the denominations. (Hamilton 2,3)

Beyond doctrinal disputes and membership maladies, ecumenism has seen its adherents struggle financially as well. Notice that in January of 2002 the National Council of Churches announced that an additional sixteen employees had been laid off. This was part of a two-year effort to try to balance the budget of the NCC. Religion News Service, Ecumenical News International published the following information about this situation by indicating that:

> The 52-year-old ecumenical agency represents 36 mainline Protestant and Orthodox churches. NCC finished the 2001 fiscal year on June 30 with a deficit of $2.1 million—far exceeding last May's official projection of $730,000. For the current fiscal year, officials trimmed NCC's budget from $6.87 million to $5.7 million. With additional cuts, the NCC will have 39 employees. Two years ago, it had 102.
>
> The agency's largest contributors, the United Methodist Church and the Presbyterian Church (U.S.A.), are reassessing their contributions. Both churches said their dues would be based, in part, on the NCC's improved fiscal outlook.
>
> NCC Treasurer Phil Young says it is crucial that the organization balance this year's budget. Otherwise, he says, "We're facing a moment of very sober truth." ("Deficit" 1, 2)

The piece stated that at the November meeting Elenie Huszagh, a Greek Orthodox laywoman, was installed as the first woman president of the National Council of Churches. Huszagh shared her belief that the NCC had turned in the right direction and that they could function effectively ("Deficit" 1, 2).

Just like the NCC, the World Council of Churches (WCC) has seen the need to push for changes to be made due to the difficulty they have encountered in terms of maintaining unity and harmony between its various Protestant and Orthodox communions. Tom Finger believes the membership has forced the WCC, "...to refocus on historic Christian doctrine at a time when contemporary theology, some of which rejects traditional Christian teaching, is a potent force within some WCC-member churches" (1).

The progression of opposition to the Ecumenical Movement can be found to include "struggles" all the way to total disagreement. The late M.H. Reynolds, Jr wrote the following two paragraphs:

> "All Christians should forget their differences and join forces to evangelize the world by the year 2000. We cannot reach this goal alone." On the basis of this attractive proposal, we are now witnessing the greatest and most deceptive push toward ecumenical apostasy the world has ever seen. Joining hands with "all" professing Christians to fulfill the Great Commission under the banner of AD 2000 Ecumenical

> Evangelism has even greater appeal because it is coupled with the false claim that the world could be completely evangelized by such a united effort by the end of this decade. This would supposedly provide a wonderful 2000th birthday present for Christ at His return.
>
> The AD 2000 Ecumenical Evangelism Program is receiving unprecedented favorable responses from those who fail to recognize the unscriptural principles upon which any such movement could possibly function. Thus, an ecumenical-evangelical steamroller is being created of unparalleled proportions. In the past, efforts by liberal ecumenical leaders to forge an unscriptural unity on the basis of "peace," "love," "social action," etc., have failed. However, it now appears that this newest tactic of Satan to produce an unscriptural, ecumenical unity through the use of "Evangelism" has a great potential for success unless God's people wake up to what is really happening in the name of Evangelism. This dangerous program should be exposed and rejected by all who truly love Jesus Christ and desire to obey and please Him. (2)

The Ecumenical Movement continues to experience a variety of emotions. These encounters include: the ebb and flow of desired changes, the basic aspiration for status quo, and progress or positive developments. Notice the transition of viewpoint, from one end of the spectrum to the other, as expressed by John Stott concerning the topic of plurality. Roy McCloughry interviewed Stott in 1996 in a cover story, reprinted in 2003 by Christianity Today. The following is a portion of that conversation when Stott declares:

> I don't mind plurality as long as it goes hand-in-hand with unity. But I've given a great deal of my life to the development and preservation of unity within the evangelical constituency. I have never believed that our differences have been great enough to warrant fragmentation. I don't mind people founding their own societies and going after their own thing—again, it's an example of specialization—provided they still recognize that we belong to one another. (7)

Stott was asked by Gary Barnes in September of 2003: "What do you believe to be some of the most critical issues needing to be addressed by the working groups preparing for the 2004 forum?" Stott's answer differed dramatically from the one he gave in 1996:

> I focus on what to me is the most critical issue, and that is the challenge of pluralism. Pluralism is not just recognition that there is a plurality of faiths in the world today. That is an obvious fact. No, pluralism is itself an ideology. It affirms the independent validity of all faiths. It therefore rejects as arrogant and wholly unacceptable every attempt to convert anybody (let alone everybody) to our opinions.
>
> In 1977 Professor John Hick's symposium The Myth of God Incarnate was published, and in 1987, ten years later, The Myth of Christian Uniqueness. All the contributors confessed that they had "crossed the Rubicon" from "exclusivism" and "inclusivism" to "pluralism."
>
> The reason we must reject this increasingly popular position is that we are committed to the uniqueness of Jesus (he has no competitors) and his finality (he has no successors). It is not the uniqueness of "Christianity" as a system that we defend, but the uniqueness of Christ. He is unique in his incarnation (which is quite different from the ahistorical and plural "avatars" of Hinduism); in his atonement (dying once for all for our sins); in his resurrection (breaking the power of death); and in his gift of the Spirit (to indwell and transform us). So, because in no other person but Jesus of Nazareth did God first become human (in his birth), then bear our sins (in his death), then conquer death (in his resurrection) and then enter his people (by his Spirit), he is uniquely able to save sinners. Nobody else has his qualifications. (Barnes 1-2)

"Where does the Community Church movement fit into all of this?" is a question that could and most likely would be answered with at least a couple of different responses. We will mention it very briefly due to the fact it is difficult not to see some type of relationship between the Ecumenical Movement and the Community Church. Steve Miller makes reference to the phenomenon in the United States that has been growing since 1900. Miller refers to "...the rise of Protestant churches without denominational affiliation" which is a movement known as the "Community Church" (Miller 13). Even though some are working for the renewal of their denominational bindings, many of the Community Church fellowship are not. They would prefer that the relationship of the local community would be valued above their previous connections with any denomination. E. Claude Gardner cites a Community Church publication from its 50th anniversary that states: "The International Council of Community

Churches is post-denominational." The high price these organizations pay (by sacrificing truth) for unity is expressed by their saying, "We may immerse at baptism like Baptists, but also sprinkle, as do the Presbyterians" (9).

The International Council of Community Churches answers the question, "What is a Community Church?" with these words:

> It is neither planted nor transplanted from outside. It grows out of the hopes and needs and aspirations of the people of the community. It is a native product of the life of the community.
>
> The community church serves all the community, and claims the whole of the community as its parish. It is in fellowship with all other Christian churches, and welcomes all who love the Lord Jesus Christ to its fellowship and membership, regardless of sect or denomination. It invites to the Lord's Table all who "truly and earnestly repent of their sins and are in love and charity with their neighbors and desire to lead a new life following the commandments of God," regardless of other affiliations.
>
> It practices ecumenicity in worship, believing that Christians may and ought to worship and serve the Lord together despite differences of theological opinion and Biblical interpretation. ("History" 1)

One of the most influential religious bodies comes from an individual Community Church congregation that has its own association. The Community Church in South Barrington, Illinois, known as the Willow Creek Community Church oversees the Willow Creek Association (WCA). The WCA is: "…an alliance of 5,200 seeker-sensitive churches" thus proving the wide-reaching effects this "unity in diversity" movement has had (Reed 21).

Though there have been struggles of "in fighting" over doctrine, methods of evangelism, and even identity crisis, ecumenism has appealed to the masses. But sheer numbers are not a complete picture. This movement continues to (even with good intentions) direct and encourage people the world over to accept and obey a plan without our Heavenly Father's approval. In contrast, we are challenged to proclaim the message of Jesus in its entirety (Matthew 5:13-16; 7:13,14; 21-23).

Confronting temptations and challenges before God is as old as humanity. God's faithful followers have had struggles to face in the past, as we do today, as will those that follow us on this earth (if the Lord wills, James 4:15). That is to say, without respect of any individual or group, once we step away from God's plan of unity (Eph. 4:4-6) we are left with error in place of truth and confusion instead of Biblical unity.

Examining the Ecumenical Movement from the New Testament2

"...that they all may be one, as You, Father, are in Me, and I in You; that they also may be one in Us, that the world may believe that You sent Me." – John 17:21

It is obvious by the prayer recorded in John 17 that Jesus viewed unity as a matter of great importance. Thus to deny the significance of unity is to deny the very teaching of Jesus Christ! We are indeed obligated to seek unity. The inspired apostle Paul wrote that we must endeavor to keep the unity of the Spirit in the bond of peace (Ephesians 4:3). This being the case, should we as Christians embrace the Ecumenical Movement? After all ecumenism seeks to provide harmony and peace for a "universal Christian community." Is the Ecumenical Movement or even the Community Church what Jesus had in mind as He poured His heart out in prayer to the Heavenly Father just prior to His trial and crucifixion? Many modern day religious leaders would have us to believe just that. Referring to John 17, Leon Morris states, "enthusiasts for the ecumenical movement sometimes speak as though the reunion of Christendom would be the answer to Jesus' prayer" (644). Raymond Brown believes that this passage "has been used frequently in ecumenical discussions with the presumption that it refers to church *unity*. For Roman Catholics, in particular, 'That they all may be one' is the ecumenical slogan" (775).

The prayer of Jesus in John 17 (as well as numerous other passages such as Ephesians 4:3; 1 Corinthians 1:10; 2 Corinthians 13:11; et al.) demands unity. This fact is beyond question. The problem arises when mankind attempts to define unity based upon personal desires and preconceived ideas. Seeking unity in diversity (meaning any doctrine will suffice as long as one will confess that Jesus Christ is their savior) has led to the sacrifice of truth. The key to the situation is seeking truth first, even if it means the sacrifice of unity. All men must realize that the need for truth is logically prior to the need for unity (Warren 177). Jesus, who did not shy away from controversy if it meant standing up for what was right. He further taught that unity could never take precedent over truth when he said, *"Do not think that I came to bring peace on earth. I did not come to bring peace but a sword"* (Matthew 10:34). To further prove that He did not approve of any and every case of unity or disapprove of any and every case of division, Jesus said in Luke 12:51, *"Do you suppose that I came to give peace on earth? I tell you, not at all, but rather division."*

The seemingly cloudy concept of unity now becomes increasingly clear. We must understand that the Son of Man prayed for *unity,* not some diverse and loose-jointed *union.* Seeking to form unions with denominations for the sake of drawing larger numbers to local congregations at the expense of truth is the exact opposite of what Jesus prayed. New Testament Christians must readily and defend the timeless truth of the Bible in a loving yet uncompromising fashion (Proverbs 23:23; Jude 3; Ephesians 4:15)! In spite of the popularity of ecumenism in this postmodern generation, we must continue to proclaim the sanctity of the one true church, of which Christ is the head (Ephesians 5:23; Colossians 1:18). Unity demands remaining steadfast in teaching the gospel plan of salvation, which includes the essentiality of baptism (Mark 16:16).

The first myth to be dispelled is that the church of Christ is "just another denomination," which is another way of saying "one church is just as good as another." Jesus Christ came to this earth to set up and establish one and only one institution (Matthew 16:18). All other religious groups are denominations that stand condemned by scripture. J. Pat McGee clearly shows this to be the case with the following syllogism:

> 1. If it is the case that the Bible teaches that there is one and only one church, then all other religious bodies are false religious bodies being under the Lord's curse (Galatians 1:8,9; Matthew 15:13,14).
> 2. The Bible does teach that there is one and only one church (Matthew 16:18; Acts 2:47; 1 Corinthians 12:13,25; Ephesians 1:22,23; 2:16; 3:6; 4:4).
> 3. Therefore all religious bodies other than the church of Christ are false religious bodies and thus under the curse of God. (23)

Cecil May, Jr. illustrates how any scripture must be studied in light of the entire Bible and that an understanding of Biblical terms is an absolute necessity:

> Men often ask, "Do you believe that you have to be a member of the church of Christ to be saved?" When the terms of the question are understood Biblically, it answers itself. When "church of Christ" has its New Testament meaning, which is its only proper meaning, then it is that "one body" (Ephesians 4:4) to which Christ adds all the saved. Since salvation is by Christ upon our obedience to the gospel, and since we are added to the church of Christ upon our obedience to the gospel, the question really becomes: "Do you have to obey the Lord in order to be saved?" Then we can turn simply to the words of Jesus: "He that believeth and is baptized shall be saved; he that believeth not shall be damned" (Mark 16:16). "Except a man be born of water and of the Spirit he cannot enter the kingdom of God" (John 3:5). "Not everyone that saith unto me, Lord, Lord, shall enter into the kingdom of heaven; but he that doeth the will of my Father which is in heaven" (Matthew 7:21). (20)

Secondly, New Testament Christians cannot compromise the doctrine of baptism. In fact, when the truth about baptism is taught and believed, it should serve as a unifying force of fellowship instead of becoming a source of division. In regard to this, Thomas B. Warren wrote:

> Two men attain Christian fellowship with one another when each one of them attains fellowship with God (1 John 1:3; Ephesians 2:13-16; Romans 6:3-5; Galatians 3:26,27). One attains fellowship with God when he is baptized into Christ (2 Timothy 2:10; Romans 6:3-5; Galatians 3:26,27 et al.) and, thus, two men attain unto fellowship with one another when each one of them is baptized into Christ. Further, two children of God (i.e., two people who both have been baptized into Christ) maintain fellowship with one another (and with other faithful children of God) by walking in the light of His word (the faith, the word of God, the gospel, the New Covenant, the truth, et al. 1 John 1:7). (178)
>
> Warren summarizes the entire matter as follows:
>
> The unity which is authorized by the New Testament should be both recognized and honored by all accountable persons. This involves (1) ATTAINING Christian unity by being baptized in the name of Christ (and, thus, being added by the Lord Himself to the church which He purchased with His own blood, Acts 20:28) and (2) MAINTAINING that unity by living faithfully as a member of the church (1 John 1:7; Ephesians 1:22,23; Hebrews 3:12,13). (173)

It is certainly an honor for us to have participated in this noteworthy project. We are thankful for all that have had a part, especially its editors who are dedicated to strengthening and defending the church.

Works Cited

Barnes, Gary. "Why Don't They Listen?" 2003. *ChristianityToday.* 4 Oct. 2003 <http://www.christianitytoday.com/ct/2003/009/2.50.html>

Brown, Raymond E. The Gospel According to John XIII-XXI. *The Anchor Bible.* New York: Doubleday, 1970.

"Deficit Forces NCC to Trim Staff Again." 2002. *ChristianityToday* wire services. 4 Oct. 2003 <http://www.christianitytoday.com/ct/2002/001/12.19.html>

Douglas, J. D, editor. *New 20th-Century Encyclopedia of Religious Knowledge*. Grand Rapids: Baker Book House, 1991.

Erickson, Millard J. *Concise Dictionary of Christian Theology*. Grand Rapids: Baker Book House, 1986.

Ferguson, Sinclair B. and David F. Wright, editors. *New Dictionary of Theology.* Downers Grove: InterVarsity Press, 1988.

Finger, Tom. "Orthodox, Evangelicals Push for WCC Reforms." 2002. *ChirstianityToday*. 4 Oct. 2003 <http://www.christianitytoday.com/ct/9T1/9T1022.html.>

Gardner, E. Claude. "The Community Church Views." *Firm Foundation*. 116 (2001): 9.

Guthrie, Stan. "Presbyterians Check Divisiveness." 2002. *ChristianityToday*. 4 Oct. 2003

<http://www.christianitytoday.com/ct/2002/009/7/15.html>

Hamilton, Michael S. and Jennifer McKinney. "Turning the Machine Around." 2003. *ChristianityToday*. 4 Oct. 2003 <http://www.christianitytoday.com/ct/2003/008/1.34.html>

Hastings, Adrian, Alistair Mason, and Hugh Pyper, editors. *The Oxford Companion to Christian Thought*. Oxford: Oxford University Press, 2000.

"History." 2001. International Council of Community Churches. 29 Aug. 2003

<http://iccc.i-go.to/pages/iccc.html>

May, Cecil, Jr. "Is the church of Christ merely a denomination?" The Spiritual Sword. 3.4 (1972): 17-20.

McCloughry, Roy. "Basic Stott." 2003. *ChirstianityToday.* 4 Oct. 2003 <http://www.christianitytoday.com/ct/2003/135/51.0.html>

McGee, J. Pat. "The challenge to refute the view that the church is merely a denomination." *The Spiritual Sword*. 11.4 (1980): 22-24.

Miller, Steve. "Is Willow Creek Community Church the Church of the Bible?" *Firm Foundation*. 109 (1994): 13-15.

Morris, Leon. The Gospel According to John. *New International Commentary on the New Testament*. rev. ed. Grand Rapids: Eerdmans, 1995.

Musser, Donald W. and Joseph L. Price, editors. *A New Handbook of Christian Theology.* Nashville: Abingdon Press, 1992.

Oden, Thomas C. "The Not-So-New Ecumenism." 2002. *ChristianityToday*. 4 Oct. 2003

<http://www.christianitytoday.com/ct/2002/009/5.47.html>

Olsen, Ted. "European Disunion." 2002. *ChristianityToday*. 4 Oct. 2003. <http://www.christianitytoday.com/ct/2002/009/32.13.html>

Reed, Eric. "Willow Creek Church Readies for Megagrowth." *ChristianityToday*. 44 (2000): 21.

Reynolds, M.H. "AD 2000 Ecumenical Evangelism: A Warning!" 1997. Fundamental Bible Church. 17 Oct. 2003 <http://www.fundamentalbiblechurch.org/Foundation/fbcad200.htm>

Richardson, William J. "Ecumenical Perspectives in the Thought of Alexander

Campbell." *Restoration Quarterly*. 40 (1998): 153-69.

Tennant, Agnieszka. "The Good News About Generations X & Y." 2002. *ChristianityToday*. 4 Oct. 2003 <http://www.christianitytoday.com/ct/2002/009/3.40.html>

"Walking the Old, Old Talk." 2003. *ChristianityToday* editorial. 4 Oct. 2003 <http:www.christianitytoday.com/ct/2003/010/36.34.html>

Warren, Thomas B. The Bible Only Makes Christians Only and the Only Christians. *Moore: National Christian,* 1986.

End Notes

[1] For more on the history of this movement, see: J. E. Choate, "The Spirit of Compromise and Ecumenicalism" *Ecclesiastes and Song of Solomon* (Memphis School of Preaching Lectureship) 1994.

[2] For more details concerning ecumenism, the Community Church, and the New Testament, see: William Woodson, "Fellowship: The New Ecumenism" (Freed-Hardeman University Lectureship) vol. 60, 1996; and *The Spiritual Sword* vol. 32.1, 2000.

Does The Church Have To Change To Grow?

Dale Jenkins

"These are times that try men's souls," so said Thomas Paine in his "Crisis Papers." And these are the days that define our mettle. Various chapters in this work have focused on an understanding of issues that challenge the Lord's church in the infancy of the 21st century. But ultimately the subject with which we will spend our time is the birthplace of each of these issues. *Must the church change to grow?*

We live in a time when many changes are occurring both culturally and globally. Think of the changes that have occurred culturally, socially, educationally, financially, and technologically in just the last twenty years. These changes can be grouped into three effects that bring anxiety and tension to our world.

1. The pace of everything has increased. Life is speeding up. Progress, in general, always causes things to go faster. We have become a quick-reflex, channel-flipping, fast-forwarding people. Today's state of the art technology will be obsolete before it hits the market.

2. Each decision is more complicated. Even simple decisions for our lives have reached new levels of complexity. One reason for this is that technology has connected everything. The world has become smaller. Things that happen on the other side of the world affect my life today. Another reason for the complications is that we are inundated with choices.

3. Every value is being challenged. We see this everywhere. Right is being called wrong. Wrong is being called right. There are people today that do not believe there is even such a thing as right and wrong. Modernism has caused us to question long held truths. Today some group is prepared in some way to challenge every value we hold. Political correctness has created all kinds of crazy ideas.

These changes have begun to affect the Lord's church. We would like to assume the best and believe that at least many of the changes we are seeing touted today began out of the desire for the church to grow. Many have turned toward these ideas because it has seemed that what we have tried must not be the best because numerical growth in many places has been sluggish. Neil Anderson of the Gospel Advocate said it well: "In an effort to energize the church, many have turned outside Scripture for direction and authority" (November, 2003).

Alvin Toffler, who wrote the best-selling book <u>Future Shock</u> says that when people go through rapid times of change they need what he calls "islands of stability." The church must be one of these "islands."

But it is apparent that in many places the church has become closer akin to a battleground than an island. The debate and conflict over various issues in the church has reached massive proportions. Congregations that for years committed to certain standards are systematically and progressively throwing aside older doctrines in favor of newer ones. I am amazed at how many congregations and schools are fast jettisoning things they have for all their life held to be biblical truths.

Books are being written by people, once known for truth, but now denying the very things they believed and are affirming new truth. They are claiming passages in the Scripture must be reinterpreted or ignored because they reflect only cultural bias. Various approaches are used to do away with what has been the interpretation of the Word of God. In fact, they are re-interpreting passages so patently obvious that even a rather brief reading of the passage leaves you in little doubt as to the intent of its meaning.

The church, in many places, which is to be the bastion of truth, is falling fast to the march of modernism. Let us assert that the teaching of the Word of God will not become victim to what is going on in the society around us. We need only return to the Word of God and affirm what it says to hold our ground.

We are aware that this kind of effort is really not the effort of men, but it is the effort of the archenemy of God, the God-hater himself, Satan who desires to use sinful human agents to attain his goals. His real goal is to overthrow the plan and design of God for His church. That is why it is so tragic when the church capitulates, when the church falls into the lies of Satan and becomes a part of his own system of attack on the plan of God. We must reaffirm our commitment to the Word of God.

All of this has resulted from the frustration that the church was not growing fast enough to suit some. Perhaps we should be reminded early on that all growth is not measured in numbers. Sometimes God brings about our greatest growth when we are "pruned" (see John 15:1-2; Hebrews 12:5-11). If Noah had measured success purely in numbers, then he would have given up his ark-building career before the first drop of rain dampened the earth. In Bible times considering numbers was often times a detriment. Remember David's sin in numbering the people (2 Samuel 24) or the famous "army" of Gideon (Judges 7)? Just because "the count and the amount" board is not flashing with a new "Record Attendance" number does not mean we are to change our direction.

That does not make the opposite of growth any more desirable. I would like to believe that all want the church to grow numerically. God actually records in clear language the growth of His Family in the first century (Acts 2:41; 47; 4:5; 5:14; 28; 6:1; 7; 8:4; 12; Colossians 1:6; etc.). Some, it seems, have an aversion to growth that makes them believe that if a congregation is growing numerically, they must be unsound. How far we have moved from the agenda to restore New Testament Christianity! Donald McGavran, professor of missions and church growth at Fuller Seminary in California, says: "For a church to claim to be a New Testament church because it has the right form, as regards deacons and elders, and right ritual in regard to communion and baptism, and right name is, to be sure, good. But the claim sounds a little hollow when the New Testament life and exuberant ability to proclaim the Gospel and propagate churches are lacking. A marble statue of a horse might exhibit all the outward forms, but lacking the ability to run and father colts; it cannot really claim to be a horse. To truly be New Testament churches, the gathering of Christians must want to grow, know how to grow, and pay the price to grow."

When the church is not growing numerically, it frustrates all godly people. Different people have reacted to the assumed stagnation in different ways. And it just seems to be human nature that when something is not working right we want to tinker with it.

Some have concluded that growth is difficult and washed their hands of it. They have turned their attention inward: some to fighting, marking and hobby riding; others to buildings, programs and constant activity.

Still others apparently have made change their god and gone about it with an agenda bent on a new vision for the Lord's Kingdom. They scour the religious landscape to "see what is working." They have joined the "fad of the month club." This month it may be lighting, next may be presentation systems and later in the year we will talk about celebration. Just hang on we will eventually market the church to a materialistic consumer-driven market. We might eventually make God so accessible that we believe Him to be just like you and me. They would do well to remember the state of those Paul identifies, *"Professing themselves to be wise, they became fools, And changed the glory of the incorruptible God into an image made like to corruptible man"* (Romans 1:22-23). Remember God's message in Isaiah: *"For as the heavens are higher than the earth, so are my ways higher than your ways, and my thoughts than your thoughts"* (Isaiah 55:9). Consumer driven churches are not producing spiritual giants, but an immaturity that pouts, whines, and may even desert when it does not get its way. We are not even hinting that it is wrong to tamper with the lighting or that presentation systems are sinful, but if we make growth our god, eventually we will be led into changes that are sinful. Ultimately we have got to offer our message, presented as God has given it, that demands repentance, true sorrow, change of lifestyle, sacrifice, and a cross for each of us. That message will never market well.

Others have made rigidity in opposition to change their banner. There are those who have deified the 1950's. If you don't believe that, just look in on some of our buildings with the design, lighting, sound systems, classrooms, teaching materials, newsletters, and presentation styles. Even the water fountains and "pulpit flowers" say we are stuck in the past. Suggest any change and you will be a marked man. These believe they are defenders of the faith when they squash an innovative approach or put a creative presenter in his place.

To both of these groups, we would say our gospel is not five days old nor 50 years old, but 2,000 years old. That ancient gospel must be preached without addition or subtraction *"in season and out of season"* (2 Timothy 4:2). When presented in its purity, it will still change hearts. God is not surprised when men reject His plan anymore than when they rejected His Son. Jesus made it clear that some would reject Him and His Words (John 12:48). We must challenge both those who seek change just for the sake of change, as well as those who hold to traditions of men as authoritative.

But maybe, just maybe the gospel is not *"out of season"* right now. Maybe we just have not tried. Perhaps it is our lack of commitment to the pure life-changing gospel. Maybe we would do well to stop keeping the faith and start sharing it. Before you slam me too hard, may I ask when was the last time you presented the gospel in clear and loving terms to a person who was not a Christian? Growth is complicated. If you do not believe that fact, survey the Dow Jones chart in your Sunday paper or ask some small business owner. Growth is hard, but we have what the world needs. They just do not know they need it.

With growth will come change because change is inevitable. The fact is, we all enjoy the changes in our world that bring convenience. Some might pine away for the good ole' days, but I find they do so while sitting in air-conditioned houses and driving fine cars instead of riding in a horse and buggy. To the Christian, change is an actual necessity. There came that great moment in time when we were translated from the kingdom of darkness into the kingdom of His dear Son (Colossians 1:13) and before that could happen there had to be a change of heart, a change of allegiance, and a change of lifestyle. Christianity is all about change (Matthew 18:1-5). It was that kind of change that led Paul to know that a man like Philemon could accept a runaway thief of a slave who had also become a greatly changed man (Philemon 10-17). When that vast throng in Acts 2 asked that question of all questions: "What shall we do?" Peter's first and immediate inspired response is "change!" Baptism requires a change in behavior toward God (vs. 42) and a change in behavior toward each other (vss. 44-45). When one obeys the gospel from the heart, the changes are very real (Romans 6:17). Great moments of change are great teaching moments. Our children need to hear of that moment when we determined to follow the Lord and surrendered our all to Him, when He led us out of the bondage of sin and into the grace of God.

When it comes to the changes in our fellowship, there have been blessings. It seems a growth in spirituality among our people has taken place. We now have direct mission involvement and service activities in many communities in the name of Christ. But many of the changes would not receive such rave reviews. Many who wear the name Christian seem more materialistic, and much of the change has produced uncertainty as to who we actually are and what we stand for.

Change is uncomfortable for some of us. We find it hard even to change those things we wish to change, like eating and exercise habits, not to mention study habits and work habits. People have been described as reacting to change as either turtles, very slow, or rabbits, jumping right into it. Change is all around us. Perhaps one of the most significant questions the people of God face in the midst of rapidly changing times is, "How are we to face the challenge of a changing world?" Change is a reality. Transition is also a reality. Will the church of the Lord Jesus Christ respond, or will she crawl back into the sand and hide?

Let me be very, very clear. The Lord's church will be OK. Even the gates of hell cannot impede its ultimate progress (Matthew 16:16-18). That is as good a promise as we have from the Lord in a day like this. Strauch wrote: "The church is the most precious thing on earth to God." He's correct. Paul said it was purchased with His own blood (Acts 20:28). The church is eternal and God-protected, and will "work" in any culture, in any time.

What must we do? Change? Then change! But here is a clear and concise warning: Change carefully, remembering God's never-changing pattern and design for His church. Remember also its message and worship, remembering His laws governing even expediencies.

The old preacher used to say: "I suppose it'd bring more people in to offer fried chicken and sweet tea on the Lord's Supper." (Shockingly, in some corners of our brotherhood it is being suggested that such a ridiculous concept would be acceptable.) It would also bring in more people to have air conditioning than not. Why one and not the other? Why a meal for our guests but not beer and pizza night? The reason seems too simple to mention. One changes doctrine and is wrong; the other is method and changes nothing of God's plan. Yes, the Bible is God's love letter to man, but it is also His law for man. To suggest that none of the New Testament is law exhibits a total lack of an even cursory understanding of plain texts. We must be prepared to rebuke strongly those who seem to effortlessly throw aside Bible instruction; along with those who speak disparagingly of the faith and/or the Lord's church.

Let me suggest five challenges that lie before us in changing times:

1. The challenge to remember those things that must not change:

In Malachi 3:6, God says, "I, the Lord, do not change." This is a theological term called the immutability of God. That means He has always been the same, He is the same right now, and He will always be the same.

Hebrews 13:8-9b speaks of the changeless Christ. *"Jesus Christ is the same yesterday, today, and forever. Do not be carried about with various and strange doctrines. For it is good that the heart be established by grace"* In the midst of transition, hold on to this: "Jesus Christ is the same yesterday and today and forever."

That means we are not going to jump on every bandwagon that comes along.

That means we will not try out every fad or fashion that comes down the pike, just because it's new or just because it works somewhere else. Hebrews says to us, hold on to the changeless Christ, watch out, and *"Do not be carried about with various and strange doctrines. For it is good that the heart be established by grace."* Do not be panicked into thinking you have to do something crazy in order to stay afloat. Do not be fooled into believing that you have to make sweeping changes just because. Remember, Jesus Christ is the Lord of the church, and He is the same, He is dependable, yesterday, today, and forever.

God's love never changes. Jeremiah 31:3: God says *"I have loved you with an everlasting love."* You were made to be loved by God. His love is continuous. It is everlasting. It is consistent. God's love is based on His character. Romans 8:38 in the Message translation says, *"Nothing living or dead, angelic or demonic, today or tomorrow, thinkable or unthinkable — absolutely nothing can get between us and God's love."*

God's Word will never change: Isaiah 40:8 says, *"The grass withers and the flowers fade, but the Word of our God shall stand forever."* It is timeless, enduring, and eternal. It never withers; it is always fresh. It does not get stale. God's Word is never out of date. If we want to build our lives in a way that is solid and significant and handles the stress and the changes of today, we had better build it on the truth of God's Word because it is bedrock. It is not going to change. Popular opinion is going to change; psychology books are going to change; talk radio hosts will change what they talk about. Everything else changes. But God's Word does not. So if you want stability, build your life on God's unchanging truth.

So in the midst of the changes we face, remember the things that will never change. New members. Yes. New methods. Yes. But: Same book, same Savior, same faith and doctrine.

2. The challenge to encourage creative methods and uses of the tools that God allows us to develop.

As we strive to avoid making changes that are not within the boundaries of God's Word, we face a danger of stifling the creativity of those around us. Is there a young Jule Miller out there? Before his death, Brother Miller told me of being a young preacher in his 20's and realizing that while all his preaching friends were telling stories of hundreds of conversions from their meetings and preaching engagements he felt useless, for he was not having that effect. So, out of his own inability, he developed a series of slides with a script which he later put on tape and filmstrips and then on VCR and now you can use it on DVD and perhaps hundreds of thousands have become Christians from his creative use of his "inabilities." Would we have encouraged such an innovative method? Is there a young Jimmy Allen full of fire and zest, a young Gus Nichols who loves local work, a young Lipscomb, Harding or Hardeman with minds as sharp as any in our world, a young Ira North or Batsell Barrett Baxter with abilities to move people to action? And will we encourage them as they grow or will we step on their youth? John Galsworthy, a writer from the late 1800's, said: "If you do not think about the future, you cannot have one."

Most of us know that in a local congregation it is easy to make the wrong decisions or to move too slowly and miss golden opportunities. Likewise, we can move too fast and cause hurt and harm when only good was intended. Let us pray for and work toward the future that our children will have wisdom from above (James 3:17). Remember the old adage: "Attempt great things for God and expect great help from God."

3. The challenge to allow true congregational autonomy.

It is obviously a greater challenge to allow autonomy when we hear of a sister congregation doing what we would not advise or even do ourselves in the congregations where we serve. It is easy to keep unity and allow autonomy when we are mirrors of each other.

Remember, I am not talking doctrinally here. Our doctrine has already been determined by God's breath. I am not talking about those who have obviously left the gospel plan of salvation, the purity of worship and the roles God has given us or those who say they have not "left their core" values while their actions prove otherwise. Howard Norton was "dead-on" in his description and evaluation, quoted in the October issue of *The Christian Chronicle:* "My heart is broken because of the unscriptural changes that are taking place in a small number of churches of Christ. The introduction of instrumental music into the public assemblies is but one example. Such changes are neither casual nor cosmetic. They are based on a fundamental shift in attitude toward the New Testament as the authoritative divine guide for the church today. Those making these changes have decided to introduce instrumental music even though there is not a shred of justification for it in the New Testament of in early church history. These people then tell us that they have made no significant change in the church's core values. What a falsehood!" (October, 2003). There has been and always will be those who deny the scriptures. But in a brotherhood of tens of thousands of congregations only a fraction of them have gone that far astray.

Let us *"Endeavor to keep the unity of the spirit in the bond of peace"* (Ephesians 4:3) and to *"Love the brotherhood"* (1 Peter 2:17). The self-righteousness, arrogance and exclusivity exhibited within either extreme are not becoming to those who claim the name Christian. You and I have both heard people who suspect others for their practices when they have already admitted that the issue under question is not a matter of doctrine, but of practice and preference. You may not like the translation they choose to use, you may not like the songs they choose to use, the direction you think their choices are heading, their use of technology and a hundred other such matters, but if you do not allow the elders to lead there, you are casting a vote toward destroying peace in God's Family choosing to mark those over non-doctrinal matters! Let us cease the maliciousness and scandalous slandering that have been the fuel of many brotherhood fires.

4. The challenge to personal spiritual growth.

Christianity is ultimately a very personal quest, for we will each stand before the judge of all the earth as individuals. In a day where there is so much instability we must not become discouraged and give up or become sidetracked (Hebrews 10:39; 2 Corinthians 4:16).

Ephesians 4:11-16 teaches that as each individual part of the body, the church, grows up into Jesus the head of the body, we individually contribute to the growth (like a joint in a human body) of the rest of the church. As we grow, this Scripture says, we cause the church to grow. If we do not grow or work properly, we impede the growth of the body. As each individual part or person in the church grows, the whole church is built up in love.

Do not join the ranks of those nay-sayers who have the Elijah complex, having begun to believe they are the only ones who care and no one else is interested in keeping the faith. The message is still working around the world. And the more we become like Christ, the more we will grow—not conformed, but transformed.

5. The challenge to remember God's promises.

I am told there are over 6000 promises in the Bible. Some seem especially comforting in light of the challenges that lie before us. *"I am with you always"* Matthew 28:20. *"Now unto him that is able to do exceeding abundantly above all that we ask or think, according to the power that worketh in us, Unto him be glory in the church by Christ Jesus throughout all ages, world without end. Amen"* (Ephesians 3:20-21). *"So shall my word be that goeth forth out of my mouth: it shall not return unto me void, but it shall accomplish that which I please, and it shall prosper in the thing whereto I sent it"* (Isaiah 55:11). Let us commit to keep our eyes focused on the Lord first of all (Hebrews 12:2). Norvel Young had it right: "The future is as bright as the promises of God."

Finally, let us remember that if the church is to grow it must change. If you want to enlist dynamic change in your congregation, get busy in the business of helping it to grow. Grow it with the only kind of real growth, God's way. Teach lost souls the pure, simple, good news of Jesus Christ and as His ambassador be a part of the process of God giving the increase as they obey His gospel. You want issues to become less divisive, then stir the waters! You want unity to become more prominent, stir the waters! Stir the waters!

Worship in Our Time

Contemporary or Traditional?

Russell L. Dyer

Worship conjures about as many personal images in mind as there are people to consider its meaning. When I consider worship, what comes to mind is the picture of the congregational assembly of my youth. I loved it. We sang. We prayed. We listened to the Word being proclaimed. We gave. We remembered the sacrificial death of Jesus in the emblems of the Lord's Supper. It was a time of recognizing the greatness of God in all His capacities. It was refreshment to our faith and to our lives. It was a reverent and desiring approach to the Father who we knew loved us.

When confronted with the temptation to receive kingdoms for bowing and worshiping the devil, Jesus refused. He referenced scripture and said, *"Away with you, Satan! For it is written, 'You shall worship the Lord your God, and Him only you shall serve' "* (Matthew 6:10). That we may come boldly before God and offer to Him the sacrifice of our praise has to be among the richest treasures and greatest opportunities we have in this world. Still, I am reminded of the bit of wisdom imparted by a seventh grade geography teacher. Mrs. Giffert wanted to make sure we understood what it meant to be in junior high school as compared to elementary school. She told us that we would be allowed more freedom and privilege as we continued to advance in our education. Then she made the statements she would repeat many times throughout the year as she taught us. She said, "Every privilege comes with a responsibility. The greater your privilege, the greater your responsibility will be." Such a statement did not make much of an impression on a bunch of twelve-year-olds. Only with the passage of time and a maturing life did the meaning of her reflective words come home with meaning. We do have the great blessing and privilege of worship. We carry with that blessing the responsibility that is not to be taken lightly.

The public worship of the church has always been a point of discussion and even division. Some of the clearly divisive points that separate denominations have to do with the conduct and constitution of worship by members as they assemble. Even within the church, there have been long-standing disagreements about worship within the church assemblies. In recent years, these disagreements have found themselves coming from greater distances of belief and practice, as members of the body seem to be farther from one another. Two descriptive words have come into common usage to represent the opposing poles of belief, "Contemporary" and "Traditional". These words have been joined with "Worship" to define or declare sides in the apparent argument.

Without clear definition or meaning associated with such terms, leaders and congregations are left wondering where they stand in the midst of such a debate. Are we traditional or are we contemporary?

A recent family vacation allowed my family to visit with three congregations as they assembled for either worship or Bible classes. Each of the congregations had some unique characteristics. The picture of worship drawn from each place allowed for some reflection on the general concept of worship, as it is perceived by some of us.

The first congregation was in a moderate sized town in southern Alabama. Their building has been in place for about three-quarters of a century. There are some members who have been a part of that congregation for most of that time span. The building has been remodeled in recent years and is very attractive and comfortable. At the time of our visit, the membership was somewhat smaller than it was thirty years ago. Other than the change in numbers, the activity of worship was very close to what has been practiced from the beginning of the assemblies there. The congregational singing of familiar songs, a scripturally based and life challenging lesson, a reverent observance of the Lord's Supper, earnest prayers, and financial giving, combined with the warm fellowship to raise attention to the value of God in our lives.

The second congregation was in a tourist area of Florida. We were present for the mid-week Bible classes, and did not have the opportunity to be present for a scheduled time that included congregational worship. We did attend a class that was engaged in a study of worship, especially relating to the assembly for worship. They were using a small paperback book as a guide for their study. As I had previously read the book, I knew that the class would be challenging for me. The class began with the question of why we worship. There seemed to be an agreement by several in the class that worship is about us. The teacher stated that through his years of study he had come to the belief that there are no required acts of worship. He stated that he was comfortable with what they did in their worship assemblies, but did not see the activity as required. The general response of the class was taken as an agreement to his statement.

The third congregation we visited was in northern Louisiana and happened to meet near the highway, making it easy to locate their building. The assembly for worship was held prior to their Bible classes. So, as we arrived and were warmly greeted, we made our way into the worship area. At the front of the seating was a man trying to get people to sing with him as he lead some newer songs. The worship assembly had a more "formal" beginning shortly after we arrived. After some introductory remarks the song leader encouraged everyone to take a few moments to greet one another and the visitors. It appeared that there were about 75 people present. Everything was conducted in a very casual manner. People were all dressed very casually. Only one man was in a suit, and even he did not formalize it with a tie. Most of the songs were newer, "praise" type songs. Comments from the song leader and the preacher during the service made me aware that they were trying to change the course of the congregation. One of the songs had a place in it where some of the people clapped their hands. Most did not. The preacher later commented about the behavior and noted, "We are not sure yet that we should do that." His tone and words implied that they were trying to see where they could change practices. The comments he made in his sermon noted that there were going to be more lessons to help them see where they could go and what they could do. At the end of the service, one of the leaders made a few announcements and then encouraged members not to give up on them. He asked that everyone be patient through the end of the year (5 1/2 months). He said, "Then we can see where we are." It struck me that they did not seem to know where it was that they were going.

We noticed that each of the congregations we visited had strengths and weaknesses. In that way they are like every other congregation of the church. There is no reason to question the sincerity or integrity of the leaders or the congregation as a whole. These three congregations are just given as recent examples of some of the things that are challenging the average congregation, especially in the public assembly for worship.

Our challenge is to carefully consider the public worship of the church. There should be no doubt that the public worship of the church provides a recognizable picture of the way a congregation sees God and His Word. There have long been protracted discussions that have considered the constitution of proper worship. Recognizing what worship is supposed to be, to whom it belongs, and how it may properly be conducted is necessary to fully present ourselves to God.

Give Worship the Meaning it is Supposed to Have

In order to do something properly; it is necessary to know what it is that is being done. It is early in the record of the historical progress of humanity that we recognize determined acts of worship. Such acts are segregated or separated from the general acts of service that are a part of living a godly life. While it is understood that our lives are to be lived in a manner that honors God, the worship under consideration is more defined in a determined pattern. In the fourth chapter of Genesis we learn that worship that is offered to God can be accepted, or deemed unacceptable by God. We read that *"Abel offered a more excellent sacrifice than Cain"* (Hebrews 11:4). It was through the nature of the practice of worship that Abel is recognized as righteous or right behaving. In contrast to his brother, Cain made an offering to God that was not acceptable. That unacceptable worship combined with his subsequent behavior, causing Cain to be recognized as unrighteous or not right in his behavior.

Doing worship right requires that we know what it is. Assigning a definition to worship is not difficult. It is applying a meaning that generates the difficulty in us and among us. The common word for worship among the Hebrews was *shachah,* which means "to bow down, to do homage." Our greater interest is given to the Greek words of the New Testament that are used to express worship. The key word is *proskuneo,* which literally means, "to kiss toward." It conveys the idea of doing humble obeisance to God. Another notable word is *latreuo,* which has the meaning of "service or ministry." It should be noticed that all worship is service, but not all service fits the definition of worship. Still, there must be something of a usable or working definition for us. According to Warren Wiersbe, *"Worship is the believer's response of all that they are – mind, emotions, will, and body – to what God says and does."*[1] I am more inclined to a practical explanation or definition of worship. I would say,

> *"Worship of God is recognizing the very nature of God for who He is and what He has done, and undertaking the activities that are designed by that nature to appropriately praise Him."*

The evolving nature of language keeps a definition from being final in all details. Still, the principle it conveys remains constant. Again, I recognize that it is not so much the defining of terms that falls into contention as it is the application of that definition. It is absolutely necessary to have a good definition as a reference if we are to have a good application. We cannot determine a practice to be right or a wrong if there is no defined principle from which it is derived.

Worship is tied to four active matters:

1. Information. We do not worship what we do not know. Worship is derived from some understanding of that which we are trying to worship. A Samaritan woman recognized the difference between the teaching of the Jews and the Samaritans regarding worship. Her question related to the proper geographic location for worship. Jesus made clear that her question arose from ignorance. *"You worship what you do not know; we know what we worship"* (John 4:22). Similarly, Paul confronted the people of Athens for their ignorance in worship. *"Men of Athens, I perceive that in all things you are very religious; for as I was passing through and considering the objects of your worship, I even found an altar with this inscription: TO THE UNKNOWN GOD. Therefore, the One whom you worship without knowing, Him I proclaim to you"* (Acts 17:22-23). Perhaps there have been many people and cultures that have tried to worship a god that they did not know. Paul told his Grecian listeners that he was making that unknown god known to them. He further told them that God had overlooked their time of ignorance, and was calling them to turn to Him. God wanted them to worship Him in a more complete knowledge of Him.

   There are certain things we need to know to even begin a course of worship. We need to know whom or what is being worshipped. There must be someone or something that is the object of the worship we offer. Once knowing who or what, we need to know how. How worship is to be offered is the practical aspect of the consideration. To be possible, worship must be practiced in activities that are understandable by the ones who are offering the worship, as well as the one who is receiving the worship.

2. Motivation. Once we are aware of whom it is that we worship and how that worship is to be practiced, we need motivation to do what is to be done. Here, we look not only at the outward form, but also at the inward heart.

   The activities we undertake in our lives fall into two primary categories. There are things that we are compelled to do, and things that we do by choice. There are activities that are forced upon us. Such activities may be as important as being for the preservation of our lives, or as simple as satisfying the plans of some outside force. Sometimes we do things just to satisfy other people. Of course, if it is to satisfy a government or a wife, that activity may tend to preserve your life. Other activities are done as a matter of choice or personal desire. We do some things just because we want to do them. It is possible for the two to be mixed.

   Worship is a choice. The devil challenged Jesus to *"fall down and worship"* him (Matthew 4:9). Jesus chose not to do so. When choice is available, we look for reasons to do or not to do. We call that reason, motivation. When there is no choice to be made the only motivation is that of force. My mother used to force me to clean my room and make my bed. There was no reasonable choice for me to make. She had the power to force me to do as she saw fit. Worship is far from force. So, there must be enough of a motivation that we will choose to worship over other things that we might desire to do.

   The very nature of God beckons us to worship Him. Jesus claimed that God seeks our worship. He desires it. The person and position of God calls for worship. The world He has made for us demands our worshipful response. The caring and benevolent actions of God for us, especially in the loving sacrifice of His Son, evoke from every observant heart the outpouring of thankful worship. In short, God deserves our worship. That is at the heart of the motive.

3. Application. Things are almost always harder to do than they appear. We may laugh at that aspect of the "Murphy's Law" type of principles. We also have to admit the truth that is contained within them. Few things are as simple as it seems they should be. Truth ought to be easy to apply. The fact of the matter is that we may well know what to do, and even have strong motive to do it, and yet not do it.

   The application of worship takes it from thinking to active working. For the Jew who lived under the Law of Moses, it meant actually going to the herd, picking the lamb, and physically sacrificing that animal. Worship is not just about the heart. It is also about the practice of the activities of worship. Paul wrote of "singing and making melody in your heart unto the Lord." To sing as worship, a person has to verbalize the intentions of the heart. The same is true of any activity that is intended to worship God. It does take heart, but it also takes action that fits the understood nature.

4. Dedication. Worship is a continuing practice. It arises from conscious recognition of what God does. Consider the dedication of Daniel. Daniel let nothing deter him from his continuing practice of praying to God. The accomplishment of anything of value takes dedication to that goal. The general living of a Christian life takes the dedication of laying aside anything that might deter or hinder the chosen course.

> *"Therefore we also, since we are surrounded by so great a cloud of witnesses, let us lay aside every weight, and the sin which so easily ensnares us, and let us run with endurance the race that is set before us, looking unto Jesus, the author and finisher of our faith, who for the joy that was set before Him endured the cross, despising the shame, and has sat down at the right hand of the throne of God"* (Hebrews 12:1-2).

In previous times, it was common to see advertisements that encouraged people to make it a practice to attend worship. Dedication to worship has been undermined by a variety of things. Our society once guarded Sunday from interfering activities. Sunday has become a day for sports at every level, household chores, and shopping. The progression of change in our living circumstances has challenged our dedication to the practice of public worship. Perceiving all of the distractions that now affect attendance at public worship, it must be understood that dedication is an indispensable ingredient.

Locating the Worship Struggles

There have always been debates concerning what elements should or should not be a part of our public worship of God. Determining what should be applied in the practice of worship may seem to be an easy matter. Really it could be. It is just that the human involvement as a part of the determining factor disrupts the applications. Preference, prejudice, tradition, and enjoyment often vie for superiority in the applications of choice. A friend was discussing with me the practice of worship. She said, "I like the fact that so much of your practice of worship is so tied to the scriptures, but when it comes to the music I like all of the stuff that is added by using the instruments." Preference was obviously important to my friend.

Recognizing the modern conflicts finds the old conflicts still alive. How we appropriately worship God has been a appreciable challenge since the earliest of days. Cain and Abel each offered sacrifices of worship to God. The sacrifice of Abel was accepted. The sacrifice of Cain was not. With such an example, and other incidences of note, we are called to carefully consider what it is that we bring to the "table" of worship. There are a wide variety of opinions to be found in just about every religious group. For the sake of space we will divide them into two basic categories. On the one side, some people suggest that worship is generally undefined and open to the flowing changes of culture and personal preference. On the other is the belief that only what can be clearly identified by direct command or example can be allowed into the worship of the church. Consider the following quote from the late Andy T. Richie, a long-time teacher on the subject of worship at Harding University.

> *"There are two extremes in attitude toward the idea of regulatory teachings from God. One of them might be described by the almost trite idea of cold legalism. The other is that of sentimentalizing and humanizing everything. The first would make anything right if it comes within the bounds of law, and the other would almost deny that God has any regulations for people today – that whatever they feel to be right is right, that whatever works is right."*[2]

No one should attempt to undermine the integrity or sincerity of either general group. Still, both cannot be right. That which is acceptable to God dictates a direction to be recognized.

By definition, worship is a prescribed activity or group of activities. "Worship is not merely a feeling, but the expression of one's devotion in actions. The critical issue is whether or not one has biblical authority for the actions he offers as divine service. Neither right acts with wrong motives, nor wrong acts with right motives, constitute pure worship. It is authorized actions offered from hearts with pure motives which constitute the worship our God deserves."[3]

There is very little question about whether we should worship. Even people who rarely or never assemble with others in an effort to worship recognize that it should be done. Even with that cognitive recognition, societal distractions have lessened the importance of worship and have taken a toll on regular attendance. As numbers decline, faithful and dedicated worshippers question what is to be done to gain the return of people to worship.

There are two main elements involved in the effort to return people to the active practice of worship. The first element is loyal pride. We do not like to lose. Being a part of a local church takes an investment of a person. An investment decline has all the markings of loss. We do not like to be seen by others in a losing capacity. The second element is honest care for souls. When we believe that we are right, we want others to be right. Believing that worship is a necessary part of the Christian life makes us want the people we love to share that belief. Seeing we are commanded to worship challenges us to pull others into line with what we see is right. That we would want people to realize the importance of worshipping God is an obviously good thing. Speaking of God's view of His people, "He delights in their corporate worship. As important as our private worship is, it must be balanced by congregational worship; and this is where the church comes in."[4] How we use the activities of worship to attract and hold people is the point at which the conflict between the "traditional" and the "contemporary" arises.

Putting a Face to the Conflict

The progression of times is one of our greatest friends, and fiercest foes. Peter reminds us that time is the friend of man in the allowance of opportunity that it beings. *"But, beloved, do not forget this one thing, that with the Lord one day is as a thousand years, and a thousand years as one day. The Lord is not slack concerning His promise, as some count slackness, but is longsuffering toward us, not willing that any should perish but that all should come to repentance"* (2 Peter 3:8, 9). The other end of the matter is that time allows for the continuing flow of cultural and generational changes to press our thinking and bend our will. Much like another deems the styles of clothing of one generation unacceptable, so does every aspect of our lives meet the time challenge. Looking at the styles of a previous generation, we may be inclined to say that they were tasteless or boring. At the same time, those who consider their style to be "classic" may see the following generation to be so radical as to be totally devoid of taste. Both perspectives may be right and wrong at the same time. There may be elements of truth in each conclusion, and at the same time be inaccurate by making such a broad generalization.

The conflict that is generally set between the "contemporary" and the "traditional" proponents needs to be carefully balanced. Consider an example. There was a time when entering a place of worship we would find a white linen cloth covering the trays containing the Lord's Supper. When someone failed to cover the elements, it was thought to be sacrilege and sinful. Even when it was determined that no covering was required by scripture, tradition bore the upper hand. For the cloth served the purpose of keeping flies from the bread and fruit of the vine. There are often good reasons why traditional practices are as they are. At the same time, we have allowed advancements in technology and sociology to greatly affect the church without challenge. Air conditioning is a contemporary pleasure that became a part of the atmosphere of most worship assemblies in the second half of the twentieth century. While there may be a few negatives associated with a closed and comfortable building, there are a lot fewer flies.

There needs to be some understanding of meaning. Rush Limbaugh says that words have meaning. I will surely go that far with him. If we are going to use defined words to apply to individual or collective practices, it is important to grasp what is meant. It can be challenging. Trying to identify exactly what is meant by contemporary or traditional worship is like trying to identify an elephant through a magnifying glass. There are two ways with which I could address identification. I could dissect all of the parts that are commonly a part of those services and surely miss some important factors. My choice is to recognize the general philosophy and application of the concept. Some of the identifiable aspects will be mentioned. In this way, the implications and categorizations may be more recognizable.

The practice of what is often called "traditional worship" is a little more easily defined. These practices are generally more structured or limited in practice. The meaning and order of tradition is something that has become an accepted practice through the continuance of use over time. Traditional worship finds its center in a strong adherance to Biblical authority. Once a practice or behavior is recognized, it is considered a permanent practice. Authorization is the common thread of tradition. Still, there are variances of traditional practices to be found even in close geographical locations. Even with some variance of practice there generally remains a symbiotic or agreeing relationship. Again, it is the guiding principles, and general applications, to which we turn our attention as we search for clear meaning in tradition.

The word contemporary carries the meaning, "coexisting; of the same age, or present." When used as an adjective, it applies to anything that is of the here and now. We are contemporary as long as we live in this age. Typically, the meaning is narrowed in application to mean those things that are drawn of the age. Contemporary clothing would not include all clothing that exists, but clothing that reflects the tastes and fashions brought by the tastes of the day. You may have a "Leisure Suit" hanging in your closet, but it is not contemporary in the limited definition applied. "Innovative" may actually be a better term to apply to something that is generated within a certain time frame and cultural setting. Music that is being written in the present era would rightly be considered contemporary. "Oldies" may continue to play on certain radio stations and in elevators, but do not conform to the generally understood meaning of contemporary.

Innovative styles stretch the borders of traditional thinking so much that there is often conflict between the two. The conflict is one of a perceived attitude. The traditional concept likes itself and considers any disruption of accepted form to be unacceptable. The innovative concept seeks a break from practiced patterns. Change and breaking from tradition becomes a driving force. Classic or traditional practices are presented as being without the kind of intellectual challenge that the innovative practices bring.

The Heart of the Matter

If worship has a definition there are limits to what can rightly be called worship. Simply because a practice is desired and done in connection to an assembly of Christians does not make it worship. Because a thing can be done by an assembled group does not make it worship. It is still good to remember that Cain did bring an offering, but the offering was not acceptable worship (Genesis 4:3-5). Vying new or innovative styles in worship against more traditional styles is an unproductive endeavor. Each must be weighed on its own scriptural merits. It needs to be remembered that worship is not about the preference or benefit of the worshipper. It is about honoring God. "God will not be involved in something that does not honor Him."[5]

Godly worship has been a vital part of the life of the church from the earliest days in Jerusalem. These were people who loved to praise God with one another (Acts 2:46-47). While the church in Jerusalem was not without difficulties, it was a great congregation. "What ultimately makes a church great is its emphasis on worshiping God."[6]

We should not infer that worship is limited to simple and subservient efforts to praise our Lord. Worship also edifies and benefits the worshipper. There are educational, instructional, and life building aspects to worship. We are stirred and reminded who we are and how we are to live, when we worship. The fellowship of other worshippers encourages and challenges us to live better lives (Hebrews 10:24-25). There is also an evangelistic thrust to worship. The public worship of the church is designed for the participation of Christians. Still, it is not a closed-door event. Visitors and strangers have been a part of gatherings from the earliest days. People were attracted in Jerusalem, and were ultimately saved (Acts 2:47). Paul stressed the importance of the impression our assemblies make on strangers (1 Corinthians 14:23-24). It would appear that these two aspects of worship are not to be disregarded, but they are not the primary consideration as the worshippers determine the details of worship. So, it is not a matter of whether an assembly is determined to be contemporary or traditional, but that the worship correctly brings glory to God and results in the edification of Christians and non-Christians alike.

The church, and our relationship to God, does not thrive amid rebellion and change. When I was seventeen, I had a pair of old blue jeans. They were patched worn and torn. I loved them. They fit the culture of my school and my anti-dress-code style of life. On a Sunday evening we prepared to attend an evening worship. I wore my jeans. My dad walked into the room and looked worried. He kindly asked, "Son, wouldn't you like to go and put on a nice pair of slacks?" I was ready. I responded, "God does not look on the outward appearance of a man, but on his heart." I couldn't tell him where it was found, but I knew it was in the Bible. He too was ready. He explained that people who could not so readily see my heart would also be looking at me. Further, he made clear that I needed to consider carefully what my heart was saying. I changed my clothes that day, because my dad was important to me. With time, I have come to know even more how important God is as we approach Him in worship.

Consider the Differences

Traditional worship derives its practices from two directions. Long held practices that have stood the test of time and scriptural practicality are the most common source for order and content of public worship. Biblical principles and demands lay a foundation that challenges the thinking of those who aspire to make sure that what is done, is done with authority. "In spirit and truth" are the words that are hammered into the thinking pattern as it draws from the source. Phrases such as "decently and in order" find a home in traditional practices. Since "tradition" implies that it has been passed from one generation or group to another, traditional worship is generally considered to be "cross-generational." Songs used for such assemblies are commonly well known to most participants. There is comfort and security that is found in recognizable patterns. While newer songs are added over time, congregational singing adapts slowly to new words and music. Preaching in traditional worship has a high volume of scripture content and reference. While traditional lessons generally use application stories, illustrational stories are secondary to the Bible references. Technology that is used is often subdued and not given much reference. Mood is left to fend for itself, as accuracy of content is pushed to the forefront. One of the strongest criticisms of traditional worship claims that it has become ineffective and lifeless. "Some of us have backed so far away from the ditch of emotionalism that we have gotten entangled in the fence of legalism and cold ritual."[7]

Contemporary worship begins with a different premise. A more flexible source and direction for the content of the innovative style supplies any form that it has. Determining that there is no clearly defined control on the activities of worship gives much greater latitude to improvise and change the direction, pattern, and content. "...there was no archetypal form or original blueprint of worship prescribed for the early church in Jerusalem or subsequent churches ... There is no evidence that Paul ever felt compelled to standardize worship according to some divine blueprint."[8] Such seems to be the concept of thinking. I will list a few of the noticeable aspects of contemporary worship that are found in some places. Keep in mind that these observations are generalized and not consistent in all places. There is a more casual atmosphere, such as would be found at a secular meeting or a concert. High tech sound and lighting equipment are obvious and used to generate a more aesthetically controlled atmosphere. Special singers, singing groups, and songs play a large role in the presentation. Sermons typically avoid doctrine and strong positional stances, choosing instead to amplify the quality of the human spirit. Distinctions that separate the church from any other religious group are generally avoided, minimized, or even denied. Modern songs known as "praise" songs are the primary source of music to be used. The difference between these songs and the more traditional songs is that of content, musical style, and generation. Older congregational style singing is supplanted by music influenced more by "Rock" and "Contemporary Christian Music" styles. Usually there are fewer words and less choral arrangement involved. Talented and professional presenters are central leaders. While most of the congregations of the church still avoid the use of instruments during the worship assemblies, some of the same songs are used at other assemblies with instrumental accompaniment. Hand waving and, clapping during songs is practiced as a sign of personal involvement and approval. No formal invitation for baptism or repentance is extended during the worship. Some have described this style as being like a box of chocolates, "You never know what kind of treat you are going to find."[9] The reasoning behind promoting a "new kind of worship"[10] is stated in terms such as, "We are not speaking the right language"[11] by sticking to traditional patterns. "Today's culture – a digital culture – no longer relies on the printed word. Learning may come from audiotapes, videos or interactive online tutorials. News comes from television or the Internet. So it's not surprising that people immersed in this digital culture have a hard time coming to church and listening to Scripture readings."[12]

There may be other activities that are distinct to either the traditional or contemporary worship assemblies. Most of the differences that have been listed are plain to see. The greater difference is the difference in the prescriptive determination of what worship is supposed to be. "While liturgical (traditional – rld) worship includes actions by the participants in response to what God has done, such as intercessory prayer, contemporary worship sees the action of the worshipper as the main event. The songs that are sung, the educational value of the sermons, the extent of the worshipper's feeling involved in the service determines the overall value of the worship. This tilts contemporary worship heavily toward subjective experience and away from the objective truth of the Gospel."[13] We need to remember that there is an acceptability problem that relates to the public worship. Determining what is acceptable and what is not acceptable sets the point of contention and controversy between these two points of view.

Caught in the Crossfire

Leaders debate the courses of whole societies as they evolve. Advances in science and technology often place us in a moral dilemma. We then look to the leaders, hoping that they will have the answers that we need. Equivocation is too often the outcome of our trust. The spiritual society must have directional answers that relate to all aspects of the Christian life.

There must be answers about the conduct of proper public worship. Many dedicated Christians are struggling to be right in their approach to God. Those Christians, who are generally a little older and familiar with the more classic approach, find themselves in a quandary wondering if they should, or should not, oppose the imposition of innovative activities.

Some groups have tried to avoid giving one direction or another by offering two forms of worship that meet at separate times, or in separate parts of the same building. On the web site of a Southern Baptist Church two worship services are offered to meet personal preference. The phrase, "If you feel that you might enjoy a more _______________ (contemporary/traditional) style of service...." Times were given for each service. Each style was a matter of personal feelings. Some congregations toy with the use of "blended worship,"[14] where elements of traditional patterns (such as older hymns and congregational singing) are interspersed with the more innovative patterns (such as Contemporary Christian Rock and praise/worship team presentations).

The practical results are mixed. Some people are willing to follow whatever worship form the leaders present. Some are loyal but struggling. A member from a congregation that is pushing such experimentation stated to me, "I really do not like what is going on, but I'll stay because that is my home." Some people are expressing a sense of being lost. Some members are leaving congregations they love in order to find one that practices worship according to their understanding. Others are angry and congregations of the Lord's church are being divided from within.

Gaining Resolve

There must be some reasonable, and above all, God-pleasing resolution to the questions surrounding the nature and activity of worship. Is the classic style of worship all there is? Must we bend to the demands of culture to be relevant? Can we have a real life involving worship and still be scripturally aligned in the doing? The answers are, "No", "No", and most definitely "Yes". Consider the following quote. "Culture changes, the gospel does not. To suggest that this generation is so different as to require a total reframing of the church seems a bit reactionary to me. Yes, the church must be fine-tuned where Scripture allows it so as to remain relevant, but this is true of the church in every generation."[15] When we have to abandon the principles and directives of scripture to be relevant to a culture, we have become that culture and offer to it nothing that it does not already have.

The only dictates to the limits of practice in worship that have any authority are those of Scripture. "Although we have neither precise patterns not a fixed order of service, the NT contains numerous passages which flag up, either explicitly or implicitly, various ingredients making up the corporate expressions of worship of the early Christians."[16] There are clearly described activities that we are taught to practice as worship. They are consistent with all principles of godly behavior, and honor God in their practice.

The question of worship is not really whether a thing is practiced out of tradition or originates in a contemporary setting. It is really a matter of personal preference and presumption acting in a submissive way to Biblical principles that are drawn from God, and that are honoring to Him in practice.

Consider the following suggestions:

1. Draw every practice of corporate worship from clear teaching that expresses an exacting action or a governing principle.
2. Determine who is the center of the action or offering. We need to know whether we are making a show of self or humbling before God. Entertainment and worship are not the same.
3. Test every new idea, practice, literary contribution, or innovation to see if it is consistent with all other acceptable worship, and non-divisive in its application.
4. Allow worship to be evangelistic, but do not turn it into a tool solely intended to attract outsiders. Remember: worship is about God's people praising Him.
5. Allow worship to be counter cultural. Lowering worship practices to the level of the culture removes any unique offering it may have.
6. Allow worship to be a "sacrifice of praise." It should be a dedicated and giving work of a humble heart or hearts to God.
7. Remember that worship is important to God in its nature, accuracy, and presentation.

The challenge for us is to make worship what it ought to be. There will be many songs sung that are yet to be written. There will be styles of presentation that are not yet practiced. There will be orders of service that vary from tradition. If we will keep God in the proper place in our minds, our worship will follow suit. I know that this chapter does not answer all worship questions. What I hope it has done is to give a more balanced look at worship to keep us from tipping to one extreme or the other.

[1] Wiersbe Warren, *Real Worship,* (Baker Book House, Grand Rapids, MI) 2002

[2] Richie, Andy T., Thou Shalt Worship The Lord Thy God, (Firm Foundation Publishing House, Austin, TX, 1969) pg. 49

[3] Shelly, Rubel, Sing His Praise – A case for A Capella Music as Worship Today, (Nashville, TN, 20th Century Christian) 1987, pg. 50

[4] Wiersby, Warren, Real Worship, Baker Book House 2000, pg. 83

[5] Dicker, Lou, *How to Start a God-Centered Contemporary Worship Service,* Central Prebyterian Church, (Baltimore, Maryland) 2000.

[6] MacArthur, John, Jr., *The Master's Plan for the Church,* (Chicago: Moody Press) 1998.

[7] Anderson, Lynn, *In Search of Wonder* (West Monroe, Howard Publishing Co.) 1995, pg. 19

[8] Patzia, Arthur, *The Emergence of the Church* (IVP, 2001), pg. 184

[9] Crutchfield, Earl, congregationalist.org, October, 2002

[10] Vail, Tiffany, *Exposing the Myths Surrounding "Contemporary" Worship,* macucc.org, November, 2002

[11] ibid

[12] ibid

[13] Contemporary Worship: Outreach or Compromise? geocities.com/scottman/Docs/cwcc.html

[14] Kunkle, Bruce, *A Practical Guide to Contemporary Worship,* contemporaryworship.net/chapter1.htm

[15] Smith, Mark, KneEmail#434, June 2003.

[16] Jack, Chris, *Understanding Worship* 16, June 2003

Instrumental Music: Tradition or Scripture?

Ron Williams

Introduction

Should instruments of music be used today in our worship to God Almighty? Listen to the answer given by one religious scholar associated with the Lord's church in years past:

> "The question concerning the use of instrumental music in the church is not to be settled by scriptural authority. It is a question to be determined by general principles and the light of experience. If it could be clearly shown that an organ tends to promote the spirit of devotion and heighten the order and praise of worship in a congregation as a whole, then it would follow that organs should be employed."[1]

Sound familiar? Does this sound like something you have either heard or read recently? Does this sound like something some elder, or preacher, or scholar, would say today concerning what they suggest is "an insignificant issue" versus matters relating to their ideas of "the core gospel?"

Would it surprise you that the above-mentioned quotation was not made by someone in our brotherhood today? Would it surprise you to know that this comment was not made during this century or even the twentieth century as well? W. K. Pendleton, editor of the *Millennial Harbinger* after Alexander Campbell's editorship ended, wrote this opinion in **1857!** Things have really changed.....or have they?

To be consistent with that dispensation of time, notice a different viewpoint given by another Restoration minister, Benjamin Franklin. When he was asked when an organ could be used in the worship services of that day, he replied sarcastically:

> "When a church has lost the spirit of Christ; when an organ is used as an expedient to a 'sorry preacher;' when a church is intended to be a fashionable society, a mere place of amusement; when a church has a large number of dishonest and corrupt men; if a church has given up the idea to convert the world; when the New Testament says anything about it; when the Apostles gave the slightest counsel to instrumental music in a setting of worship."[2]

Who is right and who is wrong? Or, is it possible, as some might suggest, that there is no real "right or wrong" declaration that needs to be made on the issue of instrumental music in the Lord's church any longer? In other words, it is suggested, the discussion is a dead issue and there is no need to either press the matter or to declare one's intentions on something that is no longer significant or important for Biblical study.

Is this true? Has the use of instruments of music in the Lord's church been relegated to an "optional" matter that can be said to be a matter of opinion or preference rather than a discussion of doctrine? Have we come so far in our intellect and learning from educational universities of man, our understanding of culture, and the effects of religious groups around us, that we are now ready to admit that Churches of Christ have been wrong all of these years? Is it the case that we ought to repent of the undue pressure and reproach that we have brought on others by declaring, "they were wrong" for their use of the instrument in worship? Is that where we are today? Are we all ready to say that culture now dictates the doctrine and not the Scriptures?

In a book written in 2001, *The Transforming of a Tradition,* Milton Jones claims that those who maintain an allegiance to a cappella singing are hurting others by their persistence and practice. He argues:

> "Why won't the ones who want a cappella music change? It is more than heritage for many. It is conviction. Even if nearly all of Christendom doesn't agree, they must be faithful. To give up the cause is to lose all for which they have been fighting. They lose identity. How would they be recognized? What would our ancestors think?"[3]

While it might be helpful to know what "our ancestors" would think on these matters, it might be more helpful for the remainder of this chapter to ask another more relevant and pertinent question. What would God think?

The New Testament on the Subject of Music

Since the New Testament is our guide today in all matters of faith, we ought to desire to notice what God ordained men of old were commanded to write down concerning His will for our lives (2 Timothy 3:16-17; 2 Peter 1:20-21) (NKJV). Jude 3 affirms that this faith has been *"once and for all"* delivered to God's people. Since God's Word is sufficient for *"all things that pertain to life and godliness"* (2 Peter 1:3), we ought to reason that God wants us to validate what we do in the name of religion with *"a reason for the hope that is in you"* (1 Peter 3:15).

In regard to the subject of music, the New Testament, without a single exception, mentions the kind of music that God desires for His Son's Church to use in worship to His Name. Since we are charged to handle Scripture reverently and are warned of the consequences of adding to or deleting from God 's Word (2 Timothy 2:15, Revelation 22:18-19), we should seriously study these relevant passages pertaining to musical worship among Christians:

> *"And when they had sung a hymn, they went out to the Mount of Olives"* (Matthew 26:30; Mark 14:26)
>
> *"But at midnight Paul and Silas were praying and singing hymns to God, and the prisoners were listening to them"* (Acts 16:25)
>
> *"And that the Gentiles might glorify God for His mercy, as it is written: 'For this reason I will confess to You among the Gentiles, and sing to Your name"* (Romans 15:9)
>
> *"What is the result then? I will pray with the spirit, and I will also pray with the understanding. I will sing with the spirit and I will also sing with the understanding"* (1 Corinthians 14:15)
>
> *"How is it then, brethren? Whenever you come together, each of you has a psalm, has a teaching, has a tongue, has a revelation, has an interpretation. Let all things be done for edification"* (1 Corinthians 14:26)
>
> *"Speaking to one another in psalms and hymns and spiritual songs, singing and making melody in your heart to the Lord"* (Ephesians 5:19)
>
> *"Let the word of Christ dwell in you richly in all wisdom, teaching and admonishing one another in psalms and hymns and spiritual songs, singing with grace in your hearts to the Lord"* (Colossians 3:16)
>
> *"Saying, "I will declare Your name to My brethren; in the midst of the congregation I will sing praise to You"* (Hebrews 2:12)
>
> *"Therefore by Him let us continually offer the sacrifice of praise to God, that is, the fruit our of lips, giving thanks to His name"* (Hebrews 13:15)
>
> *"Is anyone among you suffering? Let him pray. Is anyone cheerful? Let him sing psalms"* (James 5:13).

In every scripture, without exception, the kind of music that God desires from those who follow Him is a cappella singing. The singing of hymns and psalms, the speaking to one another, the giving of thanks, the fruit of the lips, and the other descriptive phrases given in these texts, are all indications of verbal communication of praise from the worshipper to the One who is to be worshipped.

Where in any of these passages can even a suggestion be found that would support the use of instruments of music in our worship to God? Jesus explained in John 4:24, that *"God is Spirit, and those who worship Him must worship Him in spirit and truth."*

Jesus said that God wanted a spiritual, authority-based, attitude to be given in worship to His Holy Name. The heart as well as the head is to be dedicated to the service of God in our worship to Him.

In this regard, Phil Sanders writes:

> "Instruments cannot speak, teach, admonish, give thanks, praise, proclaim, confess or make melody on your heart. These are the things God wants us to accomplish in our singing. Instruments of music fail to do any of them. This is what makes them additions; they do something different from the instruction. They go beyond the instructions in the New Testament. Jesus taught us in Matthew 7:21-27 that Christians are to do what He says in order to obey His will and enter heaven. The burden of proof for pianos and organs must be on the one who introduces them to show where Jesus has instructed this form of worship. There has never been any evidence from the Bible, from the language, or from history to show that instrumental music in Christian worship has won God's approval."[4]

Tradition or Scripture?

Those who support the use of instrumental music in worship today would suggest that the reason Churches of Christ have not used them is due "to our tradition." What tradition are they referring to? Surely they would not avow that this tradition is like unto the "traditions of men" that Jesus so adamantly condemned in Matthew 15 in regard to the Jews dedicating money to the temple rather than taking care of their own parents. Jesus chastised those of that day, who had *"made the commandment of God of no effect by your tradition"* (Matthew 15:6).

What our Lord said next is of utmost importance to our present discussion of the instrumental music issue. After calling them "hypocrites" (those who say one thing and then do another), Jesus then explained what these individuals were guilty of, in disobeying God's will. Jesus said, *"These people draw near to Me with their mouth, and honor Me with their lips, but their heart is far from Me. And in vain they worship Me, teaching as doctrines the commandments of men"* (Matthew 15:8-9). Notice the emphasis of the final part of that statement;

"In vain they worship Me, ***teaching as doctrines the commandments of men"*** (my emphasis, RW). That, in essence, is what those who are attempting to make instruments of music a "non-issue" in the Lord's church are doing. They are guilty of trying to make a commandment of God (to sing) to become "a mere tradition" and suggest we don't have a valid reason for our lack of use of instruments of music in worship.

Those who suggest that instruments of music are allowable in the worship of the Almighty are the ones guilty of attempting to make doctrine and the commandments of men to be one and the same! Regardless of what hermeneutical hat trick one might try to pull, those who truly love and respect God's Book cannot condone such actions. The very use of the phrase, "traditions of the Church of Christ" is a shame for those who love and revere the simple New Testament teachings of Christ Jesus. As Dave Miller writes,

> "Referring to the church of the New Testament-the church of Christ-as "our tradition" is sectarian, shameful, and biblically inaccurate....The simple 'five-item' worship activity of Churches of Christ was gleaned directly from the biblical text and continues to be the undeniable reality of 'true worship'—despite the recent assaults of the 'new hermeneutic' advocates among us." [5]

Biblical Authority-The Crux of the Matter

Many denominations today are offering more than one worship experience so that differing reflections of thought and culture can be expressed in one's belief and practice of religion. "Contemporary" services along with the "traditional" worship programs are among the options given to many so they can "enjoy" (they suggest) different worship styles in their practice of what they call religion.

Are Churches of Christ soon to be practicing this same phenomenon in the use and/or non-use of mechanical instruments of music? Are we going to see announcement boards that display such messages as, "Coming soon: Bible class praise group with the organ- 9 AM Only" followed by the sign that reads, "'Traditional' worship service in the auditorium to follow at 10 AM"? How inventive and creative could we imagine elderships and preachers might become in the experimentation of the occasional use of instruments in worship? (Less one forgets a lesson from Restoration history, it was this "occasional use of the instrument" in song practice in the church at Midway, Kentucky that prompted the final push for it to be used there in 1860 for all worship assemblies.)

More than ever before, it must be understood, believed, and proclaimed that all Biblical authority resides in our Savior, Jesus Christ (Matthew 28:18). In every kind of religious discussion and question, Christians must ask what it is that the Lord wills for us today in the name of religion (Ephesians 5:10, 17). Christ must have first place in everything that we do to glorify His name (Colossians 1:18). Less we forget, our Lord reminds us that it is only when we abide *"in His word"* that we are truly His disciples and thus can know the truth of God (John 8:31-32).

Phil Sanders writes:

> "The teachings of the New Testament contains God's complete will for our time, from the time of Pentecost till the Second Coming. Had God wished that Christians use instruments in worship, He would have said so. Since God gave us His entire will for our lives, the fact that He intentionally left them out is quite remarkable. Surely God was aware of their presence, for they were used in the temple. We can only conclude that God left them out intentionally, because He did not want them. Men need to have authority from God for what they believe and practice. Like Jesus, we too should ask, *'Is this from heaven or from men?'* (Matthew 21:23-27). God requires that those who worship Him must worship Him in spirit and in truth (John 4:23-24; 17:17). One must wonder how an unscriptural practice, begun centuries late by men, can be from heaven or according to the truth. Men have no right to change God's plan or His teaching on any matter. When they do so, they act on their own authority—not the authority of God."[6]

The Silence of God's Word

How should we understand Scripture? Does God have to say "everything" about a commandment for us to understand it and obey it? In other words, when God says in the New Testament, *"Sing and make melody in your heart to the Lord"* (Ephesians 5:19), should we really expect for the next verse to say something like ("By singing, I mean a cappella music alone; thou shalt not use any instruments of music in any shape, form, or appearance in worship to My Name")? Surely there is not one Christian out there that would want to be so ludicrous as to suggest that God has to spell out every do and don't for us to obey.

Just because God has not said that we should not use instruments of music in worship does not mean that He thought it would be okay for us to add to or delete something that He wants us to do. The Bible does not specifically condemn such things as incense, praying to special people (Mary), offering roast lamb with the Lord's Supper, sprinkling or pouring for baptism, infant baptism, or using a mourner's bench for confession. Using the reasoning of some, how can we find validation for instrumental music and not incorporate all of the other things we have mentioned? The question to ask is not, "Where, in the Bible, does God condemn using instruments of music?" but rather, "Where does the Bible authorize using instrumental music in worship?"

Phil Sanders writes:

> "If the Bible were to include everything that God did not want, it surely would be too large to carry. God has chosen to tell us in positive terms what His will is for our lives and our worship. He has shown us the way, which rules out all other ways. "One baptism" (Ephsians 4:5) means there cannot be other approved baptisms, and "one church" (one body, which is the church, Ephesians 4:4; 1:22-23) means there cannot be other approved churches. The specific instruction to sing means one should sing. There is no authority for other forms of music. When God instructs us through His Word, He has authorized only that which He has identified. God does not have to exclude all other possibilities with a series of prohibitions. Laws only authorize what they authorize; they do not have to detail everything they do not authorize."7

Those who use the argument to justify the use of instruments of music simply because God does not condemn it, will find themselves in peril with other examples in the Bible. If something must be specifically condemned for it to be wrong, then God certainly was in error in putting Nadab and Abihu to death (Leviticus 10: 1-2). Furthermore, God was unjust in denying Moses entrance into Canaan (Numbers 20:6-12), in unjustly removing Saul as king (1 Samuel 10:8; 13:8-14), and was also unjust in putting Uzzah to death (1 Chronicles 13:7-13; 15:2-15; 2 Samuel 6:7).

Please notice that in each of these cases, men acted on their own authority rather than listen to the simple yet evidently, important instructions of God. Anytime when men act on their own authority, they greatly err. These examples show that God expects men to follow His expressed will and not follow their own desires if they want to be pleasing in His sight.

J. E. Choate and William Woodson, in their book, *Sounding Brass and Clanging Cymbals,* wrote of the historical debate of the question of instrumental music from 1827-1960 between Churches of Christ, Disciples of Christ, and the Christian Church. Regarding the subject of the silence of Scripture and the Christian Church they wrote,

> "The Christian Churches have continued to maintain the basic stance concerning the motto of speaking where the Bible speaks and being silent where the Bible is silent as was noted in this chapter. The reaffirmation and the reformulation of this motto is the bedrock of their defense against open membership and defense of instrumental music." 8

The authors then note a dialogue between a Christian Church minister and a Lutheran acquaintance as they were discussing the issue of the amount of water to be used in baptism. Callum Beck, the Christian Church minister, objected when the Lutheran minister said that the amount of water did not really matter by saying, "I objected of course that it was relevant, the Bible specifies immersion and therefore no other form is valid." 9

Choate and Woodson then quote from the same Christian Church minister when he realized that his response was based upon the silence of the Scriptures. Mr. Callum stated:

"At that point the thought suddenly hit me, wouldn't my non-instrumental friends love to hear me now. Theoretically we independents discard the 'law of silence' but it seems that in practice we can't help but invoke it." 10

Choate and Woodson then conclude this section with the following statement: "This necessity of invoking the law of silence while renouncing it in another context is the eternal paradox of the defensive hermeneutical posture of the Christian Church." 11

I would add that not only do those in the Christian Church have a problem of inconsistency with this, but those advocates of the use of mechanical instruments of music in Churches of Christ do as well in this regard. When someone can use the silence of the Scriptures to rule out the burning of incense and other such Old Testament items of practice but then advocate the use of instrumental music using the same logic, the paradox of such reasoning is overwhelmingly skewed.

Conclusion

Since the beginning of time, God has been interested in only one thing—for mankind to trust Him, love Him, and obey Him. From Genesis on to the final book of God's authorship, appropriately called Revelation, historically, God's greatest creation have floundered often times in keeping these simple precepts of God. Since the time of Adam and Eve, when people disobeyed God, sin, deceit, and division have been the painful results. The times when men and women have followed God fully with their *"heart, soul, strength, and mind"* (Luke 10:27), they have been both blessed and in harmony with God's will. The subject of music in our worship to God is an important issue for Christians to understand today in the midst of many prevailing man made thoughts and opinions. In the New Testament, God revealed His will for our lives in the kind of music He wanted, then in the First Century Church, and now, in the Twenty-First Century Church. In essence, God has said that man needs nothing but his physical and spiritual self to worship the Creator. God made man and has wanted his devotion and praise for that reason. While some might think that it is easier for us to allow instruments of music to do the worship for us, this has never been God's desire for His New Testament church. Worship through the instrument that God made, the heart of man reflected through his voice, is where and through which He wants man's praise today. All that God desires is for mankind to trust Him, to love Him, and to obey Him. If we truly want what God wants, then we will allow Him to be God, take His Word as the final authority, and simply use that instrument He gave us (our hearts and voices) to worship and praise Him.

[1] W. K. Pendleton, "Queries," *Millennial Harbinger7,* no. 7 (August 1857):458-9.

[2] Benjamin Franklin, "Instrumental Music in Churches," *American Christian Review 3,* no. 5 (21 January 1860): 19.

[3] Milton Jones, "The War is Over," pp. 76-77, *The Transforming of a Tradition: Churches of Christ in the New Millennium,* edited by Leonard Allen and Lyn Anderson, Orange, CA: New Leaf Books, 2001.

[4] Phil Sanders, "Musical Worship in the New Testament Church and the Use of the Instrument, Unpublished manuscript, Brentwood, TN, 2003, p. 1.

[5] Dave Miller, *Piloting the Strait: A Guidebook for Assessing Change in Churches of Christ,* Pulaski, TN: Sain Publications, 1996, p. 216.

[6] Sanders, p. 2.

[7] Ibid.

[8] Choate, J.E., and Woodson, William. *Sounding Brass and Clanging Cymbals: The History of Instrumental Music* (1827-1968), Henderson, TN: Freed-Hardeman University, 1991, p. 233.

[9] Callum Beck, "If We Really Desire To Speak Only Where The Bible Speaks And Restore The Ancient Order Of Things We Will Have To Make Some Radical Changes," *One Body* (Spring 1988):16.

[10] Ibid.

[11] Choate and Woodson, Ibid.

For Further Reading

Bales, James D. *Instrumental Music and New Testament Worship.* Bales, 1973.

Ferguson, Everett; Lewis, Jack P.; and West, Earl. *The Instrumental Music Issue.* Gospel Advocate, 1987.

Ferguson, Everett. *A Cappella Music in the Public Worship of the Church.* Biblical Research Press, 1972.

Hall, S.H. *Three Defenses of Music in Worship Answered.* C.E.I. Publishing, 1960.

Instrumental Music: Faith or Opinion. FHU Preachers Forum 1991.

Jividen, Jimmy. *Worship in Song.* Star Bible, 1987.

Kurfees, M.C. *Instrumental Music in the Worship.* Gospel Advocate, 1911 (reprint 1975).

Lipe, David. *Biblical Interpretation and Instrumental Music in Worship,* FHU 1991.

McKinnon, James. *Music in Early Christian Literature.* Cambridge, 1987.

Sanders, Philip D. *Let All the Earth Keep Silence.* Ft. Worth, Tx.: Star Publishing, 1989.

Shelly, Rubel. *A Case for A Cappella Music as Worship Today.* 20th Century Christian, 1987.Wallace, Foy E. *The Instrumental Music Question.* Wallace Publications,1980.

Debates in Print:

Boswell-Hardeman. (1923) Gospel Advocate, 1957.

Highers-Blakely.

Otey-Briney. (1908)

Shelly-Dunning (1977)

Stark-Warlick (1903) Hester Publications, 1997.

Wallace-Hunt. 1951.

The Role Of Women In The Church

Neal Pollard

They are market moguls, geniuses and giants in what at one time was strictly an androcentric atmosphere. Marjorie Scardino, CEO of Pearson Media conglomerates, Carla Fiorina, President and CEO of Hewlett-Packard Co., Adrea Jung, Avon's President and CEO, Cathleen Black, President of Hearst Magazine Division (the same Cathleen Black who put USA Today on the map), Anne Mulcahy, CEO of Xerox, among scores of other business women, stand at the pinnacle of the corporate world.[1]

Women have found a place of leadership and influence in practically every area of expertise—Supreme Court Justices (Sandra Day O'Conner and Ruth Bader Ginsburg), exploration (Ann Bancroft), bioengineering (Dr. Cindy Bruckner-Lea), politics (Elizabeth Dole and Margaret Thatcher), investment banking (Muriel Siebert), the NASA program (Salle Ride, Ellen Ochoa, and Mae Jamison), architecture (Maya Min), Surgeon General (Antonia Novello), commercial airline pilots (Emily Warner was the first, in 1973), and many, many others.[2] In fact, in a March 7, 2003, speech, President George W. Bush related that currently "Women account for forty-seven percent of all employed persons" and that "women-owned small businesses are growing twice as fast as all other U.S. firms…."[3]

Women rising to such powerful business positions stand in stark contrast to the culture of their mothers and grandmothers, who lived in a day where women's occupational choices were far more limited. A program of advancement and change began in the middle of the nineteenth century. This "first wave" of feminism had, as its core issues, the right of women to vote, the right to own property, the right to enter various professions, and the right to control their earnings.[4] Modern feminism has a radically different agenda even though it was conceived and born through this original movement.

Modern, radical feminism indeed represents a revolutionized way of looking at gender issues and a woman's role in the world. Contemporary issues of the feminists include lesbianism, pro-choice (abortion)[5], as well as a broad program of indoctrination. Indoctrination, or deliberate lobbying by feminist groups such as the National Organization of Women and the Women's Action Alliance, began in earnest in the 1960's and 1970's. These efforts led to "…the unisex agenda—abolition of sex roles, devaluation of the traditional marriage and family, legitimization of homosexuality, 'free' universal day care of children, abortion on demand, and feminist indoctrination in the schools."[6]

There are many shades of feminism. Defining even its broadest ideology can be difficult. Yet, from the legitimate and needed changes that have given greater freedoms to women in this society to the most destructive proposals of radical feminism, the whole spectrum is a reminder of the new gender landscape. This new era is not only establishing itself in America but by degree throughout the whole globe. Congregations of the Lord's church around the world are being affected to varying degrees by the role of women in the secular world. Women have taken an intrinsic role in secular society. We are then left to consider how the church utilizes her power, intelligence, and spirituality without undermining her God-given role?

Of course, varying options have been given to answer this challenge. From the broader spectrum of Christendom down to the more relevant positions of those within New Testament Christianity, suggestions as to the role of women in the church cover the extremes as well as the biblical center on the subject. As the role of women has dramatically shifted, the need to give specific, thoughtful, and Bible-based answers is perhaps greater than it has ever been.

Radical suggestions that unfairly bind women have included forbidding her to teach Bible classes to even small children, make comments in a Bible class, or teach the Bible to non-Christians. Determined loosing on the matter has led to unsubstantiable grants to serve in church leadership, public preaching and positions of authority. Other efforts include gender-inclusive Bible versions, as well as recasting and reinterpreting clear scripture. Strong feelings have led to extreme stands. "But the issue here isn't feelings; the issue is objective truth."[7] Certainly, it is true that,

> First-century Christian women played an indispensable role in the Lord's work, and many passages give evidence of women working diligently in the Lord's service... yet their active role in advancing the gospel and caring for the Lord's people was accomplished in ways that did not violate male leadership in the home and church.[8]

The task at hand is to deal with the role set aside for women in the church in terms that honor God's Word. That means taking a close and careful look at New Testament passages relevant to the subject. Many chapters and books have been written to address the role of women in the church. However, it is not the purpose of this writer to review them all in this limited space. It may be noted, however, that some, though coming to a rather ambiguous conclusion, have argued arduously for a radical reinterpretation of the "traditional" view within churches of Christ.[9] Other writers, more boldly, introduce a completely transformed hermeneutic that dramatically alters the traditional exegesis and application of key texts. They have come to the conclusion that an "egalitarian" (i.e., full equality in the leadership of the church, from its organizational duties to its public leadership in the exercise of worship assemblies) approach is needed in the church.[10] The majority of writers continue to assert from exegetical and contextual examination that there are role distinctions within the body of Christ.[11] By looking at key passages on the subject, we will explore the restrictions placed upon the work and function of women in the church as well as those things she is called and permitted by God to do.

The Texts For Consideration

The role of women is specifically addressed in the following texts: 1 Corinthians 11:2-16, 1 Corinthians 14:34-35, 1 Timothy 2:8-15, 1 Timothy 3:11, and Titus 2:3-5. Other passages exemplify how first-century Christian women were functioning in the church, as in Acts 16:15,40, Acts 18:26, Romans 16, 1 Corinthians 16:19, Philippians 4:2-3, et al. Attention will be given to the commands found in the former texts, as well as brief application from the latter ones.

1 Corinthians 11:2-16

A large problem within the Corinthian church was bitter division (1:10). This division was provoked mainly by jealousy and arrogance regarding the different spiritual gifts possessed by individual Christians there (1:7; 12:1-14:40). They were also troubled with general status seeking by various Christians there (cf. 1:29; 2:5, 4:18-19, 11:17ff), persistent worldliness (3:3; 15:33-34), and a variety of individual offenses (5:1ff; 5:11; 6:1ff; 6:9-11; 10:7-10). In the midst of this relatively long letter by Paul, he specifically addresses gender roles in 11:2-16.

There Is An Ordained Model For Gender Roles (3)

Actually, Paul points out three relationships: man in relationship to Christ, woman in relationship to man, and Christ in relationship to the Father. Only one of these relationships involves gender—the second. Yet, all three are hierarchical (by which this writer means an arrangement according to order or role). In each pair, one is "head" and the other is to be in subjection to that head. Some maintain that an ambiguity exists about whether "husband" and "wife" rather than "man" and "woman" is intended in this passage. In light of the larger context it seems that these gender roles are applicable with regard to function and role within the church. To limit it to the home or stretch it to mean all situations is to do violence to the text. Paul seems to be addressing church matters, so the verse is best understood as addressing the function of men and women within church life and work.

This Model Could Be Violated (4-7a, 14-15)

Though the example seems obviously cultural in nature, Paul references it to show that the Christian man and the Christian woman could potentially be guilty of violating the gender roles established by God.[12] At the end of the thought begun in verse four, Paul gives the underlying rationale for why the cultural practice was to be observed. Yet, the mention of head-coverings here, a matter that was "obligatory and temporary,"[13] seems to serve as an example of how the

Corinthian Christians were violating their gender roles. In any age, though cultural variables and norms may change, the man or woman could be guilty of violating the biblical model for gender roles in the church.

This Model Is Established By Order Of Creation (7b-9)

The reasoning given by Paul is tied to creation. The why of the order of creation may be endlessly debated. That it is a fact cannot be denied. The very reason why woman was to recognize man as head goes back to Adam and Eve.

This Model Is Maintained For A Heavenly Reason (10)

The mysterious statement in verse ten may refer to angelic involvement and interest in the activity, obedience, and worship of Christians. Whatever it means, it is given as support for the woman to observe the cultural symbol of subjection to the man.

This Model Does Not Allow For Abuse (11-12)

While the model has certainly been abused, the scripture makes neither allowance nor permission for such abuse. Each gender is dependent upon the other. Interdependence has primary significance in the marriage relationship (Genesis 2:18.23), but it is also seen in the church. The very propagation of the human race is a matter of interdependence (12). Therefore, neither gender has cause to boast. The church is complete because of the presence of men and women. Neither gender is superior or inferior because of the roles given them by God!

1 Corinthians 14:34-35

Paul gives two commands in this difficult text. Paul tells the Corinthian Christians, "Let the women keep silent in the churches" and "let them ask their own husbands at home." Of continuous debate has been the matter of to exactly what kind of assembly Paul makes reference, as well as exactly what Paul meant by sigao (silence).[14] Many other matters in these two verses have evoked questions.[15] The second command undoubtedly speaks to husbands and wives, for widows, unmarried women, and Christian women without Christian husbands could not obey the command of this passage. The first command is directed to "women", but comes from a Greek word whose meaning is either "women" or "wives". Its meaning must be determined by the context. Nonetheless, it imposes a role restriction on the women in the context of an assembly. If it were a special assembly where miraculous gifts were exercised, it would not have a parallel in modern assemblies. If it were the general assembly of the household of God, then it would be parallel to Paul's instructions to the Ephesus church via Timothy (1 Timothy 2:8-15). The latter case appears to be the more likely. Fuller consideration will soon be given to that text. Whatever the kind of assembly was meant in 1 Corinthians 14:34, there was a forbidding of women to speak a message in the assembly because of the different gender roles they were given by God.[16]

1 Timothy 2:8-15

In this section of scripture, the Holy Spirit through Paul tells women to do three things. The Ephesian women are to dress modestly (2:9), do good and godly works (2:10), and learn in silence with all subjection (2:11-12).[17]

"Dress Modestly"

While the context gives evidence that these women were seemingly guilty of "overdressing," modesty consists in revealing the hidden person of the heart and not accentuating the body (cf. 1 Peter 3:4; v. 10). The NAS has, "I want women to adorn themselves with proper clothing, modestly and discreetly...." These women, as they came into the assembly, had a choice as to which part of their dual nature they would emphasize. Paul says that to emphasize the body rather than the spirit is to violate God's role for her there. It is no mistake that immodest dress does much to hide Christ while modest dress does much to eclipse the world with its sinful influence. God looks to the woman to display this pure orderliness.

"Do Good And Godly Works"

She was to "be good" while assembled. The NIV speaks of her adorning "good deeds, appropriate for women who profess to worship God." This teaching ties verse eight, which is legislation for the public assembly, to verse ten. Her deportment in the assembly was to be godly. A specific way for her to so conduct herself there is explicitly given in verse eleven. The call is for women to discreetly, modestly do good deeds. Such an understanding of 1 Timothy 2:9-10 brings the entire context into greater harmony, so that her function in the assembly in verse eleven is in keeping with the expectations already stated for her in the previous sentence.

"Learn In Silence With All Subjection"

After specifying her dress and manner, Paul then moves to her function in the assembly. It is one of full or entire submission ("submissiveness"). She must not teach or have authority over man in "the household of God" (cf. 3:15). Any function in the assembly wherein she would be in a leadership or teaching position over the man is explicitly forbidden. The reminder of one writer is of practical relevance here, that "...in the ancient world, teaching was by nature an authoritative act" and that "we need the reminder that teaching, in the formal sense at least, is an authoritative function."[18] Any exercise or function in the assembly where her participation would constitute exercising authority over the man is not permitted. "It is true in and out of the assembly that Adam was formed first, then Eve. In other words, though these passages have assembly contexts, the principles underlying them are broad and reach back to creation."[19] As is rhetorically asked of 1 Timothy 2, "Is it only cultural when Paul says that a woman is 'not to teach or have authority over men... For Adam was formed first, then Eve'?"[20] This includes acts where her function would clearly be one of authoritative leadership, but connotatively includes instances where her participation would be perceived as such. All the while, attention must be given to the place (assembly—1 Timothy 3:15) and the act (teach; have authority over men), both of which specify the role of women in the church.

1 Timothy 3:11

Like the preceding verses, 1 Timothy 3:11 falls within the broader section of 1 Timothy 2:1-3:16. Just prior to giving his reason for writing, Paul identifies the characteristics needed for one to serve in the church as overseer (1 Timothy 3:1-7), as a deacon (1 Timothy 3:8-10,12), and a somewhat enigmatic female group (1 Timothy 3:11). Just who these Christians are has been widely argued. Petrillo gives five possibilities: wives of elders, wives of deacons, special female servants appointed by the church, widows indeed, or all women.[21] Blackburn offers what he calls "several reasons for favoring the probability that the verse speaks of female deacons," including textual proof that 1 Timothy 3:11 was unlikely an exhortation to a deacon's wife and pointing out similarities in the list of qualifications for the deacon and those qualities urged on the women in this verse. [22] Yet, as Miller concludes, "Even if women were deacons in the New Testament church, they would not have functioned in any sort of leadership or authority position over men."[23] To force gunaikes to mean "deaconess" is to strain at both the immediate and remote contexts of the New Testament. It simply refers to Christian women, in general, as Paul had already done in the previous chapter.[24] Petrillo's summary is most compelling.

> "There are so many things Paul could have done to let us know that a special 'office' was in mind for women (such as give qualifications that would not be required of all women, or to use a word or phrase to indicate some serving capacity like he did with the deacons).... church history doesn't exactly offer compelling evidence that the early church had deaconesses - which they most certainly would have had if this had been an apostolic directive." [25]

Elders delegate specific responsibilities to a class of special servants known as deacons (cf. Philippians 1:1), but women have the responsibility to serve and can do so in almost every area that men can. Both men (who are not serving as deacons) and women can be enlisted in such areas as helpers to do the tasks outlined by the elders. The only exception for women would be in any exercise wherein she would be teaching or having authority over a man in the "household of God" (1 Timothy 3:15). Elders typically assign deacons to serve in such areas as taking attendance, audio and video taping, benevolence, building maintenance, baptistery cleaning, education, fellowship, finance, grounds, missions, aiding shut-ins, transportation, worship, youth, security, visitors centers, equipment maintenance, library, personal evangelism, Bible correspondence, involvement, visitation, bulletin boards, hospital ministry, special events, future planning, jail ministry, outreach, advertising, crisis intervention, newcomers, and the like. In almost every one of these areas, there are places for the work and assistance of women. Women, in serving through these capacities, are to conduct themselves with the qualities Paul shares with Timothy. Considering the scope of the work of the church, Paul's admonition is that Timothy impress upon it the need to be the pillar and support of the truth. Each sub-class of people in the church not only can, but must be as involved as possible in fulfilling that objective. Women generally (1 Timothy 2:8ff; 3:11) and widowed women specifically (1 Timothy 5) are fully included in that charge.

Titus 2:3-5

Paul instructs another preacher, Titus, to "straighten out" the unfinished business of helping the Cretan churches become scripturally organized. This included church leadership (1:5-11), but also much more. Part of the sound doctrine those churches needed was proper role fulfillment. These rules were almost entirely broken down along gender lines—older men (2:2), older women (2:3-4a), younger women (2:4b-5), younger men (2:6), this preacher himself (2:1,7-8), slaves (2:9-10), and then the congregation as a whole (3:1ff). Thus, Paul addresses the role of either gender and that of those of varying social status. The focus of this chapter will be put only upon the older and younger women.

"Teach The Older Women..."

Paul outlines four characteristics for older women. Interestingly, these four traits are strikingly similar to the qualities listed in 1 Timothy 3:11. The Timothy passage calls for women to be dignified. Here, the older woman is to be possessed of reverent behavior. The first carries the idea of being worthy of respect, while the second shows how that is accomplished. "Not malicious gossips" is the same word in both passages. He is urging women to guard carefully the nature of what they say about others. "Not addicted to much wine" is a negative expression of the same idea in 1 Timothy 3:11, where the women addressed are to be "sober." It is said that the expression in Titus 2 comes closer to depicting the idea of an alcoholic than any other New Testament passage.[26]

She also is to be a teacher of good things. Such an idea is inherent in being faithful in all things (1 Timothy 3:11). A core component of faithfulness is teaching truth (cf. Titus 1:9).

These traits have an enormous bearing on conduct in the home, but their impact is not limited to that realm. An instance of this application is seen in the fourth attribute that these older women were to possess. They are to teach the younger women. The exemplary conduct of the older women served as a model for the younger Christians in the church to emulate. Paul addresses her character in four traits, her attitude, her speech, her conduct, and her service as they impact church life.

"Encourage The Young Women..."

A key role of older women in the church is to instruct younger women. Too often, the older women have either abdicated or been denied this vital work. Consequently, the "hope of eternal life" (Titus 1:2) has been extinguished in the heart of many a younger Christian woman. Paul lists a seven-fold curriculum that is to be dispensed to the younger women by the older women. These points are then to become qualities incorporated into the young woman's life. Even without the benefit of hearing this from older women, younger women today can be grateful that they have Paul's inspired instruction for them. These seven traits are further subdivided into three pairs plus a seventh and more general qualification that is in keeping with her primary task in the marriage context as described elsewhere in the New Testament (cf. Ephesians 5:22-24).[27]

Young Women Are To Love Their Husbands: Men need demonstrative indication of affection and affirmation. Young married women might lose sight of the care of their husbands in everything else with which they were tasked. It cannot be overlooked that husbands might not be lovable at all times. She may need a reminder to demonstrate a quality that acts in the best interest of her husband (cf. 1 Corinthians 13:4-8a; Romans 5:6).[28]

Young Women Are To Love Their Children: Young women should be trained to utilize their natural maternal affection toward their children. Just as men are enjoined to "bring them up in the discipline and instruction of the Lord" (Ephesians 6:4), young mothers are to build within them a sense of worth and value. A church filled with children who have learned love from a mother that disciplines and restrains as well as affirms is a great church. The young woman is instructed to be family-oriented.

Young Women Are To Be Sensible: The word sophron (sensible) is directed at three of the four gender subgroups in Titus two (2:2,5,6). The word depicts one who is in her right mind or sane. It also carries with it the idea of self-control. Teamed with the idea of purity, it is the quality of trustworthiness and wisdom in interacting especially with the opposite sex. She must execute common sense in her dealings with men. Being sensible or self-controlled bears especially on her outward conduct.

Young Women Are To Be Pure: Jesus taught that purity is a matter of the heart (cf. Matthew 5:8). Paul tells young women to be inwardly clean and holy. Avoiding the potential trap of sexual sin is contingent upon beautifying and caring for that hidden woman of the heart. This second pair of responsibilities characterizes the young Christian woman's daily life and church life, too.

Young Women Are To Be Workers At Home: Working at home is unfairly disparaged and dishonored in the world and in the church.[29] The word in Greek does not make staying at home an absolute imperative. Few would suggest that it does. There are passages that identify (Proverbs 31) and situations that show such work to be legitimate and even necessary. What is urged on women is being "good managers of the household" (NRSV). It is to be her domain. She is to exemplify the character the home takes as well as maintain the orderliness of its affairs. There is a necessity for her to work at keeping that home. As she follows this admonition, she deserves the trust and confidence of her mate.

Young Women Are To Be Kind: She seeks opportunities to do good. Her winsome nature is verified in how she treats others. Great concentration is given to the deportment and attitude of younger women in Titus 2. Kindness is expressed in her benevolence, hospitality, active participation in good works in the local church, and her demeanor in interacting with all others. The text of a radical feminist "manifesto" glorifies women who are "aggressive, assertive, domineering, overbearing, strong-minded, spiteful, hostile, obnoxious, vicious, pushy, loudmouthed," and concludes by saying, "you always know she is around."[30] Maybe so, but she is anything but kind. As one preacher is fond of saying, "If you are not kind, you are the wrong kind." So it applies to the young women in the church.

Young Women Are To Be Subject To Their Own Husbands: This summary statement defines the role of woman in the home. It is not about her comparative value alongside her husband. God makes clear that men and women occupy different roles in the home as well as in the church. This idea of submissiveness is the same as that expressed in public assembly matters in 1 Timothy 2:11.

Perhaps this text in Titus two is complemented well by the words of Raye Lynn Mathews:

> "The roles of men and women in the home are not so different from the roles of men and women in the church. The men of the church provide the spiritual leadership and practical support. They are our elders and deacons. They are our spokesmen, decision-makers and special servants. The men have the privilege of leadership and the awesome responsibility that goes with it. The women of the church provide management skills and emotional support. The women have the ability to multi-task, nurture and encourage. When combined, we make a smooth-running, love-filled church."[31]

The Conclusion Of The Matter

The role of women in the church remains a sensitive issue. Ignorance and abuse are the two main causes of trouble. It may be that the subject has been neglected and scriptures have been abused. The result has distorted the role God designed for women to occupy in the church. Some extremes bind without scriptural support, while others extend unauthorized.

God has given women an honored function in the church. It is a different one from men. Why He has done so has drawn much speculation. Could it be that God has foisted man into the responsibility of church leadership because he generally tends to be less spiritually inclined than the woman is?[32] Perhaps. The predominant gender represented at the foot of the cross was female (John 19:25). The special group who ministered to Jesus' needs was women (Matthew 27:55-56). Female disciples were numerous in that difficult time between the resurrection and the church's establishment (Acts 1:14). After the establishment of the church in Acts 2, Christian women were to be found in many capacities. They were active in evangelism (Acts 18:26), providing a meeting place for the church (Acts 12:12; Romans 16:5; Colossians 4:15), aiding mission work and missionaries (Acts 16:40; Romans 16:4), and tirelessly performing good works like benevolence, hospitality, and similar service (Romans 16:1-3; 1 Timothy 5:10). Women are not now doing all that is available for them to do. It is important to realize that most of the work God expects the church to accomplish includes the work women can do. Let every faithful Christian woman be found applying herself to such activities. May congregations of God's people rededicate themselves to honestly and deliberately examining New Testament teaching on the role of women in the church. Let God's desires for the use of her abilities be the beacon. May women be fulfilled in the role assigned to her by God. Let men support women in their roles and enlist their help in the cause of Christ. As the "the pillar and support of the truth", we can glorify God in our scripturally defined service. That is the ultimate goal of our roles.

[1] www.infoplease.com/spot/womenceo1.html. Other CEOs include Mary Kay Ash, Mary Kay Products, Patricia Russo, Lucent Technologies, Cinda Hallman, Spherion Corporation, Meg Whitman, ebay, Shelly Lazarus, Ogilvy & Mather (one of the biggest ad agencies in the world).

2 www.greatwomen.org

[3] via the Comprint Military Publication Stripe, a newsource provided to Walter Reed Army Medical Center personnel.

4 Dr. Jack Cottrell. *Feminism and the Bible: An Introduction to Feminism for Christians* (Joplin: College Press, 1992): vv. 17-19.

[5] See F. LaGard Smith on the unmistakable fellowship of feminism to the homosexual and abortion special interest groups in the books *Sodom's Second Coming: What you need to know about the deadly homosexual assault* (Eugene: Harvest House Pub., 1993): vv. 87-91 and *When Choice Becomes God* (Eugene: Harvest House Pub., 1990): vv. 67-80.

[6] Cottrell: vv. 53-54.

[7] Charles Colson and Ellen Vaughn. *Being the Body* (Nashville: W Pub. Co., 2003):

v. 266. Note: This writer does not agree with all of Colson's foregoing conclusions in this chapter, but the author rightly addresses the extreme agenda in the religious world to tear down the walls concerning gender roles despite the clear truths of scripture.

[8] Alexander Strauch. *Biblical Eldership: an Urgent call to Restore Biblical Church Leadership* (Littleton: Lewis & Roth Pub., 1995): vv. 58-59.

[9] See Carroll D. Osburn. *Women in the Church: Refocusing the Discussion* (Abilene: Restoration Perspectives, 1994).

[10] Note especially the chapters by Osburn, Geer, and Blackburn in Essays on Women in Earliest Christianity, Volume 1 (Carroll D. Osburn, Ph. D., ed., Joplin: College Press, 1993).

[11] Jan Hailey seems to say, as concisely as any, this very thing: "It does not follow that there are no unequal roles in the community of faith" (Osburn, ed., Essays: 165).

12 Ralph Gilmore gives five contextual reasons why women were to wear veils in first-century Corinth: (1) Lest she dishonor her head (v.5), (2) To be modest (v.6), To show respect for creation (v.7-9), (4) To show respect for angels (v. 10), and (5) To show respect for other churches of Christ and for Paul (v. 16). *Gender and Ministry: The Role of the Woman in the Work and Worship of the Church* (Huntsville: Publishing Designs, Inc., 1990): v. 186.

[13] Warren, Thomas B. *When Is An "Example" Binding: a Treatise on Correctly Interpreting the Bible* (Moore, OK: National Christian Press, 1989): v. 124.

[14] Sigao is found three times in 1 Corinthians 14 (28,30,34). In verse 28, the tongue speaker was to keep quiet when there was no interpreter. In verse 30, one who was receiving the revelation of a prophet was to receive it in silence. In verse 34, the woman is not allowed to speak "in the church" (Paul says this in 34, then repeats it in 35). The immediate context of speaking has to do with prophetic utterance of revelations. The women, in the general assembly of the church, were not to "speak" but were rather to be in "silence." The weight of sigao meant that she could not in any way "preach" or "utter words" (laleo). She is not enjoined to total silence, including singing or confessing, just as in the case of the tongue speaker (28) and receiver of a revelation (30); rather, she was to be silent in a specific vain.

[15] Essays: v. 219.

[16] Some seek to prove that God's role for women in the church is restricted to the public worship assembly, thus asserting that in other forums, even where men and women are present together, she may teach or lead (as in small group meetings, devotionals, seminar and workshop lectures, etc.). This takes too limiting a view on what is meant by "household of God" (1 Timothy 3:15) and "in every place" (1 Timothy 2:8), etc. The household of God is not the assembly, but the family of God—the church. In every place is indicative of every place where a mixed group obtains. This seems quite clear.

[17] Incidentally, three more sets of instruction are found later in the epistle, in chapter five. The first instructions are for widows, who are told to trust in God and continue in

constant prayer (5:5). Then, widows are singled out and told to do good works, a list of which is enumerated in the text (5:10). In 1 Timothy 5:14, younger women are instructed to marry, bear children, guide the house, and live exemplary lives.

[18] Tommy South, "Paul's Motive For Forbidding Women To Teach," *Abilene Christian University Lectures: Christ and Culture: the Problem of Secularism* (Abilene: ACU Press, 1990): vv. 210-211.

[19] Lightfoot, Neil. *The Role of Women: New Testament Perspectives* (Memphis: Student Assoc. Press, 1978): v. 42.

[20] Ibid: v. 37.

[21] Petrillo, Denny. *Commentary on 1,2 Timothy & Titus* (Abilene: Quality Pub., 1998): vv. 44-45.

[22] Essays: vv. 307-310. Truly, the four qualifications for the women in 1 Timothy 3:11 are synonymous with qualifications for deacons—"grave", "not doubletongued", "not addicted to much wine", and to a lesser extent "not pursuing dishonest gain" (1 Timothy 3:8).

[23] Miller, Dave. *Piloting the Strait: a Guidebook for Assessing Changes in Churches of Christ* (Pulaski, TN: Sain Pub., 1996): v. 254.

[24] It may be appropriate here to insert a related thought. Because so many have inordinately emphasized the work of a deacon as an office, it is easy to lose sight of the fact that *diakonos* indicates a work to be done and not simply an office to be held. Somehow, through time, this special service has been reinterpreted as some sort of sub-shepherding or junior eldering. Subsequently, to some recognition as a deacon is equated with a name on a church bulletin or stationary, a picture on a bulletin board, or a title honoring one's status. This is as antithetical to the meaning of the name deacon as anything could be. The failure to view one's tasks as a responsibility to be humbly discharged bespeaks a larger problem in a culture that has forgotten how to serve.

[25] Denny Petrillo, e-mail to the author, 20 August, 2003

[26] Petrillo: v. 176.

[27] Gaebelein, Frank E., Ed. *The Expositor's Bible Commentary, Vol. 11* (Grand Rapids: Zondervan, 1978): vv. 436-437.

[28] Petrillo: vv. 176-177.

[29] Consider this quote from Lightfoot: "Scripture...does not support this stereotype of a housewife who has a boring and meaningless life. One ingredient alone makes the difference—love.... When Paul says that women are to be domestic, immediately preceding this, he mentions love for their husbands and for their children. Love transforms it all" (Role, v. 45).

[30] Osburn, *Women in the Church:* v. 16.

[31] Raye Lynn Mathews. "A Woman for God," Church & Family Summer 2003: 31.

[32] Smith, F. LaGard. *Men of Strength for Women of God: Has the Time Come for Shared Spiritual Leadership*? (Eugene: Harvest House, 1989): v. 261.

Additional Sources Consulted

Cates, Curtis A., Ed. *The Epistles of 1 & 2 Timothy, Titus: Challenges of 1st Century Preaching* (Pensacola: Firm Found. Pub. House, Inc., 1986).

Dodd, Brian J. *The Problem with Paul* (Downers Grove, IL: Intervarsity Press, 1996).

Ferguson, Everett B. *The Church of Christ: a Biblical Ecclesiology for Today* (Grand Rapids: Wm. B. Eerdmans, 1996).

Gulledge, Dennis. *Women of the Word* (self published, 1991).

Kostenberger, Andreas J., Thomas R. Shreiner, and H. Scott Baldwin, Eds. *Women in the Church: a Fresh Analysis of 1 Timothy 2:9-15* (Grand Rapids: Baker, 1995).

McWhorter, Don. *God's Woman: Feminine or Feminist?* (Huntsville, AL: Publishing Designs, Inc., 1992).

Schaff, Philip. *"Homilies On Timothy: Homily X,"* Nicene & Post-Nicene Fathers: Volume 13: Chrysostom (Peabody, MA: Hendrickson Pub., 1999).

Smith, Dennis E. & Michael E. Williams, Eds. *The Storyteller's Companion to the Bible,* Volume 13: New Testament Women (Nashville: Abingdon Press, 1999).

The Elder As A Spiritual Leader

Dale Hartman

The importance of elders who are strong spiritual leaders within the church cannot be overly emphasized. There are many that have written through the years, detailing the importance of qualifications and duties given to the men who fill the service of elders. At the same time there seems to be an inadequacy in communicating with precision a clear picture of the development involved in becoming the man who fills such a vital role. Throughout this chapter, there will be references to BAGD (Baur, Arndt, Gingrich, Danker, A Greek-English Lexicon of the New Testament), and LN (Louw and Nida, Greek-English Lexicon of the New Testament). These references are used in addition to scripture references. The importance of communicating a clear picture of the leadership to be found in elders is amplified as we grasp the meaning of the words used and the application of them in their context. Hopefully, we can gain some clarity of the beauty and importance of the lives and teaching of the men we have as elders in the church.

An elder leads by the spiritual example in his personal life.

Any time you go to a coastal area you will see piers where there is a salt crusted "high tide" mark. An experienced sailor can merely glance at the high tide mark and know how much slack to allow in his rope for his boat to safely be tied to the pier. This mark is a physical representation of the height of the tide over many years.

There is a "spiritual high tide" mark in each congregation. It is not some salt-crusted pier. It is the spirituality of the men who are the leaders and shepherds. Their leadership will determine the maturity level for that entire congregation. Their speech and their example will have a great influence on each member of that church. Through the years, their leadership and example will influence an entire generation of God's people under their care.

A church will never exceed the level of spirituality that is modeled for them by their leaders. Therefore it is incumbent on every elder to realize the importance of his personal example. Peter exhorts shepherds to be an example to the flock (1 Peter 5:3). An elder's life becomes a visual form that is designed to be copied (LN.58.58). His character is to be a model of behavior as an example to be imitated (LN. 58.59). In his spiritual life he is a pattern for all to follow. An elder's spiritual life is a pattern to the church in a similar way that what God showed Moses on the mountain was a pattern for the tabernacle (Acts 7:44).

There is a character concept that functions much like an "umbrella term" for God's spiritual shepherd. He is to be blameless (Titus 1:6) or above reproach

(1 Timothy 3:2). He is to be spiritually mature enough that there are no glaring personal faults to weaken his influence.

No one will perfectly possess all the qualities found in 1Timothy 3, Titus 1 and 1 Peter 5 when he begins serving as a shepherd. However, each of the character traits is an important quality for each shepherd to develop. A struggle always arises between the humanity of leaders and the loftiness of the qualities that God wants a leader to possess. Hopefully, a man who has been an elder for twenty years will be more mature than when he first began serving as an elder.

Problems often arise in the selection process regarding how "qualified" a man is in comparison to the qualities in Scripture. As a minimum, I believe that a prospective elder must possess each of these qualities to a positive degree. If you want to be picky, I'd say at least 51%! What that means is that we must have high expectations of our leaders, but not hold them to a standard of absolute perfection that only one man has met. They must meet a "minimum standard" but be expected and allowed to continue growing and maturing in their spiritual development through the years.

In each of the places where Paul wrote about elders, there was a critical need for elders to be men who were spiritual leaders. The new church would be known and judged in the community by its permanent leaders. In many communities the church probably met and worshipped in the households of its elders. The quality of their leadership would be critical to the future health of these congregations. For each of these places had unique needs for leadership that was to be fulfilled by its spiritual shepherds.

The island of Crete was known for a culture dominated by those who were liars, evil beasts, and lazy gluttons. In stark contrast, the influence of Jesus was to be seen in the lives of elders who were blameless (Titus 1:6). A blameless man is without accusation in his private life. He is one who cannot be accurately accused of anything wrong (LN.33.433). While he will never be perfect, an elder is to conduct himself in such a way that his life is a positive advertisement for Christ and His church. This extends to his personal life, his reputation and his family.

Ephesus was the most cosmopolitan and urban city in Asia Minor. Commercially, it was the financial gateway to the East. Within the center of the worship of Artemis and materialism, a bishop's life is to stand out. He is to be above reproach (1 Timothy 3:2). This means that his personal life is above criticism (LN.33.415). His life is lived on such a spiritual plane that he is considered 'irreproachable' (BAGD.77). There is not to be an area in his life that an insider or outsider can point to and say, "He is a good man in most areas but......."

An elder is to be seen by the entire community in a favorable light. He must be well thought of by outsiders (1 Timothy 3:7). The quality of his life is to allow him to have a good reputation by those people who are not Christians. His conduct is a positive witness to the influence of Jesus in his life. The reputation of his character allows him to have a good standing with outsiders (BAGD.619). While he will never be Jesus, the word has become flesh in the conduct of his life. Spiritual truths are effectively visualized in his attitudes and actions. He is recognized as a leader because of the quality of life that he displays to those who interact with him on a daily basis.

The first church with which I worked was in Childress, Texas. One of our fine elders had run a grocery store for decades and was widely known for his dependability and honesty. He had developed a keen interest in cars through the years. So when he retired from the long hours of the grocery business he opened a corner used car lot. He sold good quality cars and did a booming business. I was speaking to another of the elders and asked why he was doing so well. "People will drive over 200 miles to buy a good car from someone that they know is honest and trustworthy" was the reply. Here was a godly elder in a business that is proverbially known for cheating and dishonesty. His character and his word caused people to refer their neighbors, friends, and families to buy a car from an honest car salesman. A few years later he finally retired and moved to the coast. People were upset for miles around because they had lost a friend and a dependable person from whom to buy their cars. He was greatly missed by the church and the community when he moved.

This man was a leader in the church because of the quality of his personal life. His word was his bond, and his character was impeccable. The high quality of his reputation was known for miles. His life was a walking advertisement for the Lord's church. He led by his life as well as his lips.

An elder leads by being the spiritual leader of his household.

There are specific criteria regarding an elder's domestic relationships. He is to be a household manager (1 Timothy 3:4). He presides over his household in a godly manner. This means that he, not his wife, is the spiritual leader in the family. He is to be the one who is striving to influence others to cause them to follow a recommended course of action (LN.36.1).

Today we tend to think of a household as being 'mom, dad, and the kids.' New Testament households were often extended families that might also include other relatives, slaves and hired workers. Households were a primary building block of society and were often the base for family businesses. We would be closer to the New Testament concept if we thought of "household" in light of a contemporary Italian family which often includes grandparents, aunts, uncles, cousins, and other family members. This is quite a different responsibility than only looking after a wife and children. As the leader of the household, a potential elder would gain valuable skill in the art of influencing others. He would exercise a position of leadership by being at the head of his household (BAGD.870). Learning to preside and rule over one's household in a caring and graceful manner was essential training for one to preside over God's household. The oversight of children, servants, workers, and relatives should be a proving ground for larger responsibilities that God intends for him later. Louw and Nida insert an interesting footnote regarding the concept of guiding and leading. "The meanings.... imply a willingness on the part of others to be led. They also imply a minimum of control on the part of the one guiding or leading" (LN. p 465).

A good household manager has learned the importance of dealing with each person at an individual level. If something is important to a child, it must also become important to his parent. Some fathers are too occupied with "big things" when their children are small to listen to their small problems and the little people's chatter. Later, they wonder why their older children do not listen to them very well. If a father will not respect his children by listening carefully to them when they are little, why should they listen to him when they get older and mature? A good manager has learned to develop willingness within his own children to follow Jesus by the manner in which they have been led. A child will remember a father's actions even if he has forgotten his words (Luke 15:17-19).

An effective household manager would never give the responsibility of developing faith in his children to some one else. God places the responsibility of developing godly character in his family squarely on his shoulders. Regular devotions or times of personal instruction can never be replaced. If a father is to maximize the potential of teaching opportunities that arise "as you go by the way" (Deuteronomy 6), he must make time for regular teaching times with his children.

The training of the elder's children is evidenced by two passages. The first gives the principle positively. The second is a negative reflection of the same principle.

1. "He must manage his own household well, keeping his children submissive and respectful in every way" (1 Timothy. 3:4).
2. "If any man is blameless having faithful children who are not open to the charge of being wild or disobedient" (Titus 1:6).

If you diagram each of these sentences and locate the principle subject, you will find that these verses are focusing on the father's training of his children or of the children's relationship to their earthly father. An elder's children will be faithful to their father as they learn to submit to his orders or directives (LN.36.18). They have been trained to obey and submit to their father's instructions (1 Timothy. 3:4). They are not willfully defiant of their father's will. They do not set themselves up as being in control. These children have grown up in the state of submissiveness (BAGD.1041). They have learned to subordinate their will to the will of their father. If they have not learned to obey their earthly fathers, how can they give glory to God on account of their obedience to the gospel of Christ (2 Corinthians 9:13)?

Effective household management is demonstrated in a child's demeanor and approach to life (1 Timothy 3:4). Principled thought, rather than youthful emotion guide him. His behavior will have a measure of dignity that leads to respect (LN.88.46). Here is a child that will stop and think before he acts. His behavior will include elements of dignity, seriousness, and holiness (BAGD.919). A young person whose behavior could be described as dignified and respectful would certainly be noticed among his peers. This mindset would not be typical of what was known in Ephesus.

On the island of Crete Paul's instructions are that an elder's children are not be charged with being wild or disobedient (Titus 1:6). A charge is an open indictment of the actions of the child. He is describing a situation in which their behavior is such that a charge is made against them in light of their father's character. The character they are not to have charged against then is recklessness or rebellion. This term is translated a number of ways (KJV, AS- riot; NASV- dissipation; RSV-profligate; McCord- debauchery; NIV- wild). Here is behavior that shows lack of concern or thought for the consequences of an action (LN.88.96). This child refuses to submit to authority and is undisciplined in his behavior (BAGD.91). This child is a negative reflection on his father because he has become reckless to a point where he doesn't stop to think about the consequences of his behavior or how his rebellious behavior may negatively influence others.

The second type of behavior that is not to be characteristic of elder's children is that of insubordination (Titus 1:6). This word is also translated a number of ways (KJV, AS- unruly; NASV- rebellion; RSV- insubordinate; McCord- disobedience; NIV- disobedient). It describes someone who is rebelliously disobedient (LN.36.26). The idea generally denotes 'wastefulness'. It also can describe a reckless abandon and dissipation (BAGD.148). Paul uses this word to describe human behavior that is the product of drunkenness (Ephesians 5:18). Peter uses this word to describe the mindset of the pagan world. The people of the first century were so accustomed to this "wild profligacy" that they are surprised that Christians would not join them in this excess (1 Peter 4:4).

An elder's children have been trained to stop and think of their father's instructions before taking action. They have learned that their conduct is not carried out in a vacuum or in isolation. Personal behavior on a day to day basis is not only a reflection on the child, but on one's father and family. A child's willingness to submit to his parent's teaching is in complete harmony with the counsel of godly wisdom (Proverbs 10:1; 5:20; 17:25; 19:26; 29:3,15; 30:17).

An elder's effectiveness as a spiritual household manager manifests itself by godly children who have behavior that stands out to the point that they are clearly counter cultural. The faith of their father has made such an impression on their lives that they choose to live godly lives rather than be shaped by their local youth culture. If left to their own devices, or the influence of their peer group, children will never develop this kind of a mindset on their own. Having children who live godly lives is evidence of the fingerprints of faith. This type of a child is the product of an effective household manager. The quality of the child's life is a living testimony to the household management of his father.

Before a man is given the responsibility of caring for the household of God, he is to have proven himself by managing his own household. He has developed the capacity to look out for the emotional and spiritual development needs of his family. With the same tenderness that the 'good Samaritan' cared for the needs of the man left beaten by the road (Luke 10:34), he learns to care for his own household.

He has learned to deal with his children's successes and failures in life. As their father he has nurtured their faith and their soul. This requires a delicate sense of timing. Sometimes a child may need to be patted on the back. At other times the child may need to be patted further down his anatomy! Different situations and different personalities need to be treated equally, yet differently.

An effective household manager has learned to encourage, to comfort, and to urge his children in their walk with God (1 Thessalonians 2:12). He knows how to hold his children close to him and encourage them as only a father can. He has learned to embolden them in their belief or course of action that they should take (BAGD.766). He has learned to positively give words of encouragement that discipline his sons (Hebrews 12:5).

A father has also learned to comfort his children when they fall short. Nothing impacts a child's behavior more than how he is treated after he fails. It is a great blessing to have a father who has the heart to console and cheer up a child so that he will try again (BAGD.769). Paul urges the leaders of this church to use this ability to "encourage the fainthearted" (1 Thessalonians 5:14).

Finally, a father has learned to urge his children to live for God. He affirms and attests to their potential in God (BAGD.619). He is able to testify to their potential and urge them to a greater vision of what God can mean in their lives. An effective household manager may be a combination of a teacher, a coach, a counselor, and a cheerleader in every stage of his children's life.

The clearest witness of an elder's ability to shepherd the flock is the manner in which he has managed his own family. The litmus test is the willingness of the children to listen to the counsel of their father. This is the prerequisite for being charged with the care of God's family. To that end Paul writes, "for if a man does not know how to manage his own household, how can he care for God's church" (1 Timothy 3:5).

God wants children to grow up to obey their parents in the Lord and to honor their fathers and mothers (Ephesians 6:1-2). Example is crucial in this area. The way a father relates to the child and to the mother of the child will set the tone for all the relationships in the family. A child will learn a lot about obedience by observing his father obeying God. Children will primarily learn about honor by how he is treated. A child will be more influenced by what they see than merely what they hear. An elder's children have seen their father at his best and at his worst. Yet it is very clear to them who he serves and what his priorities are. His involvement in their spiritual development has made such an indelible impression on them that they want to serve the same God he serves! They want to please their earthly and their heavenly fathers. A man who has disciplined them, loved them, and cared for them has led them in their family. They have been so impacted by his management and care for their lives that they are willing to be ridiculed as social outcasts to walk in his steps of faith. Their willful obedience to an earthly father they have seen will lead them to a willful obedience of their heavenly father, whom they have not yet seen.

An elder is to be "the husband of one wife." A lot of different opinions exist on what this passage means. You will hear opinions ranging from "this is a statement against polygamy" to "an elder can only have been married one time." A literal translation gives us something to consider. Paul says the elder is a "one woman man." An elder is sexually faithful to his wife. This would apply to his mind as well as his body.

There are a lot of men who are "the husband of one wife", but that doesn't mean they are a one woman man. This American generation has heard more details than we wanted to know about political leaders who are married, but are far from being faithful to only one woman. An elder is a man who is blameless in his morality. He is not only married to one woman, he is faithful to her. He can be trusted to deal with other women without becoming physically or emotionally entangled. He will need to talk to people at all hours of the day and night without any doubt about his character or his integrity.

Godly morality was a challenge to Christians in every part of the Roman Empire. The first sin that is normally given in Paul's "vice lists" has to to with sexual immorality (1 Corinhians 5:19; Galatians 5:19; Ephesians 5:3; Colossians 3:5; 1 Thessalonians 4:3-7). The moral faithfulness of an elder and his wife is a powerful example of "walking in the light" in the darkness of an ungodly community.

Paul is interested in the 'spirit of the law' as much as the 'letter of the law.' An elder is a man who is scripturally married to one woman. However, this covenant is more than "some ink stains that have dried upon some line." He has a covenant in his heart, with God and with his wife, that will make him known as someone who is morally trustworthy. His conduct in this area advertises his difference in a world of sexual promiscuity. He is a one-woman man.

God wants a shepherd to "qualify" himself by the quality of spiritual leadership that he exercises in his own household. A major contribution to the spiritual development of a congregation will be the involvement of an elder's family. Their spirituality, example, and dedication will influence the entire church. An elder's words before a congregation will either be strengthened or weakened by the behavior of his family in the community. There has always been a need for an elder's family to be a living example before the church. Who they are in their actions will speak louder than anything that will be said by their father or husband. Their example can be one of the most powerful advertisements of the teaching of Jesus in the local community. A shepherd's family can truly be a city set on a hill that cannot be hidden (Matthew 5:14).

An elder leads by shepherding the flock.

There has been a lot of discussion concerning the actual role of elders in leading the church. The question is often asked, "how much authority do the elders have?" It may be helpful to examine the churches begun through the work of Paul. Consider the leadership in these churches before there were elders. Doing this will allow us to see the responsibilities of the leaders and their congregations to each other before elders were appointed.

My conviction in this discussion is that there are passages involving the discussion of leadership roles that do not specifically mention any of the primary words that are used for formalized leadership positions. There is no reference in 1 Thessalonians, 1 Corinthians, or even Hebrews to bishops, elders, or shepherds. These passages would apply to elders if they were present. However, the text does not indicate the existence of elders in these churches.

These passages would apply to the "in between state" of a local church. This state is between the time the church was planted and the time that there were men who were formally recognized as possessing the qualities needed to be the elders for that church. These passages have specific spiritual qualities given for the leadership in that church. They are not like the more formal lists in 1 Timothy 3, Titus 1, and 1 Peter 5. Just because a young church does not have "qualified" elders, does that mean that there is no need to shepherd and guard young Christians? Paul gives specific instructions regarding the qualities of these early leaders and he also gives specific responsibilities to the church to follow these men. I see these passages functioning as a "half way house" on the journey of an immature local church developing to the point of appointing the men we know as bishops, elders, and shepherds. If there were elders in these young churches, then these passages would obviously apply to them.

Note this list of the qualities of these men and the reciprocal responsibility of the churches to these men.

	Characteristics of leaders:	Responsibility of congregation:
1 Corinthians 16:15-16	1. first converts in Asia	1. submit to such as these
	2. devoted themselves to the service of the saints	2. submit to everyone who joins in the work
	3. they join in the work	
	4. they labor in it	
1 Thessolonians 5:12-13	5. work hard among you	3. respect those who work hard among you
	6. who are over you in the Lord	
	7. who admonish you	4. who are over you in the Lord
	8. they work among you	5. be at peace among yourselves

Paul's final petition in 1 Corinthians 16:15-16 is his local solution to their ongoing problems with unity (1:10; 4:16; 16:15-16). Rather than being divided over Paul, Apollos, Peter or Christ, he urges them to submit to their leaders who have been Christians for a while (the first converts in Asia). He wants them to work with leaders who have "devoted themselves to the service of the saints." These men have the potential to bring about order in the Corinthian church by putting things into place that will help the entire body. These men are acknowledged by Paul because they first have proven themselves by their devotion to the service of the saints (BAGD.991). These men are able to work together, and have given themselves to labor in the work of the Lord. Therefore, the church has clear responsibilities that it must fulfill towards this type of leaders.

Paul's familiar petition in 1 Thessalonians 5:12 also instructs that church to work with the local leaders that are present in this infant church (4:1; 4:10; 5:12; 5:14). They are to be mindful of those leaders who labor among them. These men are willing to exert themselves physically, mentally, and spiritually as they work with the church (BAGD.558). Paul reminds the brethren that their leaders are over them in the Lord. This means that they are either to exercise a position of leadership by being at the head of the church, or they are to have an interest in the church by showing concern and caring for the members (BAGD.870). They show their concern for the well being of the members by admonishing and working hard in the church.

These leaders are a far cry from autocratic figureheads who simply give orders to other people. They are very much in the spirit of what Jesus meant when he told his apostles, "But not so with you; rather let the greatest among you become as the youngest, and the leader as one who serves. For which is the greater, one who sits at table, or one which serves? Is it not the one who serves? It is not the one who sits at table? But I am among you as one who serves" (Luke 22:26-27).

Before the church matured to the point of having elders, these men distinguished themselves in the congregation by their hard work and service. Their leadership grew out of their maturity and concern for the well being of the church. They worked shoulder to shoulder with Paul while he was among them. They caught a vision of nurturing and encouraging those in need from Paul's example. They were men who built an interest in the spiritual development of younger members by showing concern for them and giving them aid. Their service and hard work had enabled them to be recognized as the leaders in these young churches.

The day to day life of these congregations was not a democracy where either the entire congregation met to vote on matters, or where all the men gathered to decide certain issues. The church is charged with very clear responsibilities under their leaders. In the same way that a wife chooses to submit to her husband by voluntarily yielding in love (Ephesians 5:2), the members are directed to submit to their leaders (BAGD.1042). They are also to honor them by acknowledging their high status (LN.87.12). The church is to recognize the merit of these men by showing them honor and respect.

Paul clearly says that these men are "over you in the Lord" (1 Thessalonians 5:12-13). Independent minded Americans shudder at the thought of someone being over them in the Lord. However, this is God's plan for leading a young church to greater stages of maturity before it has men who are recognized as elders. A church that has been under the guidance of 'leaders' will respond much more favorably to the leadership of new elders than will a church that has functioned as a democracy. In a democracy one uses influence to get his way, similar to a political strategy. No one is clearly "the boss" when he gets his way through political means.

God's plan was for a church to learn submission from the very beginning. It is especially important for new Christians to recognize their need to submit to the judgment of older, more mature members (1 Corinthians 16:15-16). God wanted a young church to learn to submit in the sense of voluntarily yielding in love (BAGD.1042). Rather than the young church drifting to and fro, it was to be brought under the firm control of its leaders. It would be a learning process on both sides of the equation, but it would also be a far cry from more contemporary views of 'church democracy' in the absence of elders.

At this point you may be asking, "Why talk about leaders before elders, when your topic is the need for elders to be leaders in the church?" The reason is quite simple. If the church had responsibilities to submit to their leaders before elders were appointed, how much more would these principles apply to a congregation with elders? Today, some believe that elders do not have any more "authority" than to make suggestions to the church. It is true that in some churches elders have clearly abused the position given to them by God by being tyrants and even dictators. The abuse of a few should not cause us to miss the intent of passages about submission.

Peter speaks of this unique relationship within the context of the younger being subject to the elders with humility (1 Peter 5:5). Learning to submit is one of the evidences of being filled with the Spirit (Galatians 5:21) and is a vital part of many New Testament relationships (Luke 2:51; Romans 8:7; 10:3; 13:1,5; 1 Corinthains 14:34, 15:28; Ephesians 5:4-24; Titus 2:9; 1 Peter 2:13). Humility would include the ability to acknowledge the rightful place of another without being self-righteous or resentful.

It is reasonable to question why God would go to the trouble to designate the selection of elders (older/wiser men), bishops (to oversee the church) and shepherds (to look after and tend to) if they were merely figureheads. The Hebrew writer is very clear about a church's response to its leaders, "Obey your leaders and submit to them; for they are keeping watch over your souls, as men who will have to give account. Let them do this joyfully...." (Hebrews 13:17).

It can be a challenge for those who have grown up in a culture that stresses independence and self-initiative to think in terms of submitting to their spiritual leaders. God makes this responsibility very clear by referring to this relationship as a shepherd tending to a flock (Acts 20:38). The church is to look to the example of its spiritual shepherds for leadership in the same way that sheep look to their shepherd to provide for their physical needs. The church is to follow the leadership of their shepherds as sheep follow the instructions of their shepherd. Our culture struggles with this analogy of spiritual leadership and submission. However, this is God's teaching about submitting to our leaders.

The supreme example for all leaders in the church is that of Jesus. His example in 'tending to the flock' and his care for the spiritual needs of his followers is exemplary. While he cared for the physical needs of those around him, he clearly kept a spiritual focus in his ministry. He did not get mired in the demands of the temporal to the neglect of the spiritual. His example shines brightly for all that take on the responsibility of spiritual leadership. One of those who knew him best described him as the "Shepherd and Guardian of your souls" (1 Peter 2:25). He was the ultimate 'good shepherd' (John 10:11-16). Jesus was a shepherd who knew his sheep and they knew his voice. He was the one who looked after the well being of his flock. His spiritual concern for the needs of his sheep caused him to literally lay down his life for his sheep. Here is selfless concern for the good of others at its best.

In addition to being described in pastoral terms, Jesus is also the guardian. In this capacity he has the responsibility of safeguarding or seeing to it that something is done in the correct way (BAGD.379). Here is the description of one who has the responsibility of caring for spiritual concerns. The focus of this passage is on the role of caring for believers (LN.35.43). No one has ever done this better than Jesus.

In the same way that Jesus looked after his sheep, the elders are to tend the flock (1 Peter 5:2). They are charged with the loving care, leading, feeding, guarding, and guidance of the church. Their responsibility and assignment is to take care of the flock (LN.35.49). Because they are the shepherds, Peter instructs them not to abuse this position. They are not to be domineering autocrats. They are to assume the responsibility of leadership willingly and eagerly. This is the kind of example that true spiritual leaders are to be to all the flock.

Shepherds have unique responsibilities to the flock that no one else has. They have a charge from God to be the spiritual leaders of the flock which they tend. Many elderships are becoming increasingly aware of the magnitude of this responsibility. More and more time is being spent in prayer and visitation of the sheep than in "decision making." More elderships are defining their leadership in terms of tending and caring for the sheep under their oversight. They are delegating the day to day physical matters to those whom God has equipped to do these tasks. Relief from other matters allows the elders to concentrate more on the priority of shepherding and tending to spiritual matters.

The church will never have too many men who are willing and qualified to shepherd the flock. This is not a matter where one can read a few verses and immediately become an elder. The development of spiritual leadership is something that requires lengthy preparation. We need to be talking to our teens about marrying a life partner with the potential to grow into this level of spirituality. It requires many years of walking with Jesus and working with a life partner to achieve the level of maturity that is required by God for spiritual leadership.

The church desperately needs men who will assume the responsibility of shepherding and guarding the flock. These men occupy a very special place in the plan of God. They set themselves apart by the quality of their spiritual lives. They lead the church by the splendid example of their personal lives. They lead the church by the spirituality that is exemplary in their families. They lead the church by the love and care that they demonstrate as they shepherd the flock. They lead in every aspect of their lives. They are the spiritual "high tide mark" for all to see and to follow.

The Influence of the Entertainment Culture on Worship Assemblies Today!

Stephen A. Bailey

Introduction:

Get Ready to Rumble! When I was a boy, the anticipated activity around many homes on Saturday night was for the family to gather around the television and watch "Big Time Wrestling!" Now I was never one to really *believe* all that stuff was real, but there were certain members of my family who just *knew* it was authentic wrestling!

Unfortunately, that is the dilemma many people face today as they attend worship assembly each Sunday. They do not know how to distinguish between what is real and what is manufactured. So goes the entertainment influence on the Lord's Church, as you and I know it today.

A Look at Entertainment in America Today

According to one market research firm, Americans spend $535 billion a year on leisure activities. The sporting leisure category with the most participants is outdoor jogging. Other top leisure categories include social sports such as golf, fishing, bowling and billiards. The average golfer spends $600 on green fees each year. One set of parents estimate they spend $3,000 a year on their son's soccer career.

The average citizen in America is hopelessly in love with the entertainment industry. Movies are at an all-time high in popularity. The movie industry took in $3.87 billion dollars in the summer of 2003. The average cost of attending a movie in the United States is $10 per person for a premiere movie. A family of four who attends the latest Walt Disney production, eats some popcorn, shares a box of candy, and has a soda from the fountain, could easily kiss $60 goodbye before the first preview is shown on the wide screen. This extravagant amount, of course, does not factor in the cost of being bombarded with unwholesome talk; our precious children adding such language to their vocabulary, and then the parents having to *un-teach* those new and colorful words! Yes, the world's searing influence on our kids today is like a hot knife gliding through a stick of butter!

How many of you have traveled to New York City and experienced a Broadway premiere? The average cost of a play in New York City in July of 2003 was $60 per person! A professional football game with decent seats will cost $50-60.00 each. Add a bag of peanuts, a soda pop, and you have another $100 of the family budget spent on entertainment. A professional baseball game with good parking, decent seating, hot dogs, soda pop and peanuts could easily run close to $100! You see brethren; the entertainment industry is vying for your hard-earned dollars. By Biblical example and command, we should be giving our "first fruits" to the Lord, before spending such extravagant amounts of money for our entertainment. No wonder many churches today feel they are competing for a slot in the "worship zone" on Sunday. Yes, many churches have turned to the world to dictate their pattern of worship, and take cues for the weekly service of the Church. The motto seems to be if it is entertaining, it will bring in the masses. Brethren, our worship is to God, and not for our entertainment.

Some Worship Services in America Today

Here is the scene: The stage area dims, the lights go up slowly, and voices begin to fill the sanctuary or worship center with singing. The stage area resounds with music and shouting. The lights grow dim, and a man begins to preach, while voices softly sing in the background, climaxing to a fervor so as to stir audience response to the invitation. The assembly closes with another song, and the group is dismissed until the next worship and praise time.

The foregoing scenario *could* be the worship assembly of many churches today across our land. It has all the trappings of an off Broadway production, or a performance for the approval of man.

The "That's Entertainment" philosophy influences many places of worship today. It does not take one very long to see that worship in the Lord's Church, over the years, has changed *immensely*. For example, there have been some wonderful strides made in making worship meaningful for all ages. Many of the lyrics to songs that are sung today were written with younger Christians in mind. The words are taken directly from scriptures; namely, Psalms or any number of New Testament passages. The thoughts and musical arrangements are powerful and uplifting. Nevertheless, the world of entertainment has truly made an impact on our worship services.

In the youth minister resource, Current Thoughts and Trends, September 2003, Dan Kimball wrote an article entitled, "Beyond the 'American Idol.'" In that writing, Dan stated that unchurched kids are not particularly impressed with all the glitz and glamour of high-spirited dramatic productions of worship. He went on to say that what teens were seeking was something more spiritual, with silence and worship involved in the scheduled time for worship. One sure thing they do *not* want is a worship assembly filled with flashy videos, edgy music, and smoke machines. Usually in that worship time period, there is a scheduled funny skit that makes a spiritual point, and then they all go home. All of this is to prove that Christians can have fun, too. Those things are not all bad, but these kids feel that there has got to be more to worship than just singing with a "boy band." Teens in the church of Christ want and deserve more than a contrived worship filled with drama, loud music, and technology.

Over the years, The Church has seen a progression of "entertaining" worship following after many churches in the denominational world. It is interesting to this writer that many churches in the denominational world are rethinking their form of worship and are now trying to be more biblical and God-centered. Many members of the church of Christ seem to be going the other way, following the pathway of denominationalism. May we, as a church, wake up before we make these same mistakes and lose a generation of God's Family!

A great deal can be said as to how we, as a family unit, react to our worship assemblies in the local congregation. As an adult, have you ever spoken words within your children's hearing like this: "Boy, Brother Smith really drug the song service out today!" or "Brother Bill's song selection was so boring, I could hardly stay awake!" or "I wish that Brother George would lead more upbeat songs." Admittedly, some song leaders need to speed up the singing and not make the Church feel like they are marching to Zion in a covered wagon! How *upbeat* and how *spirited* does our singing need to be? Does it need to be critiqued like a contestant's performance on American Idol? Can we not have old songs, mixed with new songs? A wise person once said, "Even Isaac Watts' famous song, *When I Survey The Wondrous Cross* was new at one time!" I wonder what people back then thought of Isaac Watts' new song? Of course, it is one of the most loved church songs around today. If a song is from the 17th Century, do we need to tear it out of our hymnals, never to sing it again? Can we not sing about *The Old Rugged Cross* anymore? Is there still not a need to sing songs that teach and admonish us to reach out to the lost? Do *all* our songs need to be songs of praise? Are there no lost souls out in the world anymore? Songs like, *Go Into The Fields*, and *Seeking The Lost* are songs that ought to stir us to reach out to a lost generation of people, young and old.

If we follow the trend today, all songs would be limited to praise songs only. Few songs, if any, would be of 4/4-time selection; and the songs must make us *feel good* when we sing them! Nothing but praise and uplifting songs are to be sung in many congregations today. Brethren, there is still a place for songs that teach us the saving message of God; songs that admonish us to reach the lost; and songs that exhort and stir the heart to praise the name of Jesus. It is this writer's belief that there must be a balance in the song selection by the worship leaders. Elders can see to it that the song leaders in the local church select a good balance of songs. Most church members believe that song leaders would prefer to lead the congregation in a well-balanced selection of new and older songs.

Worship is "to God" and not for our Entertainment

Brethren, let us always remember this important thing: God is the audience, and we are the "worshippers!" By that I mean God is the recipient of our worship. Worship must be done *"in decency and in order"* (I Corinthians 14:40). Our worship is not so much for us, as it is for God Almighty! I must hasten to say that worship does inspire us and motivate us in many ways. Singing a song with a wonderful message, or a very touching reading of the scriptures can move a person closer to God in their worship. There are some sermons we like more than others. An inspiring message on heaven or hope will affect us differently than a sermon about Leviticus, for example. Both subjects are important, but one is more inspirational than the other. That fact I suppose will never change.

My point to the above-mentioned examples is that God is the One we are commanded to worship. He alone is GOD! We are reminded in John 4:23-24, that, "We are to worship in spirit and in truth!" Does that scripture mean we are to "pull out all the stops" and do whatever we feel is good or appropriate? Should questionable and sometimes controversial issues be implemented in the worship service?

Please turn your attention to these verses of scripture:

Matthew 26:30, *"And after* ***singing*** *a hymn, they went out to the Mount of Olives."* (NAS)

Mark 14:26, *"And when they had* ***sung*** *a hymn, they went out into the Mount of Olives."* (KJV)

Acts 16:25, *"And at midnight Paul and Silas prayed, and* ***sang*** *praises unto God: and the prisoners heard them."* (KJV)

Romans 15:9, *"And that the Gentiles might glorify God for his mercy; as it is written, For this cause I will confess to thee among the Gentiles, and* ***sing*** *unto thy name."* (KJV)

1 Corinthians 14:15, *"What is it then? I will pray with the spirit, and I will pray with the understanding also: I will sing with the spirit, and I will* ***sing*** *with the understanding also."* (KJV)

Ephesians 5:19, *"Speaking to yourselves in psalms and hymns and spiritual songs,* ***singing*** *and making melody in your heart to the Lord;"* (KJV)

Colossians 3:16, *"Let the word of Christ dwell in you richly in all wisdom; teaching and admonishing one another in psalms and hymns and spiritual songs,* ***singing*** *with grace in your hearts to the Lord."* (KJV)

Hebrews 2:12, *"Saying, I will declare thy name unto my brethren, in the midst of the church will I* ***sing*** *praise unto thee."* (KJV)

Hebrews 13:15, *"By him therefore let us offer the sacrifice of praise to God continually, that is, the* ***fruit of our lips*** *giving thanks to his name."* (KJV)

James 5:13, *"Is any among you afflicted? let him pray. Is any merry? let him* ***sing*** *psalms."* (KJV)

In all of these verses, we find the words, *sing, sang,* or *sung* except once, in

Hebrews 13:15, we find the words, *"fruit of our lips."* God is saying to the Church today, "SING! That is what I want you to do for Me, and to Me! Sing with all your heart, soul, and mind!" Oh Church, if we would only sing to God like we do in the car while listening to the latest hit song on the radio; or in our room when we think no one is watching or listening. God wants to be praised and He wants that from His children today. Can you imagine what our worship assemblies would be like if each person were to sing with that kind of spirit and understanding? Our services would be such that not one so-called "praise team" would be desired. Each member of the congregation would make up a "praise team" of 300, 700 or 1000 member congregation! Oh, how I would to God that we would sing, and worship God, as we know we ought and should. For many years, people outside of the churches of Christ have attended our weddings, funerals and worship services. Consistently, without fail, the main comment visitors have about services in churches of christ is the beautiful sound of a cappella singing. Why change what is right and scriptural? Why should we be swayed just because the world says, "Entertain me." Let's stay with God's commands and sing with our voices.

Winds of Change On The Horizon—

It is disheartening to learn that some churches of Christ are exchanging a cappella singing, for worshipping with instruments on Sunday or Wednesday night, or even another night of the week with their youth.

By their decision to use instruments on one specific day, and not another, they are saying that it does make a difference to God if we worship with an instrument that is not authorized by God! When church members are enticed by the entertainment trappings of the world and try to implement them in the worship service of the Church, are we no different than Nadab and Abihu (Leviticus 10:1-2), who offered strange fire to God? Of course, we fully realize that the Old Testament is not binding on us today, but nonetheless, the lesson of Nadab and Abihu is there for a reason.

The Bible records, *"For whatever was written in earlier times was written for our instruction, that through perseverance and the encouragement of the Scriptures we might have hope"* (Romans 15:4). Paul is saying that we are to learn from the children of Israel's mistakes and not repeat them.

In September of 2003, the Oak Hills Church in San Antonio, Texas, separated themselves from churches of Christ by removing the "Church of Christ" name from their sign and stating that in early 2004, they would begin using instruments of music in their assembly once a week. That particular worship service, incorporating musical instruments, would be geared to young adults. Brethren, if the young adults begin to worship with instruments in the year 2004, once a week, how long will it be before the entire Body worships in the same manner? One year? Three years? Fifteen years? Twenty-five years?

When asked about these changes, minister and author Max Lucado said, "...although the name has changed, the church's core values will not." My question for Mr. Lucado is this: If the name changes; instruments of music are instituted in the worship; and the reason given for these changes is to draw people to the assembly; doesn't that sound a lot like people following after "whatever it takes" to entertain and entice them into the assemblies? Other churches appear to be staying away from using instruments on the Lord's Day, *for now.*

Yes, the entertainment industry has influenced the worship service of many congregations today. There is no escaping that fact. The question now is, "Where will we go with it?" The people who are worshipping with the accompaniment of a guitar on Sunday or Wednesday night with the Elders' knowledge and approval, will soon be discouraged or grow weary with singing a cappella on Sunday, because it was permissible to use an instrument when they were teens, but now that they are adults, it is *not* acceptable! Elders of the Church who are giving their stamp of approval to such "jazzed up" worship need to look long and hard at the changes that are taking place in the Church today and realize that these changes will have a major impact on the future of church worship. With the passage of time, the church will eventually "loosen up" their worship in direct contradiction to the standards of a God who demands our utmost reverence, respect and obedience to his commands! And, in the words of entertainer Ricky Ricardo, as he oftentimes said to Lucy, come Judgment Day, God will say, "You got some 'splaining to do!"

Conclusion:

Dear Reader:

Let us all make sure that we give our heart and soul to God in worship. Let us never allow the entertainment world to influence us in the form of worship, which is pleasing or "entertaining" to us, creep into the assembly of the Lord's Church. God expects us to give of our best in all that we do. He also deserves it. HE alone IS God, and we are but His servants. Let us search the scriptures daily and make sure when we worship; that our worship is directed and so motivated as to please Him and not ourselves.

Are the Fields Still White?

David Deffenbaugh

Beside a well in Samaria, the Savior of the world proclaimed to His disciples that the fields are "white for harvest." (John 4:35; all Scripture quotations are taken from the New American Standard Bible). This consequential statement, couched in agricultural terms, affirms a great spiritual truth. It relates to the mission for which He left heaven and the purpose for which He instituted the church. The fields are not of wheat or barley. They are of human souls. The time of ingathering is at hand. It is time for harvest.

There is a question. Are the fields still white? Is what Jesus proclaimed still true or was His statement applicable only to the immediate circumstance in which it was spoken? Are the numbers of conversions not as great as they once were? Is the church not growing at a rate that it once did? Are people in general more callused toward religion and is sinfulness continually growing in our world? Are the fields no longer white for harvest, or at least not as white as they once were?

Things are not always as they appear. Even if every one of the above observations were true, a conclusion that the fields are not white would not necessarily be warranted. Using the agricultural metaphor, a decreased yield at harvest may not be a problem with the crop. Yes, it may be a poor quality seed, bad weather conditions, infestations of weeds, insects, or any number of factors. It might also be a failure on the part of the farmer to do what he could, to allow for the greatest harvest. In other words, the decreased yield could be his own fault and not due to other outside influences.

Jesus' statement should not be applied exclusively to the immediate circumstance. The context of John 4:35 has Jesus visiting with a Samaritan woman at the well of Sychar. Their initial conversation led her to the conviction that Jesus was the expected Messiah. Consequently, she entered the city testifying of Jesus and many believed (v. 39). It was as "they went out of the city, and were coming to Him" that Jesus engaged His own disciples in discussion.

> Do you not say, "There are yet four months, and *then* comes the harvest"? Behold, I say to you, lift up your eyes and look on the fields, that they are white for harvest. Already he who reaps is receiving wages and is gathering fruit for life eternal; so that he who sows and he who reaps may rejoice together. For in this case the saying is true, *"One sows and another reaps. I sent you to reap that for which you have not labored; others have labored and you have entered into their labor"* (John 4:35-38).

It has been suggested that the reference to fields ready for harvest was to this group of people coming to the well from the city.[1] Also it has been suggested that the time reference (four months until harvest) is literal. It was December and harvest would come in April. Within their sight was a field of wheat literally four months away from being harvested.[2] These immediate circumstances may have prompted Jesus' terminology. It can hardly be maintained that the truth expressed was applicable only to this particular circumstance. On at least two other occasions Jesus proclaimed the harvest to be "plentiful." One was at the sending out of the 70 (Luke 10:2). The other occasion was when seeing the multitudes as shepherdless sheep roused His compassion (Matthew 9:36-37).

The idea of harvest, or ingathering, is descriptive of the entire ministry and mission of Jesus. Consider the number of parables in which this theme appears. Harvesting is not always the primary point of the parable, but the theme is still obviously present. Many of these parables are centered around and are drawn from the very familiar sowing and reaping theme. These include the parable of the sower (Matthew 13:1-9), the wheat and the tares (Matthew 13:24-30), and the growth of the seed (Mark 4:26-29). Others involve the harvest of something besides grain. For instance, the parable of the dragnet describes "fish of every kind" being gathered (Matthew 13:47-50). The parable of the laborers in the vineyard is centered around harvesting grapes, but the real ingathering of this parable is of laborers, who are called all through the day (Matthew 20:1-16). Two other parables are about gathering people. In each of these cases the gathering is to a feast. One is to a wedding and the other a great supper. In each case the intended guests do not accept the invitation. From the highways servants "gathered together all they found" and in the "highways and hedges" they "compelled them to come in" to fill the master's house (Matthew 22:1-14, Luke 14:16-24). Finally, there are the parables of the lost sheep, coin, and son. Each of these parables describes the lost being gathered and reunited (Luke 15:4-32).

The entire mission and ministry of Jesus can be viewed in terms of ingathering. He came to seek and to save that which was lost (Luke 19:10). As He ministered to the multitudes, He felt compassion for them. They were "distressed and dispirited like sheep without a shepherd." (Matthew 9:36). In the Nazareth synagogue, He applied the words of Isaiah to Himself: *"The Spirit of the Lord is upon me, because he anointed me to preach the gospel to the poor. He has sent me to proclaim release to the captives, and recovery of sight to the blind, to set free those who are downtrodden, to proclaim the favorable year of the Lord"* (Luke 4:18-19).

White fields and plentiful harvests were not merely one dimension of the ministry of Jesus. They are not simply a feature of one geographical location He visited. As Paul says, "God was in Christ reconciling the world to Himself,"

(2 Corinthians 5:19). The very process of reconciliation is ingathering. The self-sacrifice of Jesus on the cross was for all so that all might be brought back to God. What Jesus said specifically of Jerusalem was applicable to all people. *"How often I wanted to gather your children together, the way a hen gathers her chicks under her wings, and you were unwilling"* (Matthew 23:37).

Several facts leave no room for doubt with us that the fields are still white for harvest.

First, what made those fields "white" in the first place is still true. The need for a harvest, an ingathering, is because of the scattering and separation from God as a result of sin. God is seeking reconciliation with the world through Jesus Christ. The core thought of John 3:16 is that God loved the lost so much that He willingly gave His own Son that they might be saved. Jesus' own love was stirred upon seeing the multitudes "distressed and dispirited" (Matthew 9:36). Why were they in such a condition? They were suffering the effects of sin.

The only way the fields would not still be white, would be if sin were no longer a problem for man. Suggesting such a thought is blasphemous. It contrasts plain Biblical teaching and the obvious nature of man (1 John 1:8-10). If sin is no longer a problem, the sacrifice made for it is no longer necessary. God forbid that the cross be made void in any way or at any time. Our own experience and observation in this world is evidence of the ubiquitous nature of sin. People are no less distressed and dispirited today. D. L. Moody allegedly said that for two reasons he knew Satan was real, because the Bible says he is, and he had done business with him. The same can be said of sin. It is real. The lost whom Jesus came to seek and save were not only those of the first century world. The fact of sin's reality makes the fields still white.

The second fact showing that the fields are still white is God's plan for the church. God intends for the church to continue the work and ministry that Jesus initiated. Yes, God was "in Christ reconciling the world to Himself" but the passage continues, "He has committed to us the word of reconciliation" (2 Corinthians 5:19). The church is a continuation of God's work through Jesus. What is more, the church is the continuation of God's plan from eternity. Paul speaks of Jesus, the church, and the eternal purpose in the Ephesian letter, *"So that the manifold wisdom of God might now be made known through the church to the rulers and the authorities in the heavenly places. This was in accordance with the eternal purpose which He carried out in Christ Jesus our Lord"* (Ephesians 3:10-11).

Emphasis is often given to the need for evangelism in the church by appealing to the great commission (Matthew 28:19-20; Mark 16:15-16; Luke 24:46-47). This emphasis is appropriate. However, the basis for the church's evangelistic fervor precedes the command of Jesus. We ought to suspect such if indeed the church is included in the "eternal purpose." Genesis chapters 1-

11 are sometimes referred to as the "Primeval Prologue." In many ways it is prologue. Chapter 12 begins with God's call of Abraham. Events preceding that call lay the foundation for its claims and promises. Yes it is "the Lord" who calls Abraham, but this Lord is the creator of heaven and earth and all that is in them. The ancient world did not think in these terms about deity. Localized gods received their devotion.[3] But the sovereign Lord of the universe speaks to Abraham. Therefore, what He says and what He does pertains to all humanity. This is not just about one man, one family, one race, or one ethnic group, isolated in a single geographic location. What God does through Abraham is for all creation.

This prologue also identifies what God is working to accomplish. Man is in need of blessing because he is suffering under the consequence of sin. Sin entered God's good creation, and its consequences were (and are) devastating. Genesis 3-11 is a demonstration of sin's power to destroy and alienate.

Sin is a curse. God's intention is to bless man. To that end, He calls Abraham. Among the promises made to him are two of particular interest to this study. God said, "I will make of you a great nation" (Genesis 12:2). Further, He said, "And in you all the families of the earth shall be blessed" (Genesis 12:3). Considering the second of these first, God's purpose was for all of humanity. He called a solitary man, but His omniscient plan had every man in view. Paul referred to this very statement saying, *"The Scripture, foreseeing that God would justify the Gentiles by faith, preached the gospel beforehand to Abraham, saying, 'All the nations will be blessed in you.'"* (Galatians 3:8).

The second of the promises was to make of Abraham a great nation. The story line of the Old Testament takes us through the thrilling saga of fulfillment. The promised son, Isaac, was born to Abraham. To one of Isaac's twin sons, Jacob, was born 12 sons who became the heads of families that grew into large tribes. It was these descendants who became enslaved in Egypt but also whom God greatly multiplied there. Moses led them from Egypt to Mt. Sinai where this extremely large clan became a nation. There, at Sinai, God said, *"You yourselves have seen what I did to the Egyptians, and how I bore you on eagles' wings, and brought you to Myself. Now then, if you will indeed obey My voice and keep My covenant, then you shall be My own possession among all the peoples, for all the earth is Mine; and you shall be to Me a kingdom of priests and a holy nation"* (Exodus 19:4-6).

Notice three descriptive phrases regarding the descendants of Abraham; "My own possession," "a kingdom of priests," and "a holy nation." This people, the nation of Israel, were indeed God's chosen people. The implication is that being chosen is quite important. Unfortunately, these people came to consider that being chosen meant the exclusion of all others. God's intention was to choose one people that through His dealing with them, all families of the earth would witness God's glory and be drawn to Him.[4] His intention is expressed in the words of Isaiah; *"I will also make you a light of the nations so that My salvation may reach to the end of the earth."* (Isaiah 49:6). This misconstrued exclusion became a major point of contention in Jesus' day. He told Jewish leaders, *"I say to you that many will come from east and west, and recline at the table with Abraham, Isaac and Jacob in the kingdom of heaven; but the sons of the kingdom will be cast out into the outer darkness; in that place there will be weeping and gnashing of teeth"* (Matthew 8:11-12).

Closely connected to the idea of being chosen, was that of being priests. What did it mean that they were "a kingdom of priests?" It certainly was not just that they would have a priesthood. Rather, they were, as a nation, to serve as priests to the rest of the world. They would be the intermediaries between God and all humanity. So the nation of Israel was to serve as an instrument or a conduit by which and through which God intended to bring blessing upon all humanity. Considering the Jewish misunderstanding regarding their status as God's chosen people, it is no wonder that the conversion of the Gentiles became a major hurdle for the early church to overcome. Even though this issue was volatile and threatening, God's real purpose and intention would not be compromised. In Christ, there would be neither Jew nor Greek (Galatians 3:28).

With the historical purpose of God in mind, the terminology of New Testament writers is not surprising. *"But you are a chosen race, a royal priesthood, a holy nation, a people for God's own possession, so that you may proclaim the excellencies of Him who has called you out of darkness into His marvelous light"* (1 Peter 2:9). Using God's own words to describe Israel, Peter describes the church. Paul refers to the church as, "the Israel of God" (Galatians 6:16). So it is that from the time of Jesus' departure from this earth until His return, the church is to function as that instrument by which *"repentance for forgiveness of sins should be proclaimed in His name to all the nations"* (Luke 24:47).[5]

The fields are still white because the "god of this world" (2 Corinthians 4:4) still functions. Men still sin. Humanity suffers under the curse of sin, and is the object of God's compassion as well as His desire is to bless. The very existence and purpose of the church demands fields that are still white.

If this is all true, why does the zeal for ingathering appear to be waning instead of growing with each passing year? Jesus' words from John 4 give us some insight. He told the disciples, "lift up your eyes and look" (John 4:35). Perception is an issue here. Perception was a major concern of Jesus regarding those to whom He preached. Explaining why He taught in parables, Jesus said,

> In their case the prophecy of Isaiah is being fulfilled, which says, *"You will keep on hearing but will not understand; and you will keep on seeing but will not perceive; For the heart of this people has become dull, and with their ears they scarcely*

hear, and they have closed their eyes lest they should see with their eyes, and hear with their ears, and understand with their heart and return, and I should heal them." (Matthew 13:14-15).

The prejudices of the disciples kept them from being perceptive toward the opportunity Jesus had seized. They were left to wonder why He would be speaking with a woman, and a Samaritan at that. They may have never considered Samaritans as potential recipients of the gospel of the kingdom.

Time, coupled with habit and tradition, builds prejudices. Prejudice is not restricted to race and ethnicity. In the church our prejudices may extend to methodologies and practices, even ways of thinking. Two examples will hopefully illustrate the point. Historically, gospel meetings have been a primary evangelistic methodology for churches in the United States. "Protracted meetings" were productive of much good. Numerous conversions were a common result of the public preaching of the gospel in such settings. Through the years, there have been changes in general public attitudes, involvement of members in personal work, and other contributors to the success of gospel meetings. As a result of many factors, the number of conversions through gospel meetings has greatly diminished. Today, prejudices exist on both extremes. Some seem to suggest that a congregation cannot be considered evangelistic without a gospel meeting. Others maintain that gospel meetings have long outlived their useful purpose. Whether or not the gospel meeting is the best methodology for spreading the gospel in a given community, we must lift up our eyes and see what opportunities lie before us.

A second illustration has to do with demographics. The face of America continually changes. Our nation has continued unabated on the road to urbanization. The vast majority of our population now lives in large cities.[6]

The church in America has thrived in more rural settings. It sprang up and flourished when our nation was still rural in character. Much of what we do, including the procedures and methods we use, had their beginnings in the demands and peculiarities of rural life. We cannot expect to meet the challenge of reaching an urban population with the gospel using procedures and methods dictated by rural demands and peculiarities. We must be perceptive of the demands and opportunities of our urban population.

The disciples also failed to perceive because they allowed lesser concerns to take precedence over greater concerns. Their task at Sychar had been to get food. That is where they were when Jesus encountered the woman at the well. When she left Him to report her remarkable find to her friends in the city, the disciples made their first order of business to get Jesus to eat. He responded, *"I have food to eat that you do not know about...My food is to do the will of Him who sent Me, and to accomplish His work"* (John 4:32, 34).

It certainly is not that eating is unimportant. We all know it to be so. Jesus seized this opportunity to show His disciples that sometimes even good and necessary things can distract us from what is supremely important. Stephen Covey, best selling author of *First Things First*, writes:

> Putting first things first is an issue at the very heart of life. Almost all of us feel torn by the things we want to do, by the demands placed on us, by the many responsibilities we have. We all feel challenged by the day-to-day and moment-by moment decisions we must make regarding the best use of our time.
>
> Decisions are easier when it's a question of "good" and "bad." We can easily see how some ways we could spend our time are wasteful, mind-numbing, even destructive. But for most of us, the issue is not between "good" and the "bad," but between the "good" and the "best." So often, the enemy of the best is the good.[7]

Covey writes about the use of personal time. The principle holds true for the church as well. There is much good in which the church can and should be engaged. There are many needs that we can effectively help to meet. The hungry, the lonely, the divorced, the discouraged, the sick, and so many others are in continual need of help. These are the very people whom Jesus calls upon us to help (Matthew 25:31-46). Is it possible that in pursuing this good that we might neglect or minimize that thing which is of far greater importance?

Jesus faced this very challenge. During His ministry He healed many sick and demon possessed people. So responsive were the people that great multitudes sought Him. Being informed of this on one occasion, Jesus said, *"Let us go somewhere else to the towns nearby, so that I may preach there also; for that is what I came for"* (Mark 1:38). Jesus would not allow the good to displace the best. Undoubtedly the good demands our attention, but proclaiming the saving gospel of Jesus Christ, must always be kept as the top priority. It is true that sometimes we can use the "good" as an inroad to confronting people with the best. Jesus fed the multitudes. When they followed Him as a result of that benevolent act, He sought to teach them what it meant to truly follow Him. He even chastised them for following for the wrong reason (John 6).

Jesus would not allow the purpose for which He came to be clouded, even by the vast amount of good within His capacity to accomplish. In all the good that the church may do, sharing the gospel with the lost, must always rise to the top.

The very concept of restoration, though denigrated by some, is a biblical principle. The application of the restoration principle is often focused on matters of organization, worship practices, and doctrinal issues. That focus is appropriate as far as it goes. The church in God's divine purpose is to attend to fields white for harvest. Evangelism can never be viewed as an optional work. Evangelism cannot be viewed simply as something the church does, but rather it is what the church is. If restoration is a valid principle, and it is, and if evangelism is at the core of the church's identity, and it is, then nothing deserves any more of the church's commitment and energy than attending to the harvest.

The fields are white for harvest, *"Therefore beseech the Lord of the harvest to send out workers into His harvest"* (Matthew 9:38).

[1] "The 'fields' upon which the disciples were invited by our Lord to 'look' were undoubtedly the stream of Samaritans already flocking out to see him." (Guy N. Woods, *New Testament Commentary on the Gospel According to John,* (Nashville, TN: *Gospel Advocate,* 1981), 87.)

[2] "'Four months more and harvest comes' could relate to the precise time of speaking, or signify a common observation on the interval between sowing and reaping, but most consider it to be a current proverb. (George R. Beasley-Murray, *Word Biblical Commentary: John,* (Waco, TX: Word Books, 1987), 63.) "In Greek the words 'Yet four months and harvest comes' have a rhythmic form which suggests that we have to do with a popular or proverbial saying, meaning, 'Four months from sowing to harvest.'" (F. F. Bruce, *The Gospel of John,* (Grand Rapids: Eerdmans, 1983), 114.) Woods counters, "The effort of some expositors to interpret the Lord's statement as a proverb of the length of time from sowing to harvest, and not an actual date, fails because (1) there is no indication that there was such a proverb; (2) it was not four, but six months from the time the seed was sown until the harvest was garnered, and such a 'proverb' would be false." (Woods, p. 87; emphasis in original).

[3] "Since, then, God is the Creator of the universe, the earth and all mankind, we must never demote him to the status of a tribal deity or petty godling like Chemosh the god of the Moabites, or Milcom (or Molech) the god of the Ammonites, or Baal the male deity, or Ashteroth the female deity, of the Canaanites." (John R. W. Stott, "The Living God is a Missionary God," in *Perspectives on the World Christian Movement: A Reader,* ed. Ralph D. Winter & Steven C. Hawthorne, (Pasadena, CA: William Carey Library, 1981), 11.)

[4] "Whenever Israel forgot that God chose her with a view to speaking to the other nations and turned away from them in introverted pride, prophets like Amos, Jeremiah, and Isaiah lashed out at the people's ethnocentric pretension and charged them with subverting God's actual intentions (see especially Amos 7:9-10)." (Johannes Verkuyl, "The Biblical Foundation for the Worldwide Mission Mandate," in *Perspectives on the World Christian Movement: A Reader*, ed. Ralph D. Winter & Steven C. Hawthorne, (Pasadena, CA: William Carey Library, 1981), 36.)

[5] "The meaning of this vision was clear [a reference to Rev. 7:9]: the covenant that God had made with Abraham so many centuries ago—that he and his seed would bring blessing to all the world's 'families'—was the same covenant that had become

the church through Jesus." (Robert Kurka, "The Church and the Covenant" in *Completing the Task,* ed. Edgar J. Elliston and Stephen E. Burris, (Joplin, MO: College Press, 1995), 70.)

[6] For instance, the population of the state of Texas is now 80% urban.

[7] Stephen R. Covey, A. Roger Merrill, and Rebecca R. Merrill, *First Things First,* (New York: Simon and Schuster, 1994), 18.

Can The Bible Be Understood In Our Time?

Dr. Ralph Gilmore

In logical order, the issue of whether the Bible can be understood in our time is the hub to which all the other issues addressed in this book are connected. How one interprets Scripture is the hub of the wheel because any substantive changes in this area affect all other religious decisions a person makes. What I often say to students reflects this reality. For instance, one might try to change a church by re-striping the lines on the parking lot or building a new building. One might try to change a church by introducing PowerPoint into the worship environment. However, if one wishes to make a change which will make all other changes pale in significance, change the way a church views Scripture. Then you have real change.

Those Who Answer "No" to the Question of Whether the Bible Can Be Understood

Can the Bible be understood in our time? To address this question, let us assume that the law of excluded middle is valid and that this precisely stated question is either true or false.[1] Those who would answer "no" may do so from a number of perspectives. Some may argue, from an ill-advised point of view, that the Bible cannot be understood, not realizing the implications involved. They may have been convinced that the Bible has so many cultural statements that the document is robbed of contemporary relevance. They may thus view the Bible to be hopelessly antiquated, desperately needing updates available on-line @Scriptureupdate.com. If the Bible cannot be understood without modern updates then: 1) the view of the Bible being the static, final revelation of God is false, 2) those biblical writers like Jude, Peter, and Paul who claimed the Bible to be the final revelation of God are mistaken,[2] and, 3) Jesus could not be the Son of God since He was delusional.

Others argue that the Bible cannot be understood from a more academically informed point of view.[3] If I might be allowed the privilege of summarizing hundreds of pages of academic dialogue[4], many would argue that the Bible cannot be understood objectively or propositionally because there are three insurmountable barriers which cannot be circumvented. First, modern readers of Scripture can never consistently understand authorial intent. Who knows what the original authors of the books of the Bible intended? Who knows what additional information may have been added by an amanuensis (secretary) or by later scribes copying the books that veil authorial intent from us? Second, modern readers of the Bible can never understand the way the original audience interpreted Scripture when they first heard a new epistle read to them. One cannot recreate completely a first century mindset because it involves a complex nexus of too many cultural, racial, religious, gender, historical, and economic variables. Third, modern readers of Scripture cannot understand the full nature or extent to which our own contemporary biases, assumptions, cultural filters, and presuppositions cloud our own current understanding of the text. So there you have it—objective interpretation of Scripture is impossible. May I hasten to add, however, that the hole these contemporary exegetes have dug for us is expansive. Not only would the Bible be impossible to objectively understand; so would all written communication, whether ancient or modern. For that matter, those who write hundreds of pages about objective hermeneutics being impossible suffer the wrath of self-contradiction since their own writings would also be impossible to understand. So why buy their books? These same three "barriers" would also apply to their own feeble efforts at communication, would they not? Likewise, oral communication as well as written communication would be decimated. Since no teachers could teach objectively, whether written or oral, it follows that no students could understand objectively. So why teach? Denying the possibility of being able to understand the Bible alike comes at quite a significant cost, does it not.

Still others, while apparently accepting that we cannot understand the Bible alike, put the onus of understanding the Bible on the Holy Spirit. They say that the Holy Spirit, as our Counselor, works within the church today to "guide us into all truth" (John 14:26). The Holy Spirit, according to this view, works within the community of believers in an attempt to reach the unity of the faith.[5] Perhaps we might say that those taking this approach should be searching for help online **@HolySpirithelpus.com**. Let me preface my remarks by saying that I do not intend to belittle asking God for wisdom (James 1:5). Every Christian who loves the Bible should do so because he or she loves God. Asking God for wisdom is appropriate. However, asking the Holy Spirit to do my work for me in the interpretation of Scripture puts too much responsibility on Him and too little on me. If ultimately the job of the Holy Spirit is to guide the people of God into a state of perfect unity and understanding, one might say that He is doing a pretty sorry job. Why are there so many religious divisions? It must be the fault of the Holy Spirit. Some who are relying on this argument may not know that historically this argument has been problematic for charismatics (Pentecostals). If the Holy Spirit is leading one charismatic church to conclude that there are three persons in the Godhead and the Holy Spirit is also leading another charismatic church to conclude that there is only one person, Jesus, in the Godhead, who is wrong—the people involved who are reaching wrong conclusions or the Holy Spirit who is leading them into contradictory positions? Can the Holy Spirit lie? Which group is He, or is He not, leading? How can one ever know?

This whole approach reminds me of what one docent, or interpreter, at the Mormon museum in Salt Lake City said to me when I asked for an updated copy of The Book of Mormon. He said that he would provide a free copy for me, and for all the students with me, if I would agree to pray about the book to ask God if the book was from Him. He told me that God would let me know if the book was from Him. How convenient! I do not need to study diligently to ascertain the origin of a book in question; I just need to call on God to confirm or deny it. So, I told the museum interpreter that I would not accept the copy of the book in question under those circumstances. I told him that if The Book of Mormon was from God, it should stand up under scrutiny, and it should rise or fall on its own merits. Well, he gave us all copies of the book anyway! It was good that I got it free because I was already disappointed at not being able to look at examples of the "reformed Egyptian" language in person. There were none in the museum and there are none in existence.[5] In the same way, why do we have to study the Bible? Why not just ask the Holy Spirit to directly confirm the authenticity of the document, and the interpretation of it within the church?

Another major point of concern is that this view of the Holy Spirit confirming His Word within the church is based on a misunderstanding of the section of Scripture known as the paraclete section: John 14-16. Paracletos is the Greek word used several times in reference to the Holy Spirit in this part of the Bible. The word is generally translated "Comforter," "Helper," or "Advocate." The word denotes one who is called to one's side to represent the views or position of that person. Perhaps an alternate description of what the word denotes would be "a benevolent, helpful lawyer." A look at the main passages under consideration would be helpful:[6]

John 14:16-17: *"I will ask the Father, and He will give you another Helper, that He may be with you forever; that is the Spirit of truth, whom the world cannot receive, because it does not see Him or know Him, but you know Him because He abides with you and will be in you."*

John 14:26: *"But the Helper, the Holy Spirit, whom the Father will send in My name, He will teach you all things, and bring to your remembrance all that I said to you."*

John 15:26-27: *"When the Helper comes, whom I will send to you from the Father, that is the Spirit of truth who proceeds from the Father, He will testify about Me, and you will testify also, because you have been with Me from the beginning."*

John 16:13-14: *"But when He, the Spirit of truth, comes, He will guide you into all the truth; for He will not speak on His own initiative, but whatever He hears, He will speak; and He will disclose to you what is to come. He will glorify Me, for He will take of Mine and will disclose it to you."*

Notice the characteristics of this gift of the Holy Spirit. First, the world cannot receive the Holy Spirit. Since the world (i.e., those who are not Christians) did receive the Holy Spirit when He came upon the Gentiles in Cornelius' house in Acts 10, I believe one possible answer to the dilemma is that the Greek word *lambano* can mean "to grasp or seize." Jesus was predicting His own crucifixion and predicting that the Holy Spirit could not be grasped or seized. Subsequently, the Holy Spirit could not be crucified like Jesus was to be crucified. Also, Jesus was prophesying that the Holy Spirit would not be appearing in human form like Jesus had. Second, the Holy Spirit was to teach them all things and would allow total recall of the words that Jesus spoke on earth. How can this apply to the common gift of the Holy Spirit that indwells Christians (Romans 8:12-15; Galatians 4:6; Ephesians 4:32; 1 Corinthians 6: 19-20; et al.)? Is there any congregation so arrogant, or any group of people so arrogant, to claim that the Holy Spirit works within their group to teach them *all truth* and to give them absolute perfect recall of the words of Jesus? Third, this Holy Spirit gift was promised to those who had been with Jesus from the beginning. What is "the beginning" to which John is referring? As Peter explains when he informs the Jerusalem leadership of the Holy Spirit falling on the household of Cornelius, he said, "And as I began to speak, the Holy Spirit fell upon them just as He did upon us at the beginning" (Acts 11:15). Jesus promised this gift to those who had been with Him since the start of His personal ministry. Fourth, the Holy Spirit was to guide the recipients of this gift into "all truth," and this gift would involve a prophetic element to "show them things to come." Which congregations who claim that the Holy Spirit moves among them in this way are busy prophesying future events? Which ones are able to speak "all truth" without any contradiction? Which congregation has preachers or elders who, due to this Holy Spirit gift, do not make mistakes in the interpretation or application of Scripture?

To understand the context of John 14-16, we need to examine parallel accounts in the other gospels. In Matthew 26:20, Mark 14:17, and Luke 22:14, we learn that the twelve apostles were the only persons present to whom this Holy Spirit endowment was promised by Jesus in the predictions in John 14-16. The promises made by Jesus to His disciples in John 14-16 perfectly parallel his promise of the Holy Spirit gift to the disciples in Matthew 10:18-20. This Holy Spirit gift is not promised to each Christian, nor is it promised to the church as a corporate group. My opinion is that some of our people, having been taught about the direct operation of the Holy Spirit in the context of the church from universities associated with other churches, have been influenced to interpret the Counselor's work of the Holy Spirit in a way that is at odds with the context of John 14-16.

The current emphasis in "reading and interpreting the Bible in community"[7] is a revision of the same belief that the Holy Spirit will exegete Scripture for the community of believers who worship together. I completely admit to the advantages of Bible study within a group of believers. However, it is possible that an entire Bible class full of believers could misunderstand a passage of Scripture their whole lives. If this were not so, how could one explain 1500 different denominations officially recognized in the United States today? Why do charismatic groups, who believe in the direct operation of the Holy Spirit, contradict one another on basic matters of Christian doctrine, such as the Godhead, the nature of baptism, etc.? Why would the Holy Spirit not work in every community of believers and thus bring every group together in the unity for which Christ prayed in John 17:20-21? It is right to tout the advantages of group worship and group study; it is dangerous to base correct exegesis of Scripture on this arrangement.

Although I do believe in the common gift of the indwelling of the Holy Spirit in Christians, and although I do believe that this gift does help Christians in ways which I may not fully understand (Romans 8:26), I do not believe that the Holy Spirit will exegete Scripture, for me or for the church, that we are supposed to interpret for ourselves. The job of exegesis of Scripture belongs to each Christian although I may call upon God to help me in any way that is consistent with His will.

The Current State of the Hermeneutical Problem in the Church

If we can ever claim that it is possible to understand the Bible in today's world, we must be able to reconcile different ways of interpreting the Bible among the churches of Christ. Not only has a significant struggle developed among our people between two paradigms of Biblical interpretation; we can't even agree on what to call them. From mainstream churches of Christ, it seems that the preferred labels would be "pattern theology versus the new hermeneutic." I personally find the expression "new hermeneutic" to be ambiguous and misleading since some seem to think that the introduction of a newer translation as a pew Bible is evidence itself of a "new hermeneutic." It is not true that every change suggested in every congregation is due to some mass conspiracy of those who are trying to dismantle the church with a "new hermeneutic." Another way of expressing the paradigm tension is "pattern theology versus grace-centered theology." This approach may also mislead because, as a person who does believe that there are patterns in Scripture, I do not like the implication that I am not grace-centered. Nor do I want others to think that the only authority I perceive in Scripture must be in the form of a "pattern." However, I have chosen this latter designation for this section of the chapter because I find it less misleading than the first. If better descriptive terms become apparent, I can certainly adjust.[8]

Therefore, paving the way for understanding the Scripture in today's world now focuses on the two paradigms of Scripture: pattern theology and grace-centered theology. To some, pattern theology rests upon the concept of accepting the Bible itself as an overall pattern and upon justifying certain definite principles of interpretation that will direct the way to finding patterns for Christians within the overall pattern of Scripture. This is not the form of patternism which I will advocate later in this chapter. To many holding an alternate approach to Scripture, most effective exegesis is grounded in the discernment of the theological, literary, and historical context of each Scripture under scrutiny.[9]

Entire schools of thought, with accompanying Bible Departments, lectureships and printed materials, have arisen to express the thoughts of each respective paradigm. Some writers who write from outside the advocated position of the other writers are not thought worthy to be in a serious dialogue on the matter or, worse yet, are not thought to be intelligent enough to understand the issues involved. Others dismiss the validity of a certain view based on the label itself—e.g., "that is a liberal point of view and cannot be taken seriously." May I confess my personal frustration with this increasingly tense situation among brethren. I have friends from within each paradigm, but I am not personally committed to any person more than I am committed to a search for truth on this matter. Is it possible to be brought closer together? Is it inevitable that a schism must deepen? I pray not.

In the hopes of being heard by honest-hearted people on both sides, I wish to suggest a modest proposal for unity. To give this proposal due consideration, we must be willing to temporarily put aside the list of pattern principles, and the teachers of them, which we have accepted in the past in order to give a suggestion a fair hearing. After hearing the suggestion, please feel free to discard it if it does not bear up under close examination. Accordingly, we must also be willing to temporarily put aside the principles of interpretation inherent in grace-centered theology, along with the teachers of them, in an effort to understand the Bible in our time. So, here we go.

A Suggested Approach Toward Understanding the Bible Alike

There are some things about patternistic interpretation that I really do not like. The Lord's people (the church) have been fragmented by division in the past based on the philosophies of those who have found "patterns" in Scripture where no patterns exist.[10] Secondly, although it is true that the church has been "instituted" or "set up" in history according to Old Testament prophecy (Isaiah

2, Daniel 2, and Joel 2), we should not view the church in an institutionalized way or in a denominational way. We often use the descriptive phrase "church of Christ" as though it were a denominational name. This situation often arises because of patternism gone awry. Third, abusive patternism leads to a misguided paradigm of Biblical interpretation. Although the Bible does contain rules, the Bible is not a rulebook, or a constitution, or "the system of annotated codes given by God from Mt. Sinai to the present." The Bible is far richer and heterogeneous than that and simply undeserving of simple platitudes. The Bible as a whole is indeed a pattern for our lives. It is God's communication of His heart to us. The genuine issue that divides the disparate camps among us is not about whether the Bible is a pattern. Both groups agree that it is. The genuine issue is whether there are patterns within the divine Word, and, if so, how one goes about identifying such patterns. Third, abusive patternism encourages people to consider the plan of salvation as being a pattern of obedience to a system or catechism or creed. It is not belief in obedience that saves us; rather, it is belief in and obedience to the living Savior who paid the ransom for my sins (Titus 3:5; Romans 5-7; Galatians 3-4). I still believe in faith, repentance, confession, and baptism, but I do not view the plan of salvation as being a constitution or catechism. I want to be able to recognize patterns in Scripture when they occur, but I do not want to search for a pattern in every verse.

There are some things about grace-centered interpretation that really concern me. To illustrate, please note selected quotations from a grace-centered theologist:

> "Copying first-century structures, organization, patterns and rituals became for us the best and necessary means for restoring the vitality and performance of the primitive church" (Woodroof 7).

> "We believed that by becoming students of the early church and by adopting those ancient patterns of life for ourselves, we could restore the ancient church in modern times" (Woodroof 13).

> "For a new generation in our churches, . . . a critical decision has been made: function comes first, not form" (Woodroof 18).

> "Get the functions right and God will provide the forms we need to do His business effectively" (Woodroof 19).

> "It's why I call into question our reliance on "pattern theology" (rather than a thoughtful Christology) for shaping the church" (Woodroof 29).[11]

I am on record as saying that those who spend so much time disavowing any relationship to pattern thinking so often introduce another "pattern" for understanding the Bible after they have attempted to destroy the dominant existent "pattern" of interpretation which they so seem to hate.[12] For instance, the above quoted grace-centered thinker tries to argue that there are no forms, or patterns, binding on the contemporary church. However, in the process, he does argue for seven "functions" of God's church. Inquiring minds want to know: what is different about seven "functions" that must be present for the church to be the church, and admitting that to this writer these seven "functions" become an essential "form" or pattern to identify the contemporary church? Has he not substituted one "form" for another? Is he not still, at least to this extent, a "pattern theologist"?

Contrasting Paradigms for Understanding the Bible

Several years ago, I was teaching a class about my understanding of the "pattern" of pattern theology (i.e., direct statement, implication, expediency, and account of approved action) when a friend and fellow faculty member where I was teaching asked, "I can see that there is Scriptural support for the application of the four principles that you are discussing, but where did they come from?" My first mental response to her question was, "I got them from my teachers in Christian education." Somehow, I was sure she would not be satisfied with this answer, so I mumbled through another response without really answering her question.

Many of us who have been brought up being taught pattern theology have dutifully accepted the three-element (direct statement, apostolic example, and necessary inference) or four-element (direct statement, implication, expediency, and accounts of approved actions) pattern principles that we have been taught. Can they be justified? Where did we get them? These are legitimate questions.

The attempts at alternate paradigms have been varied. Some have proposed a new emphasis on Christ-centered hermeneutics; some have thought that an understanding of the theological, literary, and historical backgrounds of the text is the way to correct a patternistic approach; and some have argued for function over form. A common denominator for all alternate approaches is an extremely negative opinion of patternism.

To simplify the contrasting methods of interpretation of Scripture, I am choosing to use the phrases "pattern theology" versus "grace-centered theology."[13]

Is there any hope to avoid further schism among us? Is it impossible to understand the Bible alike? It will be impossible to understand the Bible alike if we cannot find common ground between these contrasting paradigms of Bible interpretation. The remainder of this chapter will lay the foundation for such an approach.

First Principles of Bible Understanding

Are there any first principles, or apriori, principles of biblical interpretation?[14] The problem is primarily a logical one. Logically, how can I endorse any paradigm of hermeneutics (i.e., "principles of interpretation") that I claim to come from the Bible without first having reached the conclusion that the Bible is the inspired Word of God? After all, why should anyone trust the message of Scripture unless it is what it claims to be? And yet, how can I reach my initial logical conclusion that the Bible is from God without applying principles of interpretation to it? The Bible should be able to speak for itself, but not if it cannot first be interpreted. In this process, it seems that I am begging the question (a logical fallacy known as ***petitio principii***) because I am accepting something as being true which is logically connected to the conclusion that I am claiming. So, the premises prove the conclusion, which in turn proves the premises, ad infinitum. Are there reasons for accepting some principles of interpretation for the purpose of evaluating the message of the Bible prior to one's conclusion that the Bible is from God? I believe there are.

Laying Out a Case for First Principles of Bible Understanding

The case that I wish to lay out for first principles of biblical hermeneutics (hereafter abbreviated "first principles") is based on conclusions drawn in an apologetic vein (i.e., Christian evidences). The first step is the existence of God as demonstrated by moral arguments. Moral arguments for God's existence are based on the "moral" dimension of mankind. One form of a moral argument is as follows: If humans have a sense of moral oughtness which cannot be explained on the basis of organic evolution, then God must have given it to us. For present purposes, we will need to assume that this argument is sound. I would be pleased to argue for its soundness in other contexts. Therefore, since we are assuming that this God does exist, what can we learn about Him? The way that I like to explain it, in simple terms, is this: If God has given us an "itch," then he is morally obligated to give us a way to "scratch" it. Why is this so? A God who has anticipated all the other needs of his special creation (which can be demonstrated with logical or design arguments for God) would likewise want to meet our needs in a moral realm. To summarize, God would want to reveal His will to us in a special way in order to meet the needs of this sense of oughtness that He gave us. Thus, the first step is God would specially reveal himself to us.

The second step is this conditional: Since God would want to reveal Himself to us in a special or supernatural way, this special revelation would be either written, oral, or subjectively appropriated. By listing these options, I am not limiting God in any way, but I would argue for a God who cannot do the logically impossible because it would be contrary to his nature and to the physics of the universe he has given to us. If God gives special revelation that is subjectively appropriated within each of his subjects, then this process is "subjective" in the true sense of the term. This would eliminate the possibility of transmitting an objective special revelation, and, although it might be of personal benefit to me, it would not benefit others in any teaching process. Thus, I would argue that since God wants to communicate himself and his will to us in a special way, he would choose ways that we have designated "written" or "oral." If "written" or "oral," these options fit in better with the nature of a special revelation that God wants to give on the basis of a universal sense of moral oughtness given to humankind.

The third step is: If God specially reveals himself in a writing, or in a way that is objective (i.e., communicable) as well as relevant to each individual (i.e., communicable, to each person), then this revelation would be propositional. "Propositional," in logical terms, means having objective logical content the validity of which can be measured either by testing the validity of the form of the argument or by testing the truth of the premises.[15] If God intended to give a special revelation that was to be communicated to others, then I would submit that it would have to be propositional in nature. If one believes in principles of correct thinking and in the testing premises on which conclusions rest, there is no escape from this conclusion.[16]

The fourth step is that if God did reveal himself propositionally (as we have argued that he would), then principles of critical thinking would apply to the interpretation of (i.e., hermeneutical approach to) this document. Let the reader be aware that the steps laid out thus far have application not only to the way one may read the Bible to test its claim as being the special revelation from God, but also the way one would read any document or candidate claiming to be special revelation from God. Thus this process is both logically and aesthetically pleasing to me because one does not have to assume that the Bible is God's inspired Word before one can logically test the claims of the book. These principles of critical thinking mentioned above can lead us to the "first principles of Interpretation for special revelation" for which we are searching! Then once the Bible is authenticated as exactly what it claims to be, these same "first principles" can be used to further understand God's message to us through his special revelation, i.e., the Bible.

The First "First Principle": Implication

The first "first principle" which I wish to examine is that of implication, or in some contexts known as "necessary inference." Why is this principle of implication so basic to all interpretive understanding? First let us define the principle. Statement one (1) is said to imply statement two (2) if, when statement one (1) is true, statement two (2) is also true.[17] Implication may take two forms: the weak form is one based on the correlation between two statements and the strong form is based on a causal relationship between two statements. In other words, statement two (2) may be implied from statement one (1) if whenever statement one (1) is true, then statement two (2) is also true. This is the weak form of implication. The strong form of implication is: the truth of statement one (1) causes statement two (2) to be true. Implication is basic to all rationality.

At this point, the reader may notice that I have chosen not to use "direct statement", or some equivalent phrase, as the first "first principle." This requires some explanation because of the departure from the orthodox explanation of principles of Biblical interpretation.

Why should "direct statement" not be listed first as it traditionally is? For that matter, should "direct statement" be listed at all? The first reason I have opted for a change is because "direct statement" cannot be logically first. As before intimated, even the conclusion that the Bible is the inspired Word of God rests upon some interpretive principles. One cannot possibly rightfully conclude that there are any direct statements in Scripture if one does not first conclude that the Bible is from God. Direct statements (i.e., statements made directly to an individual interpreter) cannot confirm inspiration. Such conclusions can only be reached from logical principles which rely on implication.

Secondly, every "direct statement" which an individual in the twenty-first century concludes is specifically to him is a conclusion based on implication. No statement in Scripture is directly written to any contemporary individuals. My name is not attached to any directive in Scripture, i.e., "Ralph, you should be baptized." How did I reach the conclusion that baptism is a command of God that is personally applicable to me? It requires implication. Implication comes before any direct statement for this reason.

A third reason why implication should be mentioned first is because implication is so basic to the entire area of logic, the foundation of which I believe is based on the very unchanging nature of God. Regarding of the complexity of the logical argument or the number of the premises involved, all deductive arguments can be reduced to implication, i.e., an argument is valid if the premises *imply* the conclusion. Thus ALL deductive arguments can be boiled down to an argument based on implication.

A fourth reason for the emphasis on implication is because implication puts the focus where it belongs—on the logical principles themselves and not on the persons who make inferences based on the implications involved. Thus "necessary inference" should not be a first principle for Bible understanding.

Regarding the older expression "necessary inference," Thomas B. Warren used to tell us that if (X) is a matter of justifiable inference, then the adjective "necessary" is redundant. From logic classes I have taken, it has been taught that propositions imply, but people infer. So, one of the keys to accurate interpretation of any document written in propositional form is for the interpreter to infer what has been implied by the language itself. Thus "implication" is a first principle to apply in understanding any special revelation from God because all documents or conversations are to be interpreted in this way. All nontrivial declarative statements imply something. For instance, "If I have a coin in my hand, and I put my hand in my pocket," what are implications from this sentence? Obviously, some implications are that I have a hand, that I have a coin, that I have a pocket, and that the coin in my hand is now in my pocket. If anyone tries to defeat this argument, he or she must use implication in order to attempt to refute implication. Since the principle has been used in a vain attempt to refute it, then the disputant has begged the question.

I try to teach the concept to students by comparing the concept to a piece of double adhesive tape that one wishes to discard: it sticks to whatever one tries to use to throw it away. Such is the case with implication. Anyone who tries to compare implication as a hermeneutic principle to a "Church of Christism" is grossly misinformed and does not understand "wherewith he speaks." To summarize, I have attempted to show how both direct statements and implication are "first principles" or apriori principles of interpreting any document which claims to be from God. Therefore, these principles can be trusted in helping us to reach the initial conclusion that the Bible is the inspired Word of God and in helping us to understand what the Bible teaches us to do to establish and maintain a saving relationship with God. Another matter of beauty is that this principle is not a principle of biblical interpretation exclusively, but it is purely a principle for interpreting any document containing statements with truth content (propositions). Therefore, this principle cannot be simply an unfounded tradition.

A final reason why implication should be preeminent if we want to understand the Bible in our time is because implication allows us to avoid "abusive patternism" in interpreting Scripture. In the current "hermeneutics wars" among our brethren, it seems that the major alternative proposed to "patternism" is what I have termed the "TLH approach." By "TLH approach," I mean to denote the approach of those who insist that the proper interpretation of any text is impossible without understanding the "theological, literary, and historical" backgrounds of the text being studied.[18] I agree. I believe that the understanding of the "TLH" of each text is crucial to its understanding.[19] To the extent to which any of us in the mainstream of the churches of Christ have violated this method by "proof-texting" or "finding patterns in passages where patterns do not exist," I definitely agree. However, the "TLH approach" rests solidly on the current first principle we are considering—implication. Without implication, proper interpretation is impossible because all rationality would come to a grinding halt.

In a discussion with James Walters and Randy Harris on the topic of "Postmodernism and Hermeneutics,"[20] Walters presented a paper in which he articulated the importance of the concept of "resident alien communities" in Rome as a backdrop for a better understanding of two texts: 1 Corinthians 6 and Romans 13. His historical research was enlightening, bringing to life aspects of the texts difficult to know without it. He applied the "TLH approach" in a scholarly way to the two texts. In my response to his paper, I noted that the "TLH approach," though helpful, will not answer such questions as: in modern times, is it wrong to go to law with your brother?; or, may a Christian today serve in the military? The "TLH approach" is impotent to answer such questions. Examination of the theological, literary, and historical matters in the text is critical to understanding the text, but the "TLH approach" is only a necessary step to understanding the text—not a sufficient condition for proper exegesis and correct application to our time.

The Second "First Principle": Direct Communication

If propositional special revelation is the type of communication that God would use, if principles of critical thinking would thus apply to it, and if the special revelation is expected by God to be understood by people as the Bible passes through time, then one can predict that direct communication would characterize this document. Why is this so? Let us consider it in this way. Would the God of creation hide himself from the subjects of his special revelation in secretive statements, in ambiguous symbols, or in total subjectivism? Would he anticipate that His children would fail to understand which statements were made directly to them even though He had inspired the document so that they could understand what He wanted them to do with their lives? I do not believe so. If he did this, it would smack of a violation of his sense of justice demonstrated in other areas. Also, what good would a special revelation be if it could not be objectively interpreted? Even in the case of the apocalyptic literature in Scripture (the book of Revelation, parts of Daniel, etc.), which comprises only about eight percent of its total volume, the message of apocalyptic literature was meant to be understood, primarily by the people to whom it was written and secondarily to those of us who read it today.

However, this principle of direct communication, or "personal directives," cannot stand alone. As before explained, we could never conclude that any communication was directed to us without implication. So, this principle is logically dependent on implication.

Without a revelation that was "direct" in some way to the recipients, one could not conclude that the Bible was written to us. By the nature of special revelation, it would be better for the reader to assume that the book was written to him unless the context indicates otherwise, than to assume that the book was not written to him unless the context indicates that it is. This principle of "directness" flows from the concept of special revelation and an understanding of the God who gives it. Without direct communication, no objective exegesis would be possible. Therefore, direct communication is a necessary part of understanding God's special revelation and is the second of our "first principles" of interpretation.

Let us review. The concepts of implication (the first principle) and direct communication (the second principle) are NOT catechistic statements of "Church of Christ" belief.; nor are they principles for a pattern of interpretation applying only to Scripture because these two principles apply to all communication, both written and oral. These principles are not worn out traditions simply handed down from generation to generation without thought or justification. Why? First of all, I do not believe in "Church of Christ" beliefs. Beliefs are justified on the basis of their truth value, for one thing. Also, I do not believe in using "Church of Christ" in a denominational sense. Thus, implication and direct communication are principles of interpretation that all should honor in ascertaining and interpreting special revelation from God. Whether one classifies himself as pattern theologist or a grace-centered theologist does not matter in this context because one cannot avoid the impact of these two interpretive principles.

The Third "First Principle": Expediency

A third "first principle" often overlooked is expediency. The identification of true expedients is a logical process which, like personal directives, likewise rests on implication. An expedient matter is one that is "appropriate to the purpose at hand" or "something contrived to meet an urgent need." Often we simply refer to expedients as "aids" toward achieving a goal. Of course, we would classify things such as songbooks, communion disposable cups, etc. as aids to given purposes. I believe that a mistake often made by some is to say that expedients do not come under the umbrella of biblical authority. This conclusion is not technically correct. No Christian should be proud of admitting that he or she is doing something in the absence of biblical authority.

There must be a better way. If God did reveal himself in a special way involving propositions, then expedient conclusions can be anticipated. Why is this the case? First, no propositional revelation can be exhaustive in such broad areas covered by special revelation. The document would be too large. God would never have fully explained to Noah about building the ark if he did not allow Noah to make expedient decisions such as where to find the gopher wood, how to cut it, how to shape it, how to transport it, etc. Theoretically, a virtually endless number of expedient decisions were left to Noah's discretion in the command to "Go build an ark of gopher wood." Noah would not have lived long enough for God to explain what Noah was to do in all matters involving expediency. Instead, God left these procedural decisions up to Noah.

A second justification for expediency is related to the first: the use of expedients increases the practicality and enduring nature of the revelation. What if Jesus had said, "Go preach the gospel to all by riding on a donkey's back"? This command would have been unnecessarily restrictive in modern days of faxes and email. So, expedients allow for the perpetual relevancy of the gospel as we pass through time awaiting the final coming of Jesus, and they allow for documents of a length appropriate and practical for stated purposes. Therefore, expedients are not outside the realm of God's authority; rather, expedients that are true expedients the status of being approved by God in fulfilling God's direct statements to us or implications of these direct statements. And, expedients are not applicable only to the Bible, but to any document which authorizes directive behavior to its recipients. Again, we see that this "first principle" of expediency is not characteristic of a pattern theologist only, but of all people who believe God has specifically given directives to them by means of special revelation.

As important as the principle of expediency is to understanding the Bible in today's world, this principle, like direct communication, cannot stand alone and does not apply only to interpreting the Bible. It is logically dependent on implication as well. We could never separate expedient factors from factors essential to carrying out God's will if we could not use implication.

The Fourth "First Principle": Prescriptive Actions

The fourth and final "first principle" to be discussed is that of accounts of binding action, or "examples" as some view it. If there are any actions in the category, God is prescribing that we should continue to practice these same actions in the church. Thus, I prefer to call this category "prescriptive actions." This is the principle that has come under the severest scrutiny by grace-centered theology.

It seems to me that this concept is essentially different from the other three because any special propositonal revelation involves interpretive principles of implication, direct communication, and expediency. However, this is not the case with prescriptive actions, or the accounts of action that we should be doing today by virtue of their prescriptive nature. God could have chosen not to reveal himself through approved or disapproved actions of people in history, if that had been God's choice. But, given God's legitimate reasons for giving us a special revelation with direct references to historical actions, God would be expected to give us ways by which we could ascertain which of these actions apply to us today and which do not. Therefore, I believe that an interpreter of a historical special revelation should expect to find some methodology of differentiating binding from non-binding actions.

To put it more simply, the Bible contains many accounts of people doing things in history. Which ones are binding on us today? Warren used to teach that actions which God included in the Bible for us to follow might be either optional or obligatory, and either temporary or permanent.[21]

Even though this principle is the "hot issue" for those who oppose pattern theology, the end result of such efforts, in my judgment, is counterproductive. God does expect his people to discriminate between historical actions that he wants us to follow and those he does not, whichever paradigm of interpretation one uses.

At this point, a confession is in order: I do believe in patterns in Scripture and thus technically I would be classified as a pattern theologist. Yet, I do not believe in interpreting the Bible through the blinders of abusive patternism. To illustrate: I believe in absolutes, and I believe in absolute truth. I thus also believe that there are moral absolutes which cannot be broken.[22] However, I also believe that there are "gray areas" in ethics. Some actions are morally neutral, and some actions are neither intrinsically right nor intrinsically wrong.[23] My belief in "gray areas" does not disqualify me from being an absolutist. Likewise, I believe that there are patterns in Scripture. But, there may not be as many patterns as we have claimed in the past, and we certainly are not justified in viewing the mosaic of Scripture from the exclusive paradigm of Rule Book. The Bible contains rules, but the Bible is not a Rule Book exclusively.

It is ironic, and a bit frustrating, to read some contemporary writers who often spend dozens of written pages blasting patternism only to replace the "patternism" they seem to hate with another form of "patternism." This process smacks of interpreting the Bible with blinders on. One grace-centered theologist earlier noted does exactly this. He blasts away at pattern theology, but later in his book he admits that we must accept the patterns of baptism and the Lord's Supper because of the "loss of theological significance" if we do not accept them.[24] Well, fine, be that way if you must. But if one reaches this conclusion, he is qualified as being a "patternist" whether or not he admits it.

A related issue that is bothering God's people presently (and has done so throughout the centuries) is: how does one separate culture from God's enduring principles? Or, how does one distinguish between extraneous details from the essential details in any given action that we believe to be binding?[25] This may appear obvious to some, but apparently not obvious to others: when one is considering an action in question (X), one should search for any signs of permanence in the midst of the cultural setting in which the action occurs. In 1989, I was one of the participants in a discussion about the role of women in the church today.[26] At that time, I defended a hierarchal view of the role of women in worship based on a principle of permanency found in 1 Timothy 2:12-15, 1 Corinthians 11:11-12, and perhaps 1 Corinthians 14:34-35. This permanency is due to the role of women being tied to the creation, especially the created order of man and woman. Since the instrumental roles of women in worship are founded in God's creation, at which time no human culture was in existence, I believe that these same gender roles are in effect today and cannot be dismissed by appealing to the cultural aspects of the five basic texts in question (1 Timothy 2, 1 Corinthians 11 and 14, Ephesians 5, and 1 Peter 3). This answer of how to separate culture from command of God is cursory at best, but perhaps a foundation is laid for a better understanding.

In concluding this section, let me demonstrate how a "TLH" approach, instead of admitting patterns when they do exist, runs into barricades in understanding the Bible. Although there may be reasons to be frustrated with patternism as practiced by some of our brethren, at the end of the day each Christian still needs to know whether a Biblical action under consideration IS or IS NOT prescriptive. Does God want me to continue this action today either in my personal spiritual life or in the life of the church? The TLH (theological, literary, and historical), also known as the critical-historical approach, will give one no answers here. For instance, the Passover (paschal) lamb would have been eaten by Jesus and the Twelve Apostles prior to Jesus' setting up the perpetual observation of the Lord's Supper. Using the TLH approach, Jesus *was* the Passover lamb when he died (John 1:29,36; Isaiah 53:7; Acts 8:32; 1 Peter 1:19; Revelation 5:6, 8, 12; 6:1). Using this approach, one might justify eating roast lamb for the Lord's Supper. Why not? Only a "pattern" approach would restrict it to the two elements Jesus mentioned.

Conclusion

In returning to our initial question, can the Bible be understood in our time? Obviously, it can, whether or not we are doing it well. Although I have no "pattern of biblical interpretation" to offer, I have justified four principles to help us to understand the Bible alike. The four principles are not independent: the basic principle is implication, and the principles of direct communication, expediency, and prescriptive actions each depend on implication in order to function effectively. I have also emphasized that each of these principles can also be applied to interpret all written documents thus causing one to resist the conclusion that these are "pattern" principles. I have tried to make a strong case for each principle so that if one tries to deny any of the four, one is either led to a contradiction or to an untenable position.

Now for a final appeal. I am so tired of the strengthening "us versus them" mentality among our brethren. I am so weary of discussions that begin with "have you heard what they are doing now at congregation (X)?" I am aghast at the group paranoia eating away at our unity. If I know my heart, I am not interested in defending the "pattern theology" of any teacher who has mentored me. On the other hand, I am heartbroken to see the extent to which some are going in order to find "a new vision" for their congregation, a direction that is fueled by the discarding of crucial principles of interpretation of Scripture in favor of principles that are not defensible. The postmodern culture is a two-edged sword: there are many searchers for truth in this culture, but these searchers face the formidable task of searching for truth in a document (the

Bible) which they are taught cannot be understood in today's world. It will be our opportunity to show that the Bible can be understood by introducing them to the Jesus of Scripture and teaching them to yield to His will in their lives.

Works Cited

Allen, Leonard. *The Cruciform Church.* 2nd ed. Abilene, TX.: ACU Press, 1990.

Carter, Cordell. *A First Course in Logic.* New York: Pearson-Longman Books, 2004.

Childers, Jeff, Douglas Foster, and Jack Reese. *The Crux of the Matter, Heart of the Restoration* Series. vol. 1 Abilene, TX.: ACU Press, 2001.

Cukrowski, Kenneth, Mark Hamilton, and James Thompson. *God's Holy Fire.* Abilene, TX.: ACU Press, 2002.

Fee, Gordon and Douglas Stuart. *How to Read the Bible for All Its Worth.* 2nd ed.

Grand Rapids, MI.: Zondervan Books, 1993.

Foster, Douglas. *Will the Cycle Be Unbroken?* Abilene, TX.: ACU Press, 1994.

Gilmore, Dr. Ralph. *Gender and Ministry,* Freed-Hardeman University Preachers and Church Leaders Forum. Huntsville, AL.: Publishing Designs, Inc., 1990.

Osborne, Grant. *The Hermeneutical Spiral.* Downers Grove, IL.: InterVarsity Press, 1991.

Settled in Heaven, the 1996 Freed-Hardeman University Lectureship book. Henderson, TN.: FHU Press, 1996).

Thiselton, Anthony. *New Horizons in Hermeneutics.* Grand Rapids, MI.: Zondervan Publications, 1992.

Warren. *When is an Example Binding?* Delight, AR.: National Christian Press, 1973.

Woodroof, Tim. *A Church that Flies.* Orange, CA.: New Leaf Books, 2000.

[1] This is a shaky assumption in a postmodern culture where all rationality is questioned and thus up is down, and down is up. To this concept we will return later in this chapter.

[2] Jude 3; 2 Peter 1.20-21; 2 Timothy 3.16; et al.

[3] Grant Osborne's *The Hermeneutical Spiral* (Downers Grove, IL.: InterVarsity Press, 1991) and Anthony Thiselton's *New Horizons in Hermeneutics* (Grand Rapids, MI.: Zondervan Publications, 1992).

[4] This view is quite complex and would take more space to critique than this chapter would allow. For a fuller explanation of this point of view and their defense of it, see God's Holy Fire, pp. 205-207.

[5] According to Joseph Smith, he interpreted *The Book of Mormon* from a language he called Reformed Egyptian. The problem is that Reformed Egyptian is not a language that any independent Egyptologist knows anything about. If the language exists, one

should be able to do textual criticism of Smith's interpretation of the language. Of course, this cannot be done. Thus, if you accept the authenticity of the book, you must do so on blind faith.

[6] All Scripture citations, unless otherwise noted, are from the New American Standard Version Update.

[7] *Crux of the Matter* 168-170; *God's Holy Fire* 205-211.

[8] Obviously, this is not the first time such indecision about appropriate labels has appeared among us. Regarding the issue of what I view to be extreme patternism among some of our brethren, we have not agreed on descriptive terms. I grew up describing these congregations as "anti," a term which caused derision among those of this persuasion. They prefer to be called "non-institutional," a term which causes me personal problems since I do not agree that I am a member of the "institutional church of Christ."

[9] Jeff Childers, Douglas Foster, and Jack Reese's *The Crux of the Matter, Heart of the Restoration* Series, vol. 1 (Abilene, TX.: ACU Press, 2001), 158-185; Kenneth Cukrowski, Mark Hamilton, and James Thompson's *God's Holy Fire* (Abilene, TX.: ACU Press, 2002) 170-174; 227; Douglas Foster's *Will the Cycle Be Unbroken?* (Abilene, TX.: ACU Press, 1994), 89-97; and Leonard Allen's *The Cruciform Church,* 2nd ed. (Abilene, TX.: ACU Press, 1990), 25-41.

[10] I believe that the impetus behind the split between non-institutional brethren and the mainstream churches of Christ was the fact that non-institutional brethren thought they found patterns for benevolence, edification, and evangelism in the church which I do not believe are patterns at all.

[11] Tim Woodroof's *A Church that Flies* (Orange, CA.: New Leaf Books, 2000); 33-50.

[12] *Settled in Heaven*, the 1996 Freed-Hardeman University Lectureship book, 153-160.

[13] In the search for neutral terminology to describe the different groups, one often offends one party or the other. I do not choose to identify "grace-centered" believers by the phrase "the new hermeneutic" because the term is so ambiguous and so misused by our brethren so as to render it ineffective. However, by choosing "grace-centered" over "the new hermeneutic," I do not mean to imply that pattern theologists know nothing about "grace." I do recognize that what some "grace-centered" writers mean by "grace" amounts to nothing more than "cheap grace," as Bonheoffer described it, because grace does not cover all doctrinal error. I have tried to reach an acceptable compromise in the use of terminology.

[14] Some of the material in this section of the chapter appears in the 1996 Freed-Hardeman University lectureship book *Settled in Heaven*, pp. 153-160. However, I have changed the order and some of the basic concepts of the first principles substantially.

[15] Appeals to logic in order to build a case for first principles of Bible understanding are not politically correct in these days of postmodernism. However, to discard a rational approach to understanding Scripture comes at a great cost, the cost being

the paralysis of all thought. Our brethren have no business being paranoid about logic. The proper use of logic has never been an enemy of Christianity; the lack of sound logic will be the death of Christianity.

[16] In my experience a frustrated logic teacher is one who is an atheist but still believes in principles of correct thinking with no metaphysical reason for believing that these principles exist since an evolutionary atheist has no external standard by which to measure "correct thinking."

[17] Cordell Carter's *A First Course in Logic* (New York: Pearson-Longman Books, 2004), 222.

[18] *Crux of the Matter, God's Holy Fire, Will the Cycle be Unbroken?, The Cruciform Church*, et al.

[19] Gordon Fee and Douglas Stuart *How to Read the Bible for All its Worth*, 2nd ed.

(Grand Rapids, MI.: Zondervan Books, 1993); 13-27.

[20] At Harding University Graduate School of Religion in Memphis, Tennessee in 1994; tapes available through the HUGSR bookstore.

[21] Warren , *When is an Example Binding?* (Delight, AR.: National Christian Press, 1973).

[22] Galatians 5.19-21; Revelation 21.8; Malachi 3.6; John 8.42; John 17.17.

[23] 1 Corinthians 8.13; Romans 14.23.

[24] Woodruff 30.

[25] The study of the difference in culture and principle has occupied volumes in the history of Christianity. Presently, I offered only a modest illustration of a workable method.

[26] Gilmore, *Gender and Ministry*, Freed-Hardeman University Preachers and Church Leaders Forum (Huntsville, AL.: Publishing Designs, Inc., 1990).

APPENDIX

Meet the Writers

Stephen A. Bailey is the pulpit minister for the Mesquite Church of Christ in Mesquite, Texas. Steve is married to Keitha Crawford Bailey, and they have two grown children, Erin Bailey of Oklahoma City, and Beau Bailey currently doing mission work in Dublin, Ireland.

Greg Clark is the pulpit minister at the 29th & Yale church of Christ in Tulsa, Oklahoma. He is also an instructor at the Owasso School of Biblical Studies. He and his wife, Carol, have two daughters and two sons. Greg received his B.Th. degree from Bear Valley Bible Institute of Denver, a B.A. degree from Oklahoma Christian, and the M.Div. degree from Southern Christian University.

David Deffenbaugh and his wife, Tanya, have two children, Alissa and Dalton. David has been preaching full-time since 1984 and is currently serving the South College Church of Christ in Tahlequah, OK. David serves as the Director of Libre Press, a translation and printing ministry in Donetsk, Ukraine and leads evangelistic campaign groups to Ukraine each year.

Russell L. Dyer is a graduate of Harding University who has preached and done local work for 28 years. He has been a minister for the Southern Ridge Church of Christ since 2000. He and his wife Paula (Wright) have been married for 26 years. They have three children: Joshua, Talsie, and Mandi.

Ralph Gilmore preaches for the Campbell Street Church of Christ in Jackson, TN. He teaches in the department of Interdisciplinary Studies and Bible at Freed Hardeman University. He attended Freed Hardeman University, Harding Graduate School of Religion, and the University of Tennessee. He is married to Joyce (Thornton) and they have three daughters; Jennifer, Jill and Deidra Rachel.

Dale Hartman has been in local work since 1971. He has taught in brotherhood schools in Australia, New Zealand, Canada, and at Oklahoma Christian. He has worked with the Eastside Church of Christ in Midwest City, Oklahoma for 25 years. Twelve of those years were as a missionary to Australia. He has been married to Sheila for 30 years, and they have three children.

Tommy Haynes began preaching in 1976. He has been serving the Central church in Moore, Oklahoma since 1987. Tommy and His wife Kathy have three children. Tommy is a graduate of the Brown Trail School of Preaching in Fort Worth, TX. He is the co-host of the Abundant Living Television Program.

Dale Jenkins is an alumnus of Freed-Hardeman University and Southern Christian University. He is married to Melanie (Romine), and has two sons, Philip and Andrew. He is presently the minister for Granny White Church of Christ. He has been preaching for 25 years. He currently serves on the Board of Maywood Christian Camp, the Freed-Hardeman Advisory Board and the Board of Directors of Heritage Christian University.

Jeff A. Jenkins preaches for the North MacArthur Church of Christ in Oklahoma City. He and his wife Laura have two children, Amanda & Jeremy. He is a graduate of Freed-Hardeman University. Jeff is the co-host of the Abundant Living Television Program. He is the director of the School of Bible Emphasis.

Chuck Monan is the pulpit minister for the Pleasant Valley Church of Christ in Little Rock, Arkansas. Prior to moving to Little Rock, he preached for congregations in Michigan and Oklahoma. He is a graduate of Oklahoma Christian University. He is married to Susan (North), and they have two sons: Nate and Charlie.

Kippy Myers is a graduate of the Brown Trail School of Preaching, Freed-Hardeman College, Harding Graduate School of Religion, University of Dallas, and University of Tennessee at Knoxville. In addition to full-time preaching work in Hooks, Texas and Colleyville, Texas, Kippy has taught part-time at Brown Trail School of Preaching, the University of Tennessee at Knoxville, and the University of North Alabama. He is Chairman of the Department of Interdisciplinary Studies for Freed Hardeman University. Kippy Myers has been married to his wife Debi (Claunch) for 28 years. Their daughters are Randa and Megan.

Neal Pollard has been the preacher for the Cold Harbor Road church of Christ (Mechanicsville, VA) since 1994. He has preached in evangelistic efforts in 17 states, Ukraine and Tanzania. He was the founding editor of Glad Tidings, and director of Cold Harbor Road Lectureship. Speaker, "God's Wonderful Word" TV program since 1999. He and wife Kathy have three sons (Gary--10, Dale--8, and Carl--5).

Tim Pyles is the preaching minister for the Church of Christ on McDermott Road, a church planting in Plano, Texas. He has previously served with churches in Australia and Hawaii, as well as with congregations on the U.S. mainland. He received B.A. and M.A. degrees from David Lipscomb University. Tim and his wife, Kim, have two children, Hannah and Coleman.

Bart Warren graduated from Oklahoma Christian. He is currently completing an M.A. in New Testament at Freed-Hardeman and he serves as the preacher for the Antioch church of Christ in Ramer, TN. He is married to Laura (Hanstein).

Lindsey Warren has been in fulltime ministry since April of 1974. For seventeen years, he preached for the Southern Ridge Church in Oklahoma City, Oklahoma. He now teaches in the Communication department at Freed Hardeman University. He currently serves as the minister at the Christian Chapel congregation in Henderson County, Tennessee. He has been married to his wife Susan since May of 1973. They have one son Thomas Bart.

Ron Williams is a graduate of Freed-Hardeman University and Southern Christian. He has served in ministry for the past twenty-six years and has been the pulpit minister for the Lincoln Church of Christ in Huntsville, Alabama since 1997. He is the co-author of the book, *Walking with Those Who Weep: A Guide to Grief Support.* He has been married to his childhood sweetheart, Bonnie (Lawler) for 25 years, and has two sons, Jon Michael, and Stephen.